PERIOD PASTIMES

A Practical Guide to Four Centuries of Decorative Crafts

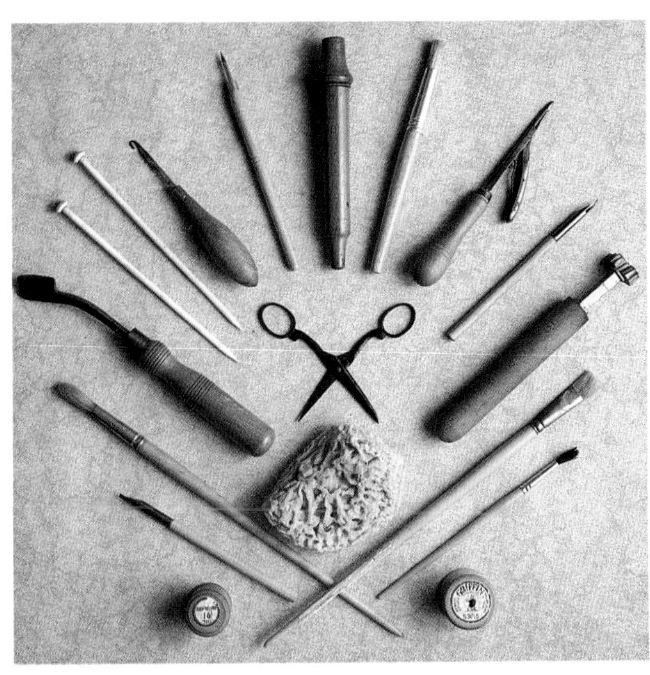

PERIOD PASTIMES

A Practical Guide to Four Centuries of Decorative Crafts

FELICE HODGES

WEIDENFELD AND NICOLSON
LONDON

CONTENTS

CONTENTS

THE LADY'S WORKBOX: NEEDLES, THREADS AND YARNS

FANCY WORK: FROM FISH SCALES TO PORCUPINE QUILLS

INTRODUCTION

For centuries, a gentlewoman was regarded by society as little more than a decorative appendage to her husband. Certainly, she was expected to run his household, which often required considerable administrative flair. More than anything else, however, her worth was judged by the skills with which she executed the 'pretty' arts such as needlework and painting, paper crafts and even wax modelling. Times have changed, but to dismiss such a leisured lifestyle simply because it has little bearing on a contemporary way of life is to lose sight of the great ingenuity, imagination and dexterity possessed by women in times past, attributes which resulted in the creation of a wealth of decorative and practical objects.

The value of these artefacts is two-fold: from a historical perspective, they add immeasurably to our understanding of the lifestyles and fashions of previous centuries. Secondly, on a practical level, they are models which can be copied today. For, while times have changed, there is an ever-increasing interest in following period pursuits. Raw materials and specially designed kits for crafts of all kinds are available in abundance and enormous pleasure can be gained from making such articles, however simple they are to construct.

1. Drawing room displaying a variety of pieces of handiwork, both period and contemporary. On the wall, *clockwise*, a picture of the Menai bridge made from cut and flattened straw on a painted background, nineteenth century; sampler worked in silk, eighteenth century; feltwork picture with traditional motifs of flowers and parrot, each padded and oversewn in silks, nineteenth century. The quilt, folded on the chaise longue, comprises large repeating patchwork and quilted panels. Made in 1920, it uses a traditional mid-nineteenth-century basket design. On the chair, the contemporary appliquéd cushion shows a nineteenth-century-style arrangement of fruit and flowers.
(The Crane Gallery, London)

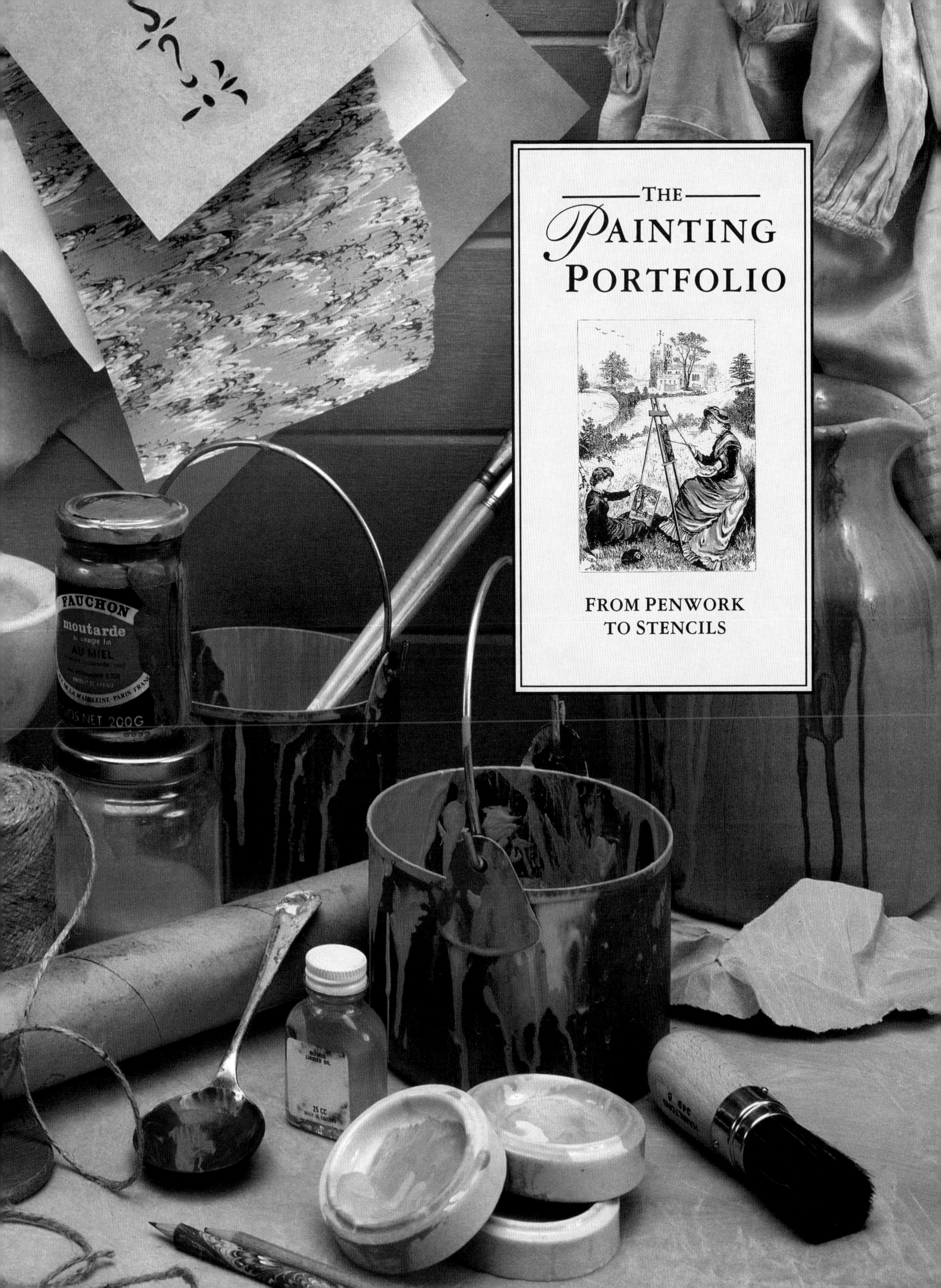
THE
PAINTING
PORTFOLIO
FROM PENWORK
TO STENCILS
FAUCHON
moutarde
AU MIEL

INTRODUCTION

. . . In fading silks compose
Faintly, the inimitable Rose,
Fill up an ill-drawn Bird, or paint on Glass
The Sovereign's blurred and undistinguished face.

From a poem by Anne, Countess of Winchilsea, *c.*1715[1]

Unlike many accomplished women of her time, for whom painting and embroidery were the mainstays of their leisure hours at home, the poetess Anne, Countess of Winchilsea found little fulfilment in the established female pursuits. She preferred writing and 'the creative privacy of a country life'[2] to the sedentary occupations of her contemporaries, and remained disdainful of the frivolous diversions recommended for 'ladies of taste'. Her progressive views, however, were not shared by the majority, and the education of well-bred girls continued unabated on its course of 'pretty arts' instruction, with its specialization in its own peculiar brand of the three 'Rs': refinements, recreations and reading novels.

Amateur painting was by no means new to the eighteenth century. Indeed, wealthy young women of previous generations, who were fortunate enough to receive some tutoring at home, had individual masters for dancing, music and art. Tuition in the latter was confined mainly to the rudiments of draughtsmanship (using pen and ink, or pastels) and painting (in brushworked sepia tints) since oil paints were considered too messy and malodorous for female tastes. Engraving on glass or copper was another easily grasped technique (and one which was

2. *Painting room in our house at York*, a self-portrait executed in watercolours by Mary Ellen Best, *c.*1838.
(York City Art Gallery)

3. Detail from a faux-bamboo cabinet with hand-painted floral motif and borders, nineteenth century.
(The Crane Gallery, London)

taken up by George III's talented daughters who had their own private press at Frogmore for printing plates).

Not only was the selection of artistic media offered to a lady's 'fair hands' limited but also the choice of subject matter was rigorously confined by what was deemed suitably 'genteel'. Hence, the lady painter of the seventeenth and eighteenth centuries embarked on a series of miniatures, still lifes, romantic landscapes and genre scenes, which she copied frequently from popular, contemporary engravings. Promising students might invent subjects of their own, under the vigilant guidance of tutors, while others turned to japanning and painting furniture, painting on velvet, on silk (to ornament a petticoat or apron) and penwork decoration.

In the 'polite' conversation of the educated classes, a knowledge of the arts was considered as important as one's own accomplishments in drawing and painting. The eighteenth-century lady was expected to be well versed in literature, music and drama, and bound to attend exhibitions, concerts and plays during 'the season'. At supper parties, when the gentlemen remained seated after the meal to discuss politics, their wives retired to the drawing room, taking with them a small workbag of embroidery and, perhaps, their latest sketches to display to their admiring friends. By the late 1700s, most fashionable women could show off their portfolios of hand-painted scenes. The staple ingredients in the execution of the gentlewoman's *oeuvre* were watercolours and pastels, and after Thomas Reeves's successful manufacture of the latter (from *c.*1766), the tedious task of preparing pigments vanished.

While artistic talent was both admired and encouraged in female education, any attempts to progress into the prodigious ranks of professionalism were sharply curtailed. The Royal Academicians Mary Moser and Angelica Kauffmann broke the rules to a large extent when they launched their successful careers in England, as did others such as Mary Beale, Sarah Curtis, Anne Killigrew, Anne Damer and Catherine Read. Their steadfast determination, however, paid dividends financially – as long as their contributions adhered to the permitted course of pretty subjects (still lifes, allegoricals and elegant portraits) and went hand in hand with their being 'an ornament to Society . . .'[3]

Nevertheless, the professional lady artist was frequently the target of unrelenting gossip, and she had also to contend with the jealousy and indignation of her ambitious male colleagues (particularly when her success was assured by the offer of a prestigious commission). It is little wonder that most gifted lady amateurs went no further than accepting the odd invitation to show a favourite work at one of the Royal Academy's summer exhibitions. The pages of Rudolph Ackermann's *The Repository of Arts* – the layman's guidebook *par excellence* to the latest trends in art, literature and fashion – were littered with references to their readers' fleeting debuts: 'Miss Wiggins of Piccadilly . . . (awarded) the silver Isis medal . . . for a copy in India ink of a landscape . . .',[4] was a typical entry, demonstrating the fashionable interest in the 'polite arts' among the cognoscenti of the early nineteenth century.

4. One of a pair of folded paper, hand-painted, candle-screens mounted on a wooden stand, *c.*1830.
(The American Museum in Britain, Bath)

Given the quantity of work produced, it may seem surprising how little real progress was made during the 1800s regarding the subordinate status of the female artist, until the general role of women in society at that time is considered. Amateur work continued to be applauded ad infinitum in ladies' magazines of the period, and the virtues of industry praised as a means of beautifying one's home (and pleasing one's husband). Just as the seventeenth-century writer John Evelyn boasted of his daughter Susannah's accomplishments '... in all the ornaments of her sex ... (her) peculiar talent in designe ... painting in oile and miniature', so the nineteenth-century gentleman bragged of his wife's, or daughter's, indefatigable (but largely unexceptional) achievements. Such sentiments were summed up in a letter which was published in the correspondence columns of the *Ladies' Magazine* (1813) in which a Mr

Benedict accounted for his good fortune 'for having a pretty wife, always at home, and always industrious'.[5] Under these coercive conditions, there was little opportunity for a woman to explore life outside her homely niche. Indeed, of the few female professionals, most gave up their careers after marriage. As the author of *The Habits of Good Society* (1859) put it: 'All accomplishments have the one great merit of giving a lady something to do; something to preserve her from ennui; to console her in seclusion; to arouse her in grief; to compose her to occupation in joy.'[6] Such was the perceived potential of women's artistry, serving more a therapeutic purpose than one of self-improvement.

John Ruskin's derisory views of the Victorian woman artist only compounded her fate. In his series of lectures on 'The Art of England', however, he revised his opinions when he admitted '... For a long time I used to say, in all my elementary books, that, except in a graceful and minor way, women could not paint or draw. I am beginning, lately, to bow myself to the much more delightful conviction that nobody else can.'[7] New opportunities for lady amateurs – both to study and exhibit their works more freely – were encouraged during the 1860s. The Society of Lady Artists (founded in 1861) and The South Kensington School of Art both offered instruction for gentlewomen, while the prestigious Royal Academy admitted a few female students from the mid-eighteenth century onwards (although they were prohibited from attending life classes until the 1890s). In America, too, modifications in art education for women were beginning to take place during the latter part of the nineteenth century. Candace Wheeler, for example, an accomplished painter of floral still lifes, exhibited at the New York Academy of Design, and did much to inspire her peers to venture into the real world '... fit ... for public as well as private patronage'.[8]

Despite the tendency towards change and controversy, not to mention greater commercial awareness, the majority of Victorian gentlewomen remained conservative in attitude. While few would have subscribed entirely to Mrs Sutherland Orr's inflexible tenets that 'women are intelligent; they are *not* creative',[9] many followed the advice offered in ladies' magazines and remained productive at home, in the pursuits recommended for delicate hands and minds. Painting, as a parlour art, fell into that much-loved Victorian category known as 'fancy work'. The sketchbook was abandoned for the cherished 'token' album, its pages bursting with handwritten poems in exquisite calligraphy, autographs, sketches and paper scraps. Painting on glass, wood, china, ivory, vellum and ribbon became the mainstays of domestic creativity.

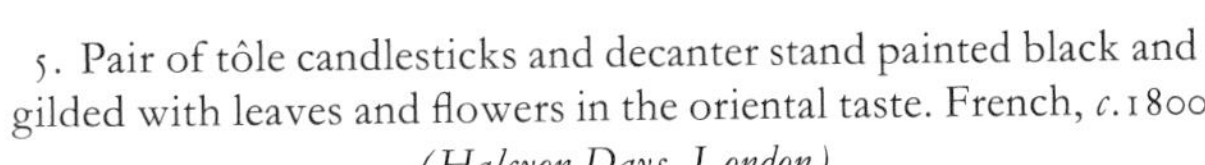

5. Pair of tôle candlesticks and decanter stand painted black and gilded with leaves and flowers in the oriental taste. French, *c.*1800. *(Halcyon Days, London)*

THE AMATEUR ARTS

Do you draw? . . . What, none of you (girls)? That is very strange.
But I suppose you had no opportunity. Your mother should have
taken you to town every spring for the benefit of masters.

(Lady Catherine de Bourgh addressing Miss Elizabeth Bennet)

Jane Austen, *Pride and Prejudice*, 1813[1]

6. *The Artist and her Mother*, a self-portrait executed in oils
*c.*1820 by Rolinda Sharples (1793–1838).
(City of Bristol Museum and Art Gallery)

The notion of the budding artist appealed greatly to the aristocracy and gentry of the late eighteenth and nineteenth centuries, whose daughters' 'polite' accomplishments would not have been complete without a smattering of French, a pianoforte on which to perform and a portfolio of their own 'landskip' drawings. By the early 1800s, the majority of girls' finishing schools featured regular tutorials in drawing and painting in their 'pretty arts' syllabuses. For those educated at home under the guidance of a governess or able parent, a drawing master could usually be found for private lessons (who needed little persuasion to take a new pupil, given his frequently impoverished circumstances.

The eight-year-old Princess Victoria received an hour's instruction twice weekly in the rudiments of draughtsmanship from Richard Westall RA, who visited her at Kensington Palace over the course of nine years. In spite of his own financial difficulties, Westall refused any remuneration for his efforts, and Victoria recorded in her diaries, with considerable remorse, that when he died in 1836 it was in 'the *greatest* state of *pecuniary* distress'.[2] Victoria's talent for drawing was demonstrated throughout her long life, and she filled numerous sketchbooks with charming portraits both of her children and the places she visited (now in the Royal Collection, Windsor Castle). Her natural abilities may well have been inherited from her mother, the Duchess of Windsor, who before her marriage, painted a trompe-l'oeil conservatory for her residence at Coburg. Her grandfather, King George III, had also been a competent draughtsman, and he instigated a fairly rigorous course of tuition for his clever daughters, the Princesses Mary, Elizabeth and Augusta Sophia, engaging the services of such distinguished artists as Thomas Gainsborough and Alexander Cozens.

While female talent was encouraged and discipline instilled, there was never any question of a promising young girl turning professional. Although her achievements may have embraced a keen eye for still lifes or genre scenes, she was seldom permitted to exhibit her works publicly and most certainly forbidden to sell them. Nevertheless, there were a small number of ambitious and gifted amateurs who,

7. Detail from a contemporary folding screen, the panels decorated with a selection of mid-eighteenth-century, hand-coloured engravings of birds by George Edwards.
(Mallett and Son (Antiques) Ltd, London)

braving the scorn of 'polite' society, chose to pursue a career in the fine arts – either because they needed the money, or for reasons of self-fulfilment. One of the first of these 'blue stockings' was Mrs Mary Beale, whose exceptional aptitude for portraiture during the mid-seventeenth century earned her several important commissions from King Charles II and the Restoration Court. Her efforts were well rewarded (with the sum of £10 for a standard three-quarter-length portrait) and she was praised for her capabilities, not only as a fine artist and teacher, but also as 'an admirable mother and wife'.[3]

During the eighteenth century, the Honourable Mrs Anne Damer embarked upon a career as a sculptress after her husband committed suicide in 1776. At a time when even oil painting was considered too indelicate for a lady's 'fair hand', she specialized in modelling portrait-busts from wax, bronze, marble and stone – materials which, even more than oils, came within an exclusively male domain. Fortunately, her success as a sculptress led to her receiving the patronage of both royalty and the aristocracy, and a number of lucrative commissions followed. Mrs Damer, however, was not totally dependent on her earnings. On his death, Horace Walpole had left her his 'Gothick' estate, Strawberry Hill, in Middlesex, complete with its resident spiders and an annual income of £2,000.

8. *Lady holding a mirror*, a drawing executed by Penelope Carwardine (1730?–1801?), probably as a preparatory sketch for a miniature, *c.*1780.
(Courtesy of Dr A. K. Brown FRCP)

Although Mrs Damer had been invited to exhibit at the Royal Academy in 1804, this was not the first time that a woman had been awarded such a privilege. The distinguished painters Angelica Kauffmann and Mary Moser had been honoured some years earlier by the Academy when they were elected Founder Members in 1768. Nevertheless, their intrusion into what was otherwise an essentially male institution was not met with unanimous approval. Zoffany, for example, excluded them from his group portrait of the Academy's members, relegating them instead to a dimly-lit part of the composition in which they could be seen on paintings hung from the wall. In addition, ladies were not permitted to enrol in the Academy's life classes but were instructed instead in the genteel arts of painting flowers and romantic landscapes – a policy which continued well into the 1890s.

Under such restricted conditions, a few women turned to the delicate art of portrait miniatures, which, by virtue of their dainty size, at least gave the impression of being better suited to 'female taste'. Sir Joshua Reynolds's sister, Frances, embarked upon a career as a miniaturist 'in spite of the contemptuous opinion expressed ... by her brother',[4] as did Penelope Carwardine, a little-known artist (and friend of George Romney) who flourished in England during the 1750s and 60s.[5]

From the late eighteenth century onwards, painting in watercolours remained the firm favourite for ladies of artistic ability. Amateurs practised their colour-wash techniques at home using both tinted Indian inks and the new dry bricks of pigment manufactured by firms such as Thomas Reeves. The latter only required moistening with a few drops of water and gum arabic. Elegant, caddy-shaped paint-boxes could be purchased from artists' supply shops, among them Ackermann's 'Repository of the Arts'

9. Pole screen adorned with a hand-painted memorial scene, in keeping with the vogue for mourning decorations during the late eighteenth and early nineteenth centuries. Inscribed and dated 'In Memory of John P. Brant 1799'.
(The American Museum in Britain, Bath)

in the Strand, London, which provided all the materials necessary to deck out an 'artist's or amateur's apartment'.[6]

Armed with her portable paintbox, pencils and sketchbook, ladies ventured outdoors to record impressions of their surroundings, and, of course, the places they visited abroad on the Grand Tour. Jane Austen subscribed to the fashion and wrote to her sister, Cassandra '... of my talent for drawing, I have given specimens in my letters to you'.[7] None of her illustrations are known to have survived,[8] but Cassandra's lively watercolour studies of her family and acquaintances demonstrate her own talents for accurate observation.

The gifted amateur Mary Ellen Best was another accomplished painter in watercolours (see plate 2). During the 1830s and 40s, she executed numerous scenes of her native Yorkshire, recording daily events in the lives of those around her. She favoured interior views, from the opulent drawing rooms of the aristocracy, to the sparsely decorated and cramped quarters of their servants. Her meticulous eye for detail and flair for colouring provide a rare glimpse of the furnishings and fashionable period tastes of early Victorian design.

During the nineteenth century, self-taught amateurs could rely on the instructions published in books and manuals such as Charles Hayter's *An Introduction to Perspective, Practical Geometry Drawing and Painting – Properly Adapted for the Instruction of Females* (1816). Ladies' magazines also provided step-by-step guides to painting, including directions for mixing and blending colours, as well as suggestions for suitable subjects. 'Take our advice, fair reader, keep your eyes open', was the inspiration offered by the *Elegant Arts for Ladies* (*c.*1856), whose writers recommended that even '... the most trifling incident, chosen and treated with taste, makes a picture'. The merits of art education were perhaps best summed up in the article entitled 'The Lady Artist', which was published in 1890 in the popular journal, *The Woman's World*: 'Of all the intellectual pursuits ... (for) the civilised and cultivated person ... Art, it appears, is that which at first sight is considered most adaptable to feminine faculties and conditions. The work ... is ... eminently genteel.'[9] Thus encouraged, the amateur turned to painting with the knowledge that while she may not 'become Titian or Claude in a day ... (she) may acquire a delightful and interesting employment'.[10]

PAINTING ON GLASS

Rosamund, though she would never do anything that was disagreeable to her,
was industrious; and now more than ever she was active in sketching
her landscapes and market-carts and portraits of friends, in practising her music,
and in being from morning till night her own standard of a perfect lady.

George Eliot, *Middlemarch*, 1871–2[1]

Painting or 'limning' (as described in *The Ladies' Dictionary* of 1694) was encouraged as a suitable alternative to fancy sewing, and tuition in landscapes, still lifes and miniatures was advertised frequently in the curricula of finishing schools in England and America. Painting on glass was a particular favourite for, as a novel medium, it permitted a variety of lustrous surface effects which were not easily achieved by the otherwise obligatory adherence to watercolours – the staple ingredient of every schoolgirl's portfolio.

Reverse-painting on glass – by which the design was executed on the underside of the pane, to ensure protection – was very fashionable during the second half of the eighteenth and the early nineteenth century. Examples could be mounted either as wall pictures, or as decorative panels to adorn clockcases and looking glasses. Mirror-back painting was a popular version of the style, and involved scraping off designated sections of the silver-foiled ground and filling in the 'blank' spaces with pictorial designs. Oil colours, both transparent and matt, were usually selected, and brushed onto the underside of the glass. This method necessitated a reverse order of working: the details of the composition were applied first and the background areas last, so as to build up the intended subject in layers, for viewing from the 'correct' side. In keeping with the vogue for back-painting, commercial productions were exported from China during the period *c.*1765–1820, and their oriental subjects provided inspiration for amateurs with a taste for chinoiserie.

In America, reverse-painting on glass figured prominently in the traditions of folk art, since it was a colourful yet relatively inexpensive means of ornamentation. Girls instructed in the technique followed a well-established collection of subjects, consisting characteristically of vibrant still lifes of fruits and flowers and pretty rural landscapes. This decorative repertoire had a wide application, and appeared with little variation on the whole gamut of 'fancy works', from quilts to paintings on velvet.

During the second half of the nineteenth century, painting on glass embraced several new styles of presentation (although the basic process of reverse-execution remained the same). Perhaps most striking was the method referred to as 'Oriental' or 'Pearl Painting'. The designs, invariably of naturalistic flowers and fruits set in urns, were painted on glass in transparent oil stains against backgrounds covered in a rich opaque shade or, more often, a lamp-black tint for dramatic contrast. The individual motifs were then backed with metallic foils to create sparkling accents when viewed from the other side (not dissimilar, in effect, from papier-mâché, with its hand-painted flowers and shiny, mother-of-pearl inlays).

Other stylistic variants were described in the Victorian handbook, the *Elegant Arts for Ladies* (*c.*1856), which included directions for making 'transparent glass paintings' to adorn windows and glazed doors. These stained glass imitations had been extolled some years earlier in Ackermann's *The Repository of Arts*,[2] in which it was stated that '... the perfection ... (of) this art, after having been supposed to have been lost for centuries ... is beyond all praise'. The writers of the *Elegant Arts* also suggested painting glass serving dishes, by which even the plainest services could be ornamented 'as well as any china', while the panelled exteriors of writing desks and chess tables could be decorated with small painted-glass roundels. This approach, referred to in the text as 'illuminated glass painting', differed little from the 'oriental' styles described previously, since both incorporated tinselled papers as backings. As was often the case, however, identical techniques were re-labelled by writers keen to introduce something new to their readers.

Another 'fascinating occupation' was described in the *Needlecraft Monthly* magazine, whereby glass miniatures could be painted and applied to the exteriors of glove boxes and other accessories. Directions for the technique were summarized briefly under the fanciful heading, 'The Alstona Method' (named appropriately after the Alston Gallery of New Bond Street, London, where all the requisite materials and *The Alston Book of Instruction* could be purchased). Although the exercise involved little more than tracing outlines from a photograph onto a sheet of glass, its 'educational' merits were applauded as a '... means of developing artistic tendencies hitherto unrealised!'

10, 11. Pair of late seventeenth-century reverse-painting on glass in naive style, *Europe*, *left*, and *America*, *above*, *detail*. (*Private collection*)

PAINTING ON RIBBON

As the novelties of painting on glass wore off by the late 1800s, so other decorative possibilities were explored by ladies' magazines devoted to home crafts. The writers of *Needlecraft Monthly*, for example, promoted the 'art' of painted ribbonwork to '... give ... dainty handiwork just that touch of individuality'. The only materials required for the task were ribbons, needle and thread, and a selection of paints (either watercolours or oils), to ornament all manner of accessories from 'theatre bags' to linen-backed photograph frames. The designs conformed to the ubiquitous floral sprays so favoured at the time 'for modelling in ribbon and paint(ed) direct from nature. Wallflowers lend themselves particularly well to reproduction .... A shade of bright yellow giant ribbon is used, and is sewn on the design in double loops, caught down with invisible silk stitches to form the four petals of each flower .... When the flowers are all sewn on, they are ready to be painted. If oil paint is used, take brown madder or burnt sienna and crimson-lake, and thin down very slightly with paraffin.... Paint in stripes and splodges, leaving the splendid material for painted ribbonwork, as it takes the colour so easily'.

Ribbonwork, if nothing else, relieved the tedium of painting on canvas, paper and glass, and provided the Victorian lady with yet another 'fancy' to add to her already burgeoning list of charity bazaar contributions.

12. Reverse-painting on glass, the drapery folds of the dress are made more lustrous by the use of oil-based pigments. English, *c.*1780. *(Mallett at Bourdon House Ltd, London)*

PAINTING ON VELVET

Among the various accomplishments of the present day, no fancy work is perhaps more elegant, produces a better effect, and is, at the same time, more easily and quickly performed, than painting on velvet.

*Elegant Arts for Ladies, c.*1856

During the early 1800s, instruction in painting and drawing was advertised frequently in the curricula of fashionable girls' boarding schools, at a time when needlework, for once, appeared to take second place. Although the rudiments of draughtsmanship and of creativity were undoubtedly stressed under the guidance of inspired tutors, the majority of art lessons adhered to a 'learning-by-rote' system, which offered few opportunities for originality. The limited repertoire of set pieces consisted invariably of pretty landscapes and still lifes, which were considered suitable subjects for the 'fair hands' and minds of young ladies. Portraiture was strongly discouraged for its overly intimate nature, a sentiment shared by Dr Samuel Johnson, who found it '. . . improper . . . for a woman . . . (as) public practice of any art and staring in men's faces is very indelicate in a female'.[1]

Watercolours and pencil sketches formed the basis of a schoolgirl's portfolio, along with paintings on velvet, which enjoyed immense popularity in America (and to a lesser extent in England) during the first half of the nineteenth century. These were executed by means of stencils or 'theorems', which were cut according to the desired pattern, be it a simple floral spray or formal still life of foliage, fruit or exotic birds. Depending on the complexity of the composition, it was usual to cut five or six individual sheets of stencils as a means of separating the various parts of the design. For girls who were unable to make their own, it is more than likely that ready-made stencils were provided – either prepared by the tutor, or purchased from specialist craft shops. The pierced sheets were held firmly, one by one, over the fabric grounds until all the outlines and contours of the subject were filled in by painting through the holes. Flat washes of colour soon gave way to the technique of shading, whereby each tint was dabbed lightly over the velvet using a short stiff brush or rag, to create a range of subtle effects. The outlines of petals and leaves, for example, might be picked out in a darker tone, which faded gradually into a barely perceptible hue towards the centre of each form. This delicacy of colouring was considered fundamental to the exercise, as described in Matthew D.

13. Nineteenth-century paintbox containing camel's hair and stiff 'poonah' brushes, palette, rags, tablets and bottles of pigment – all the accessories needed for painting on velvet. *(By courtesy of the Trustees of the Victoria and Albert Museum, London)*

14. Nineteenth-century American theorem painting in characteristic schoolgirl style, of a bowl of fruit shaded in colours on a white velvet background.
(The American Museum in Britain, Bath)

Finn's instructive volume, *Theoremetical System of Painting, or Modern Plan, Fully Explained, in Six Lessons* (1830). In Lesson IV he advised that 'the brush should be held perpendicularly to the paper, and worked with a circular motion of the wrist'. Small details could be added freehand, using a fine sable brush and Indian inks.

While theorems conformed admirably to the principles of 'formula painting' (as upheld by the majority of school instructresses) they offered, nevertheless, some scope for creativity. Talented girls might not only invent their own designs, but also trace and cut the stencils themselves, using sheets of heavy drawing paper coated with linseed oil and turpentine. Some were even permitted to prepare and mix their own colours, according to the 'recipies' published in books. In J.W. Alston's second edition of *Hints to Young Practitioners in the Study of Landscape Painting* (1805) a chapter devoted to the 'Art of Painting on Velvet' was included, while later, Maria Turner's *Young Ladies' Assistant in Drawing and Painting* (1833) proved a popular source of instruction.

In the portfolio assembled during the mid-nineteenth century by the amateur artist Lucy McFarland Sherman of Peekskill, New York,[2] the methods of theorem painting were set out step-by-step in a series of practice sheets (not unlike the rows of stitches found on the typical schoolgirl's sampler). In the first lesson, which she inscribed, 'The Gamut of Painting', some twenty different styles of brush stroke and colour-shading were demonstrated, followed by several pages of detailed tracings, cut stencils and study notes. Such a theoretical approach to painting excluded any notion of spontaneity, and yet the purely mechanical aspects of theorems were often transcended by their exquisite arrangements of carefully juxtaposed colours and forms: 'some lush and elegant, others misty and almost dreamlike'.[3]

As the vogue for theorem painting gained momentum during the 1830s and 40s, so ladies' magazines of the period – ever keen to increase their circulation – devoted lengthy articles to promoting the technique as a novel means of home decoration. The *Elegant Arts for Ladies* suggested that the stencilled designs would '... look very handsome ... (on) music-stools, the front of pianos, ottomans, banner-screens, pole-screens and borders for table-cloths'. Other journals provided small paper patterns from which the theorems could be cut and used to adorn all manner of personal accessories, the most popular of which was the reticule or drawstring bag which accompanied every lady of fashion.

Liquid colours could be purchased for the first time, relieving the amateur of the tedious task of grinding and mixing the pigments herself. White or cream-coloured velvet remained the most popular background for painting by theorems, since its pale, neutral tones and soft 'pile' were found to be the perfect accompaniment to colour-shading. Other fabrics such as satin and silk, however, were also recommended for wall pictures and soft furnishings, and even wood was suggested as a pleasing alternative if 'made very smooth ... by a good cabinet-maker'.[4]

As late as the 1880s, the amateur art of theorem painting continued to be promoted in English publications, long after its demise as a classroom exercise for well-bred American girls. In *The Young Ladies' Journal Complete Guide to the Work-Table* (1885), for example, instructions for a 'Damask Rose Poonah Painting' were provided, complete with its own numbered diagram for cutting the various stencilled sheets. In spite of its new title (derived from the so-called 'poonah' brush which was used in conjunction with stencilling), the fundamental techniques remained the same.

By the end of the century, however, theorem painting had lost its appeal. The simple charm and naivety characteristic of early examples had become stifled by the over-fussiness and grandeur of 'high' Victorian design. What had once figured among the finest traditions of folk art had now degenerated into a parlour display.

15. Detail from a nineteenth-century American theorem painting of a basket of flowers, displaying subtle colour-shading achieved by the use of a stiff brush or rag. *(The American Museum in Britain, Bath)*

STENCILLED VELVET CUSHION

Velvet painting by stencils provides a relatively easy method of achieving a charming picture without having to be a gifted artist. Once the stencils or theorems have been cut they can be re-used time and again, varying the colours and positions of the pieces to create a range of decorative compositions.

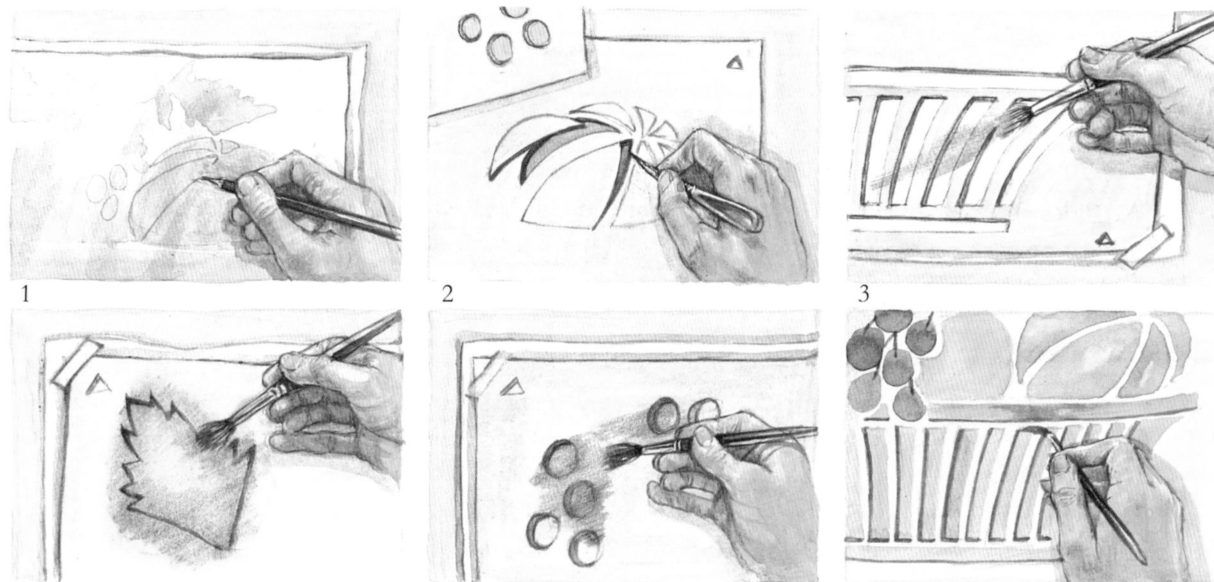

Materials
paper
tracing paper
stencil card
pencil
scalpel or craft knife
cutting board or several old newspapers
a piece of cream cotton velvet
small stiff paintbrush
fine sable brush: size 2 or 3
artists' oil colours
white spirit
rag
old plate to mix paint on
masking tape

Method

1. Select a design to copy or invent your own, avoiding anything too fussy or intricate, since this will be difficult to cut out. Trace the outline of the picture onto a piece of tracing paper. Decide how many stencils to cut by working out how many colours you will need to use. Three is probably the minimum, although antique examples may well have employed up to ten different pieces. Remember that you can also vary the colour within each stencil. For this cushion you will need one for the basket, one for the fruit and leaves and one for the grapes. In order to register the different stencils, draw a small triangle in each corner of the tracing paper.
2. Trace each of the three parts of your picture onto a separate sheet of stencil card, making sure that the lines of the design do not touch each other as this would result in the stencil falling apart while cutting. Cut each of the stencils with a sharp craft knife or scalpel, going as smoothly as possible round the curves in clear, clean lines. Use a cutting board or sheets of old newspapers to avoid marking the table underneath. Cut out the register marks in the corner too.
3. To paint the stencil picture, lay the piece of velvet flat on a surface and tape down the corners. Tape down the first stencil – the basket – and pencil in the register marks lightly. (They will be hidden later under the hem of the cushion.) Squeeze some oil paints round the sides of the plate and put a little white spirit into an old tin. Mix the colours on the plate – for wickerwork baskets combine raw sienna with a little raw umber and thin it with a few drops of white spirit. Dip the stiff bristle brush into the paint and then wipe most of it off, since very little pigment is required, and gently stroke the paint onto the velvet. Avoid bouncing it on, which would produce a heavy, muddy tone. Practise on a scrap piece first to create a variety of subtle effects and remember that by rotating the bristles of the brush different shades can be achieved, graduating from light to dark.
4. Repeat with the other two stencils. For the fruit and leaves use greens and yellowish browns, making the fruit look rounded by leaving the centre paler than the edges. Darken the top sides of the leaves to make them appear as though light is falling on their lower halves. Paint the stalks of the grapes in a brownish green and the melon in an orange-yellow colour (raw sienna and cadmium red).
5. Paint the last stencil – the grapes. Mix a dark purple-red with ultramarine, crimson and black and again stroke the paint on through the holes so the edges of the grapes are darker than their centres, to appear as if they are catching the light.
6. Although very small quantities of paint have been used, the picture requires at least twenty-four hours to dry. Final details, however, may be painted in before completely dry, taking care to cover the rest of the picture with a cloth to prevent smudging. Take a small sable brush and mix a dark brown for the basket. Paint in shadows in fine lines below and up the sides of the cane work. Use the same sort of colour for the stalks of the fruit, making it greener to shadow and vein the leaves and the melon. Add light and delicate flicks to emphasize the shapes without letting the brush strokes become heavy or laboured.
7. Finally, after leaving the picture to dry, it can either be framed or made into a cushion cover.

PENWORK

... quaint scrolls and arabesques, flowers of extraordinary forms ...
birds of marvellous plumage, and devices which
have only their oddity to recommend them.

*Elegant Arts for Ladies, c.*1856

This style of 'black-on-white' ornamentation appealed greatly to gentlewomen of artistic leaning during the late eighteenth and nineteenth centuries, since its execution required both a proficiency in drawing and a meticulous flair for design. The delicate monochrome patterns were created by using a sharp quill pen and fine camel-hair brush to apply black Indian ink or 'lamp-black' watercolour onto a white wooden surface, in imitation of the costly, inlaid ivory and ebony furniture imported during the period from India. Indeed, several early references to penwork described the technique as 'imitation ebony and ivory' or 'inlaying', and surviving examples of Georgian workmanship reflect the exoticism and influence of the Indian craft.

Workboxes, tea caddies, games boards and small cabinets appeared with profuse decoration in ink depicting, in miniature, fierce swordsmen, scribes, elephants and flamboyant foliage, of which the majority were portrayed in immense detail using fine etch-like lines. Chinoiserie motifs also figured largely in penwork and Chinamen carrying parasols, pagodas, phoenixes, prunus blossoms and stylized palm trees were all conveyed in a lively 'primitive' fashion. Often interspersed among these eastern devices were borders and emblems of Neoclassical inspiration, creating a somewhat incongruous mixture of patterns.

Sources for penwork designs appeared in ladies' journals devoted to the usual handicrafts, and in magazines such as Ackermann's *The Repository of Arts*. In the December issue for 1816, the technique was described with enthusiasm as 'among the many pleasing recreations of the fair sex ... which at once becomes an elegant and useful amusement'. Ackermann's Repository in the Strand, London, supplied the various materials required for penwork (as well as other accessories for numerous ladies' pursuits, such as Berlin wool work), while S. J. Fuller's 'Temple of

16. Pair of face-screens with penwork decoration depicting elegant ladies, exotic birds and foliage in Regency taste. English, *c.*1815.
(Halcyon Days, London)

17. Jewellery cabinet with lift-up lid and three drawers decorated with penwork chinoiserie. English, *c.*1815. *(Halcyon Days, London)*

Fancy' advertised an 'extensive collection of handsome screens ... Screen-poles, elegant Stands for Table Tops and Chess-Boards, Card-Racks, Flower Ornaments, and white-wood boxes ... for painting the inlaid Ebony and Ivory'. Specialist outlets such as these were invaluable sources of both materials and patterns, and it is likely that several had the facilities to instruct ladies in the 'art' by means of introductory demonstrations.

For economy, however, almost any item of domestic furniture – perhaps worn with age or no longer fashionable – could be adapted readily to the surface treatment, and in articles devoted to penwork, frequent mention was made of the preparation of the wooden object prior to its decoration. In *The Handbook of Useful and Ornamental Amusements and Accomplishments* (1845) by 'A. Lady', 'a coat of isinglass diluted with water' was recommended as a

18. Chinoiserie design for penwork, in keeping with the popularity of oriental stylizations during the late eighteenth and early nineteenth centuries.
(By courtesy of the Trustees of the British Museum, London)

protective surface coating '... previous to sketching the pattern ... and if the wood is not very white, or has a coarse grain, a little flake white in powder should be added to it'. A similar recipe appeared some years later in the *Elegant Arts for Ladies* (*c.*1856) which instructed that '... it is not absolutely necessary that the wood should be white, if it be hard and close-grained, for the whole surface can always be covered with a body-colour or grounding'.

Once the wood was prepared and primed, and the desired pattern selected, the artist's skill was called upon to sketch freehand the outline and details onto the surface. For those lacking confidence, tracing designs was recommended as an alternative method: '... over ... a piece of thin transparent paper ... draw the outline with a pencil, then lay it upon the wood or card-board with a sheet of black or red tracing paper underneath, and with a very fine pointed pencil pass over the lines of the outline, which will by that means be transferred to the object to be painted'. Tracing, however, could not achieve the finesse and subtlety of free-hand workmanship, and its practice was confined largely to less gifted amateurs and those seeking a quick 'finish'. In the case of large and ambitious designs, penwork executed entirely by hand was a time-consuming and arduous task, and one which might easily take several years. Perhaps for this reason, small decorative objects of limited surface area were preferred 'subjects'.

Fine patterns were produced with the aid of 'a very hard pen, after the manner of a line engraving', while background areas were filled in with brush work. Variations of the technique, however, occurred during the nineteenth century, the most engaging of which appeared simply as black drawing over the white ground with no subsequent over-wash, to create crisp and delicate outlines resembling the meticulous stitchery of Elizabethan blackwork[1] (see pp. 104–109). Other deviations introduced gilding into the monochrome schemes for added richness, or adopted red or green coloured inks in place of black.

The 'art' of penwork ceased to be a fashionable pastime by the late 1880s, and its stark monochrome patterns were gradually discarded in favour of other exotic presentations, in particular, those executed in lustrous black papier-mâché with inlays of shiny mother-of-pearl.

19, 20. Casket-shaped tea caddies decorated with penwork figural scenes depicting Chinese mandarins, temples and foliage, recalling the European fashion for exotica. English, *c.*1815.
(Halcyon Days, London)

PENWORK JEWELLERY OR NEEDLEWORK BOX

Penwork box in the nineteenth-century style, created from outlining pressed leaves

One of the later references to 'imitation ebony and ivory' was a simple project for a penwork chessboard which appeared in *Cassell's Household Guide* (1875). Adorned with foliage, the naturalistic designs were created by tracing the outlines of pressed leaves onto the wooden surface, leaving the finer details to be filled in later. The same technique is used for this small box, which would make an attractive case for jewellery or needlework when lined.

Materials
cigar box of pale, stripped wood
fine sandpaper
small tin flat white oil paint
white spirit
flat 1 in (2.5 cm) bristle brush
hard pencil
black Indian ink
fine-nibbed artist's mapping pen
piece of paper
fine sable paint brush
tin of semi-gloss varnish
artists' tints: raw sienna or umber
variety of small pressed leaves – around 25–30 specimens with finely serrated edges.

Method
1. Press the leaves overnight between sheets of newspaper under a heavy weight. The leaves do not need to be pressed until dry, as long as they are flat.
2. Seal the surfaces of the box by painting with a coat of flat white oil paint diluted with a little white spirit. Leave to dry and sand lightly. Apply a second coat and sand again to give a smooth finish.
3. On pieces of paper cut to the same size as the top and sides of the box, practise arranging the leaves into sprays and border patterns until suitable designs have been found.
4. Taking the leaves one at a time, and following the pattern, place each on the box and trace its outline lightly and very carefully in pencil. Then, with equal care, draw over the pencil outlines in Indian ink, using the mapping pen.
5. Fill in the background with Indian ink using the fine brush. In the areas immediately around the leaf shapes it may be easier to use the pen, to avoid losing the fine detail of their edges. Once the background is dry, use the pen and ink to draw in the leaves' backbones and veins very lightly, to create a delicate, intricate effect.
6. Finally, apply three or four coats of semi-gloss varnish tinted with raw sienna or umber. These will not only protect the surface but, being a yellow colour, will also produce an 'antique' look.

PAINTING ON FURNITURE

Furniture has become the principal object of luxury and of expenditure. One changes furnishings every six years so as to obtain everything inspired by the latest fashion.

Louis Sébastien Mercier, *Tableau de Paris*, 1781–90

The second half of the eighteenth and the early nineteenth century saw the heyday of painted furniture, when all manner of furnishings were ornamented according to the latest fashions in interior design. While a great deal of work was executed by commercial and freelance artists, amateurs showed little hesitation in painting pieces themselves, following the instructions published in crafts manuals in Europe and America. Chairs, tables, chests, cupboards, clock cases, mirror frames and fire boards were popular subjects for the surface treatment, and appeared in striking variety, from the *faux* wood grainings and painted chinoiserie of the Prince of Wales's Brighton Pavilion, to the rustic stencilled designs of colonial America.

Simple country furniture in pine, deal or maple became the artist's 'blank canvas', and even the humblest of cottage furnishings could be transformed into something richly decorative. For the upper and middle classes, who could afford luxury woods such as mahogany, walnut and satinwood, the taste for painted furniture was promoted by the leading cabinet makers of the period. Thomas Chippendale favoured painted motifs of Chinese inspiration, and created a wardrobe for the actor David Garrick which was ornamented with green landscape vignettes, pagodas and oriental figures on a cream-tinted ground. The grandiose interior schemes of Robert Adam were complemented by his chairs and settees painted with allegorical scenes, while Thomas Sheraton and George Hepplewhite adhered to the restrained imagery of Neoclassicism, and featured painted ribbons, flowers, acanthus leaves and medallions on the arms and legs of seat furniture.

The distinguished artist Angelica Kauffmann was a frequent contributor to the lavish interiors designed by the Adam brothers, and many of her paintings graced the chairs and commodes commissioned by their patrons. A table of *c.*1780 attributed to her hand (see plate 24) is painted pink, over which small portrait medallions and Antique urns are arranged as miniature pictures within a border of colourful

21. Pennsylvania-German painted dower chest, *c.*1785.
(The American Museum in Britain, Bath)

22. Faux-bamboo chair, *c.* 1830.
(Mrs Monro, London)

garlands of flowers. Kauffmann's highly polished style was eminently well suited to the refined sobriety heralded by Neoclassicism. Bartolozzi's engravings of her work ensured the widespread popularity of her subjects, and copies soon appeared on tables and the tôle surfaces of trays, painted freehand by gifted lady amateurs.

The vogue for painted furniture was given greater impetus during the Regency period with the publication of several handbooks devoted to its techniques. Most important among these were Nathaniel Whittock's *The Decorative Painter's and Glazier's Guide* (1827) and J. Stoke's *The Complete Cabinet Maker* (1829). Whittock's manual gave step-by-step instructions for painting furniture, using either oil paints or distemper. Although the latter was cheaper and easier to apply, oils were generally preferred for their durability. Before painting, the wooden surface was primed with a coat of chalk, gesso or lead white. A wide range of colours could then be selected, most popular among them being king's yellow, verdigris (for green), ultramarine and prussian blue. Bright tints were used sparingly, while a selection of muddy earth shades – sienna, ochre, umber, vermilion and red lead – were reserved for covering large background expanses.

The imaginative (and sometimes whimsical) paint finishes created for the Brighton Pavilion, in imitation bamboo and ebony, set the fashion for *faux* furniture among the upper classes. These decorative pieces were used to furnish bedrooms and the entrance halls of country residences, and also combined well with the informal, interior schemes of villas and the flamboyant settings of shellwork grottoes. Pine was usually deemed the most suitable material, being soft and easy to carve, and could be rendered variously: marbled, stained or painted in solid blocks of colour; grained to simulate the natural markings of mahogany or rosewood; or modelled as fake bamboo with its coats of creamy-yellow paint segmented with black lines and flecked with brown speckles. Rush-seated chairs (made frequently in pairs) and small tables of Regency design were adorned characteristically with painted bands and pictorial emblems, brushed in turquoise, black and cream, in imitation of relief mouldings. Larger items such as dressing tables, washstands, desks and blanket chests featured scrolling foliage, bouquets and ribboned swags, painted in pastel hues, or *en grisaille* for a muted effect.

Whereas examples of English painted pine conformed to a decorative approach which was largely subdued, American productions were boldly colourful and buoyant. In the Pennsylvania-German tradition, pieces were painted in brilliant primary shades of solid colour. Tulips, hearts, doves, mythological beasts and the symbolic 'tree-of-life' pattern were the most pervasive designs, many of which were executed freehand by commercial artists, as well as by keen amateurs. For those lacking confidence, there were always stencils to rely upon, to steady shaky hands.

Dower chests (made for storing a young girl's handiworks, and her dowry of fine linens) frequently displayed exquisite workmanship. Such pieces were often lovingly painted by the girl herself, or by a talented member of the family, and were presented as gifts upon her marriage. Pictorial devices and small

23. Wardrobe decorated with exquisite, hand-painted oriental scenes and motifs. English, *c.* 1820.
(Alistair Sampson Antiques Ltd, London)

24. Angelica Kauffmann's half-table, displaying lavish decorations of flowers, medallions and antique urns, *c.*1780. *(By courtesy of the Trustees of the Victoria and Albert Museum, London)*

landscape scenes were the most popular decorations, and were sometimes applied to multicoloured backgrounds, sponged or combed with abstract patterns. The surfaces could also be finger-painted into giant swirls and wave-like configurations in bold, free-flowing style.

For accomplished young ladies, the fashionable seminaries in New England provided instruction in painting techniques, and furniture decoration was often included in the tuition. A fine drop-leaf table (in the Shelburne Museum, Vermont), painted with floral still lifes and an elegant landscape, exemplifies the schoolgirl style. In common with the majority of painted furniture, it is unsigned.

Housewives, too, took to ornamenting small kitchen accessories such as candle- and knife-boxes, which they painted in brilliant colours. The usual presentation consisted of a solid background, over which a range of lively motifs of contrasting shade was applied. American journals such as *Petersen's Magazine* and *Godey's Lady's Book* kept their readers informed of the latest fashions and decorations, while in England, recipes for mixing colours and instructions for their application appeared regularly in Victorian manuals. In *Cassell's Household Guide* (1875), for example, directions for marbling 'tables . . . or the panels of pilasters, etc., in chimney-pieces' were included. Imitation malachite was also recommended, and could be rendered easily by '. . . taking a little black paint, very much thinned, and working it round with the tip of the finger, so as to form concentric rings, and then painting it over with emerald green'. Watercolour drawing on wood was suggested as a commendable exercise, and one which afforded 'amusement and instruction hand in hand . . . for . . . taste cannot be too earnestly cultivated'. Directions for painting wooden salad servers and *bonbonnières* in the oriental style, using watercolours or tinted sepia, were accompanied by line drawings so that, 'with the exercise of a little ingenuity with which we credit our readers, these designs can be adapted to any size or shape required'.

Today, painted furniture has lost none of its appeal, and specialist paint finishes and trompe-l'oeil techniques are the bread and butter of every interior decorator. Indeed, the fashion for amateur painting has turned full circle and the present day enthusiast, like the Regency gentlewoman, can pursue her hobby armed with a wealth of ready-cut stencils and instructional handbooks.

BAMBOOING A CHAIR

Chairs moulded with carved rings for 'bambooing' can sometimes be found, although almost any piece of simply designed furniture may be employed for the purpose, particularly if composed of dowel-shaped sticks of wood. Chairs are an excellent subject for faux bamboo, and look especially effective if the colours selected follow those used during the early nineteenth century – the heyday of painted furniture.

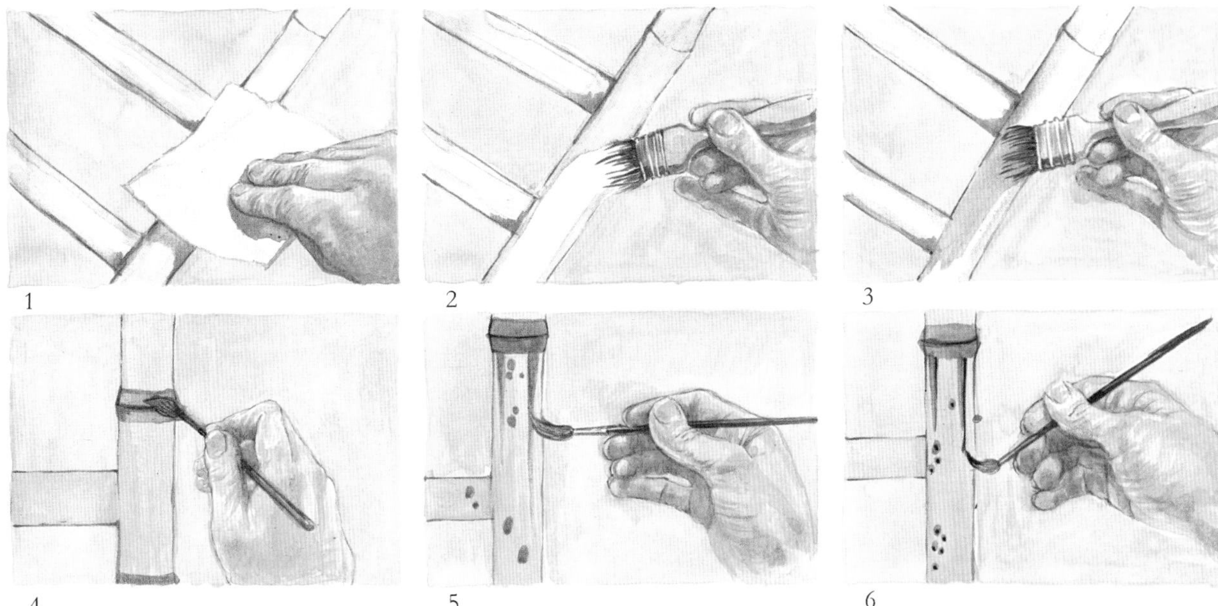

1 2 3 4 5 6

Materials
white eggshell paint – silk finish oil based
flat white oil paint
white spirit
oil colours: raw sienna, raw umber, black, ultramarine
linseed oil
silk finish polyurethane clear varnish
rag
flat bristle brush
sable brushes: sizes 3 or 4, and 5 or 6
containers, (non-plastic) to mix paint in
medium-fine sandpaper

Method

1. If it is already painted, the chair should be rubbed down with sandpaper to provide a 'key' for the new paint. Rub down the surface with a rag dipped in white spirit to clean off any grease. For new wood, undercoat the chair in a mixture of flat white oil paint thinned down with white spirit. Leave overnight to dry, then sandpaper the surface as the grain will have been raised by the paint.
2. In either case, now undercoat the chair with white eggshell paint. Two coats will probably be necessary, leaving each to dry overnight. Sand lightly again to remove any uneven areas.
3. Mix up the glaze in a creamy-brown bamboo colour:
   1 tsp flat white oil paint
   $\frac{1}{2}$ tsp linseed oil
   raw sienna and raw umber oil colours
   white spirit to thin it to a milky consistency

Apply the glaze as thinly and evenly as possible, using a flat bristle brush. Always brush in the direction of the wood grain. Paint up and down and around each 'stick' or part of the chair then finish off by dragging the paint lengthways, leaving fine lines made by the bristles of the brush. Work round the chair in this manner, up one leg and along the back, then down the next leg so that there is only one wet part to continue from. Leave to dry overnight. Apply a coat of varnish thinned down with white spirit to protect the chair. Again, leave to dry overnight.

4. Mix up a slightly thicker glaze in 'antique blue' for the bamboo rings:
   1 tsp flat white oil paint
   squeezes of ultramarine and raw sienna
   a dash of black
   white spirit to thin it

Paint the bamboo rings with a no. 5 or 6 sable brush at four or five-inch intervals around the legs and frame of the chair. The rings should be about $\frac{1}{2}$ in (1.2 cm) wide and as even as possible.

5. Paint the 'spines' of the bamboo at right angles to the rings – they should be about $1\frac{1}{2}$ in (3.7 cm) long and taper to a fine point away from the rings. Add a few round spots to represent the 'eyes' found in real bamboo. Vary the arrangement around each band to create a random, natural effect. Leave the chair to dry for a few hours.
6. Finally, add more black to the blue mixture to make it very dark. Using a no. 3 or 4 sable brush paint fine lines through the centre of each of the rings and down the middle of the spines. Put a dot in each of the 'eyes' and add a few more fine speckles around the centres. This shadowing defines and sharpens the trompe-l'oeil effect, making it look more realistic. Leave to dry overnight.
7. Apply a coat of eggshell varnish thinned down with a little white spirit to the whole chair for protection.

STENCILLING AND SPATTERWORK

When, with an old toothbrush, cardboard, and ink,
and with the ferns one has gathered and carefully
pressed, one has made a spatterwork lampshade,
one has done something delightful and useful.[1]

Frances Lichten, *Decorative Art of Victoria's Era*, 1950

The art of stencilling flourished in Europe and America in the eighteenth and nineteenth centuries, during which time the style was to become one of the most enduring and pervasive of traditional 'folk' decorations. Although the technique was known prior to this period, its application was restricted to a relatively small number of interior furnishings and objects. Textiles featuring stencilled patterns were inspired by their prototypes in silk and cotton which were produced in the Orient, and brought to the West along the well-established trade routes. Other subjects for decoration included monochrome woodcut illustrations, playing cards and flock wallpapers, whose repetitive designs during the seventeenth century were particularly suited to this method. The decorative potential afforded by stencilling – as a simple and inexpensive means of adding colour and ornament to any plain surface – was not fully exploited until the early 1700s, when new designs for interior schemes and furnishings were implemented.

The stencil decorations, of pictorial or abstract form, were first drawn onto a background of waxed paper, stiff fabric, wood or metal. The pattern was then cut out and the surrounding sheet either held firmly or fastened to the object to be ornamented. The cut-out sections could then be filled in with paint, using a stiff brush. Several colours could be applied to the same design by cutting an individual stencil for every shade employed, thus leaving each section to be worked separately, according to its tint.

By varying the colours and style of brush stroke, a rich diversity of effects could be achieved: from bold geometric configurations (such as those arranged on ceiling cornices and wall panels), to delicately mottled still lifes of flowers and fruit.

Among the most inventive patterns were those created in America by both professional stencillers and keen amateurs, who looked to the technique as a means of transforming even the most humble of rustic interiors. Due to the expense and scarcity of woven carpets, printed wallpapers and textiles from

25. American dower chest with stencilled flowers and painted scrolls on its top and sides, 1807.
(The Crane Gallery, London)

26. Early nineteenth-century American bedspread stencilled in bright colours with a basket of flowers, green foliage and red roses. The lower corners have been cut to accommodate bed posts. *(The American Museum in Britain, Bath)*

Europe, the early settlers of the 'new frontier' had few luxuries to relieve the starkness of their home environments. Stencilling provided an ideal medium with which to enliven the bare wooden floorboards and plain plastered walls with vibrant colours and rich patterning – at relatively little cost. Large canvas cloths imported from England (and later manufactured in America) could be stencilled readily and made attractive floor coverings, having the additional advantage of being moved easily from room to room. This replaced the arduous task of painting designs freehand, and since the stencil sheets could be re-used, identical motifs could be applied to various elements of the interior to create coordinated schemes of striking effect.

It was not unusual for small American homesteads to be decorated almost entirely with stencils, with their walls, floors and furnishings covered with well-defined areas of dense patterning. Floral bouquets and ribboned swags, pineapples and bowls of fruit, birds and animals were all popular subjects. In the nineteenth century, much of the work was executed by travelling professionals who, in exchange for their efforts, were provided with free room and board. Undoubtedly, the most ambitious projects were undertaken by skilled stencillers such as Lambert Hitchcock, Seth Thomas, George Lord and the Eaton brothers (several of whom employed women to cut the stencilled sheets to their own designs, or to those commissioned by the householder). It is likely, however, that small domestic objects were worked by lady amateurs, who also turned their hands to the stencilling of textiles such as tablecloths, coverlets and quilts (see pp. 118–25).

A fine example in 'reverse'-style is the pieced patchwork quilt in the Shelburne Museum (see plate 28), consisting of various spatterwork motifs of fern leaves, flowers and birds, all inspired by the paint-splashed, stencil techniques employed commonly for the adornment of floor coverings. By this method, a solid template is fastened to the surface and the paint colours flecked all around it, resulting in a 'negative' impression, with a background of delicate stippling.

Spatterwork was favoured during the Victorian period to ornament numerous domestic furnishings, from curtains and screens, to novelty lampshades and napkin rings. Pressed leaves and ferns were preferred 'templates', in keeping with the vogue for decorative woodland foilage. Their delicate shapes were pinned to a plain surface, over which a fine mist of paint or Indian ink was applied with the aid of a bristled brush and wire sieve. The negative impressions were highlighted by the profusely speckled backgrounds, sometimes executed in two or more colours for added richness.

With the recent revival of interest in country crafts and furnishings, stencilling has again become fashionable. Ready-made stencils can be purchased from interior-design shops, or traced directly from the patterns published in books devoted to the subject. Spatterwork, however, has remained comparatively obscure, in spite of the fact that its materials and methods of working are both simple and effective.

27. Detail from American wicker chair, one of a pair, painted with traditional fruit and flower motifs, nineteenth century. *(The Crane Gallery, London)*

28, 29. Nineteenth-century American patchwork quilt decorated in a bold diamond pattern displaying, alternately, geometric piecework and spatterwork. The 'negative' impressions are outlined by dark blue ink, 'spattered' through a sieve. *(Shelburne Museum, Shelburne, Vermont, USA)*

SPATTERWORK LAMPSHADE

Spatterwork can transform an ordinary lampshade into something richly decorative, especially if the colours are chosen to complement the setting. This one in deep green and gold is particularly elegant.

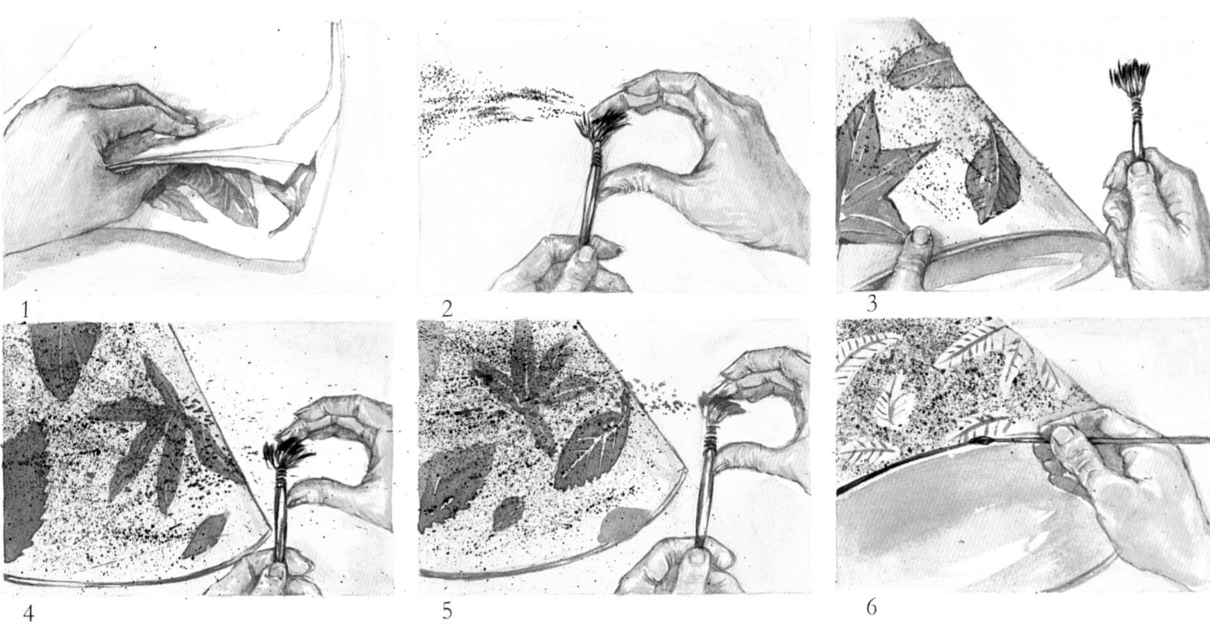

Materials
selection of leaves – ferns, maple and different serrated shapes if possible
newspaper
sheet of white cartridge paper
cream-coloured card or paper lampshade. Do not use one made of cloth or with a very glossy finish.
removable spray adhesive
2 stiff bristle brushes
artists' oil colours: black, lemon chrome, viridian, raw sienna, raw umber
flat white oil paint
white spirit
cotton rag
surgical rubber gloves
old plate for mixing paint

Method

1. Press the leaves overnight between sheets of newspaper under a heavy weight.
2. Practise the spraying technique by trying it first on a sheet of paper. Arrange some leaves on the sheet, fastening them down with a light coat of spray adhesive. Then mix up some paint on the plate. For a very dark, smart green, use just a dash of flat white oil paint to give it body, then add a combination of black, lemon chrome and viridian. For a muddy colour, add some raw umber. Thin the paint with white spirit, making it about the consistency of cream. Holding the paintbrush in one hand use the index finger of the other to pull the paint through the brush so that the paint spatters around the leaves. The range and depth of the spattering can be controlled by the amount of paint on the brush and by the distance between the brush and the surface. The size of the actual spots of paint depends on the consistency of the paint mixture. Thick paint produces small, light spots, while thinner paint will give larger spatters. Thin the paint with white spirit as necessary. If possible, work with the surface to be spattered in front of rather than below the brush as this reduces the risk of accidentally dropping large splodges. If very big drops are spattered by mistake, they can be blotted off carefully with a piece of rag. Spattering is a messy business. Do make sure to protect any nearby surfaces with newspaper and wear surgical rubber gloves to protect your hands.
3. Once the basic technique is mastered, start on the lampshade itself. Position the leaves lightly as before with the spray. To obtain the dark green-and-gold look, start with the dark green mixture as described, rotating the shade to get an even covering of paint.
4. Next, add some black oil paint to the green, plus more raw umber, again thinning it with some white spirit, and spatter the shade again to add depth and interest to the green.
5. Finally, using a clean brush and plate, mix a golden colour for the highlights. To a dash of flat white oil paint add raw sienna, plus a little lemon chrome and raw umber, to create a rich gold. Repeat the spattering process with this colour, until you have a lively contrast against the dark background. Leave the lampshade to dry overnight.
6. Remove the leaves carefully. The negative images left on the shade can be filled in by painting details such as backbones and veins using a sable paintbrush and the dark paint mixture. Start at the base of each shape and lift the brush away towards the tip. Apply each stroke as confidently as possible to create a light, spontaneous (rather than a laboured) look. To complete, paint the top and bottom edges of the shade in the dark green colour with a sable brush.

—PAPER—
PURSUITS
WITH SCISSORS AND
A POT OF GUM

INTRODUCTION

. . . O'er thee, my child, the good Delany bends
Directs thy scissors, and reveals her art . . .
Then mark the kind instructress, watch her hand
Her judgement, her inspiring touch attain;
Thy scissors make, like hers, a majic wand . . .

A poem for Mary Delany's niece, Georgina,
by George Keate, *c.*1778

While the artist relied on paper for drawing and sketching, the industrious gentlewoman of the eighteenth and nineteenth centuries turned to the material itself – not merely as a surface to paint on but also to create all manner of interior decorations. For those dexterous with sharp scissors and accomplished in meticulous cutwork, paper afforded an almost unlimited range of rich surface effects. Cut into thin strips, it could be rolled into elegant swirls for filigree work. Alternatively, pieces could be arranged into pictorial collages, or set under varnish, as in découpage. Sheets could be pierced into lacy valentine cards, or pricked with needles for subtle patterning. Profiles could be cut freehand as silhouettes, scraps mashed to pulp for modelling and tiny fragments glued into intricate mosaics.

As a schoolroom exercise, paperwork figured among the educational pursuits required of girls of good breeding in Europe and America. Tutors advertised their skills in filigree, découpage and cutwork, while enthusiasts at home relied on the instructions published in ladies' magazines and the designs published in pattern-books. An early recipe for 'paper-ware' appeared in the *Universal Magazine* in 1752, for modelling and decorating domestic items in imitation of oriental lacquer. The papier-mâché was made by boiling pieces of paper in water, mashing the mixture when soft, stirring in gum arabic and pouring the contents into a prepared mould. Once hardened and dry, the object was coated in 'strong Japan varnish', whose ingredients were also listed for brewing at home. Directions for découpage were included too, and appealed to those seeking an alternative finish for furniture and small objects.

From the recipes published in crafts manuals, it would appear that women were happy to slave over a hot stove to boil paper concoctions and dyes – perhaps their one and only time in the kitchen, which otherwise came under the exclusive domain of the cook and servants. For ladies not wishing to soil their hands, however, the fancy-work repositories such as Ackermann's in the Strand, London, provided all the requisite materials for paperwork, including a selection of coloured sheets and, for those completely lacking inspiration, patterns ready for tracing.

30. Page from a Victorian lady's scrap album, inscribed on the fly leaf 'Beatrice Allen from Aunt Georgina, May 27th 1872'. *(Christie's, London)*

31. Portrait of Princess Elizabeth (third daughter of George III) depicted with scissors and paper in hand. Pencil and wash, signed Henry Edridge, *c.* 1804.
(Copyright Her Majesty The Queen, Royal Library, Windsor Castle)

During the Victorian period, paper enthusiasts found new sources of design as ladies snipped their leisure hours away to fill the pages of their scrapbooks. Handscreens cut from thick card and painted with flowers made elegant displays, particularly when held 'to shelter a fair complexion' from the heat of the fireplace. As a young girl, Queen Victoria cut her own handscreen, which she decorated with gilded leaves under the guidance of her governess, Fräulein Lehzen. Others turned to the charity bazaar to which they contributed their paper wares, as Mrs Trollope described in her satirical account, the *Domestic Manners of the Americans* (1828):

> She enters the parlour appropriated for the meeting, and finds seven other ladies, very like herself . . . she presents her contribution, which is accepted with a gentle circular smile, her parings of broadcloth, the ends of ribbon, her gilt paper, and her minikin pins . . . with which the table is already covered . . . . She also produces from her basket three ready-made pincushions, four ink-wipers seven paper matches, and a paste-board watch-case; these are welcomed with acclamations, and the youngest lady present deposits them carefully on shelves, amid a prodigious quantity of similar articles.

FILIGREE PAPERWORK

'I am glad,' said Lady Middleton to Lucy, 'you are not going to finish poor little Annamaria's basket this evening; for I am sure it must hurt your eyes to work fillagree by candlelight.'

Jane Austen, *Sense and Sensibility*, 1811

32. One of a pair of early nineteenth-century flower pictures worked in paper filigree in gold and pastel shades.
(Mallett and Son (Antiques) Ltd, London)

The style of rolled paper decoration known as 'filigree' or 'quilling' was a popular ladies' pastime during the late seventeenth and eighteenth centuries. It required little technical expertise other than patience and a certain dexterity with scissors, paper and glue, and the relative ease with which it could be worked made it a source of entertainment and diversion at social gatherings. In *Sense and Sensibility*, Elinor Dashwood offered to assist Lucy with her 'fillagree', remarking '... Perhaps ... if I should happen to cut out, I may be of some use ... in rolling her papers for her ... I should like the work exceedingly, if she would allow me a share in it'. Such joint efforts were not uncommon and it is likely that a number of intricate compositions were created by several pairs of hands – perhaps with one girl to paint, cut and roll the papers, and another to glue and apply them to the ornamental design.

The decorative art of quilling emerged during the medieval period in Europe, when it was employed chiefly to adorn ecclesiastical ornaments. The tinted papers were cut into thin strips and rolled tightly around a quill or similar implement, and then released to form freestanding coils and swirls. These were then assembled and stuck down to the surface piece by piece in 'mosaic' fashion, to create compositions of pictorial or abstract content. Gilded papers were used to imitate the rich filigree surfaces of burnished gold vessels and brocade embroideries, while cream-coloured vellum was rendered skilfully to resemble carved ivory and wood.

The technique of paper filigree was one of several exercises to be taken up in the late seventeenth century by well-bred young girls educated in the 'pretty arts', along with fancy needlework, music, dancing and 'limning'. Like the raised embroidery of the period, the process of quilling involved a form of cutwork and appliqué and in a few rare instances, the paper swirls were combined into surprisingly innovative, 'high' relief compositions. The portrait of Queen Anne, for example (see plate 122) depicts the wax figure dressed in a robe of coloured paper coils which extend in profusion onto the deep folds of the draped canopy and columns of the background. Other common enrichments included the use of small shells, metallic spangles, pieces of mica and paper cutouts of birds and animals, which appeared scattered among densely swirled sections of paper to adorn the exteriors of workboxes, jewellery caskets and baskets. The paper itself could be shaped into a

33. Cabinet decorated throughout with paper filigree and hand-painted plaques, described in contemporary sources as 'imitation mosaic'. English, *c.*1780.
(Lady Lever Art Gallery, Port Sunlight)

34. Hexagonal-shaped tea caddy decorated with glazed panels of paper filigree depicting stylized flowers and leaves. English, early nineteenth century. *(Phillips, London)*

number of curvilinear forms, such as spirals, volutes, scrolls and cone shapes, and their precise arrangement gave rise to many striking motifs and designs. Bold geometric and lacework patterns of radiating circles and squares were popular, as were urns and baskets overflowing with large blossoming flowers. The most accomplished pieces achieved an effect of great refinement, emphasized by their seemingly 'fragile' constructions and colours in gold and delicate shades of blue, pink, red and cream.

By the early 1700s the fashion for rolled paperwork declined in England, although its popularity in America appeared to remain intact throughout the eighteenth century. Its 'educational' merits were rated highly by the private schools established for well-to-do girls in Boston and throughout New England, and many fine panels of 'quill-work' (as the technique was referred to there) were created under the watchful guidance of tutors. Ornamental boxes, mirror frames and candle sconces in shaped wooden frames were worked with free-flowing filigree swirls during the period *c.*1710–30, adorned typically with vases of flowers, scrolling foilage and spiked cone motifs in burnished gold paper. Other materials such as pieces of mica, wax, shells, spangles and metal wires were added to the American designs, recalling the English Restoration style. Once complete, the girls dated and initialled their compositions with coils of stiff paper, or signed their names on labels which were attached to the reverse side of the object.

During the 1760s, the art of paper quilling returned to vogue in England, and remained popular for several decades thereafter. The publication of numerous articles and handbooks devoted to the technique helped to foster the creation of novel patterns. In *The Ladies' Magazine* of 1786, the exercise was recommended highly as '... an amusement to the female mind capable of the most pleasing and extensive variety; it may be readily acquired and purchased at a very trifling expense'. Precise instructions for making paper designs, accompanied by line drawings of filigree motifs, appeared alongside the text, both for the benefit of beginners and those lacking the confidence or artistry to create their own. Indeed, the revival of interest in quilling was given greater impetus by its embrace of a new challenging approach which, in its enthusiasm, appeared to demand the ingenious cramming together of hundreds of minute paper coils onto the surface. This exercise was alleviated only by the addition of a small, hand-coloured engraving or painted miniature, executed on silk, framed by a pen work border and panels of filigree paper.

The profuse patterns were applied to the surfaces of numerous objects. Trays, tea caddies, workboxes, wine coasters and mantelpiece ornaments made ideal subjects for decoration, although larger pieces of furniture such as fireside screens, tables, cabinets, picture and mirror frames were also selected by those advanced in the art. In keeping with the fashion for quilling, a number of cabinet makers constructed furniture in the popular Sheraton style especially for the purpose. Their designs featured single or multiple panelled sections, which could be 'filled in' subsequently with paper ornaments. The recesses were often later glazed to protect them from dust and damage. A fine cabinet and stand adorned with filigree designs (see plate 33) was described in *Macquoid's Catalogue* of the period as '... decorated in imitation of mosaic with birds, butterflies and flowers, in the centre of which are coloured prints after Morland'. Small wooden objects were also constructed sympathetically and featured, for example, attractive boxwood stringing around the panels to highlight the paper designs within. A box '... made for filigree work, with ebony mouldings, lock and key', accompanied by sixteen ounces (450 grammes) of coloured and gold papers was presented to George III's daughter, Princess Elizabeth, in 1791. Ready-to-assemble 'kits', complete with materials and instructions, were produced in large numbers to satisfy the demand for paper quilling, and examples could be ordered direct from specialist firms such as Davis and Elliott of New Bond Street, London.

The finest antique specimens dating from the period *c.*1795–1820 were adorned in the elegant Regency style with ribbons and bows, swags, wreaths and floral bouquets. Surface texturing was reserved for background areas, using tinted papers selected for their subtle gradations of tone. Occasionally, small chips of mica or mother-of-pearl were added for contrast and sparkle.

35. Detail of paper filigree work, from a nineteenth-century picture of a floral bouquet, one of a pair.
(Mallett and Son (Antiques) Ltd, London)

A Filigree Flower Picture

Based on a Georgian design, *c.* 1800

The art of 'quilling' can be practised readily by enthusiasts today. The basic techniques are relatively simple and, once made, the delicate paper coils can be used to great decorative effect. Creating and arranging the paper coils does require some patience and dexterity, but there is, however, no need either to make or use all the quills at once. This project makes an ideal starting point for beginners, since it is made up of only a few basic shapes.

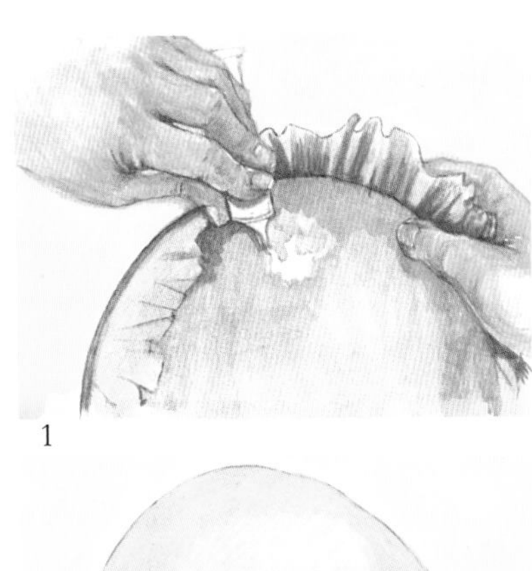
1

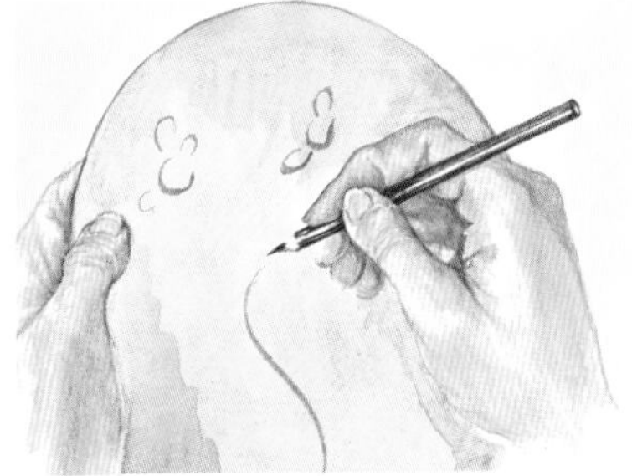
2

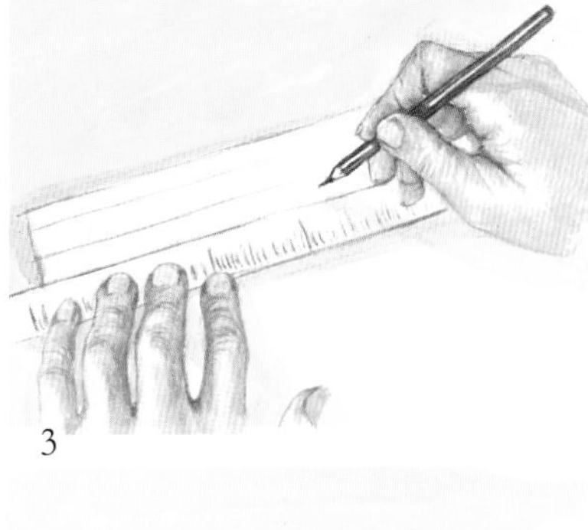
3

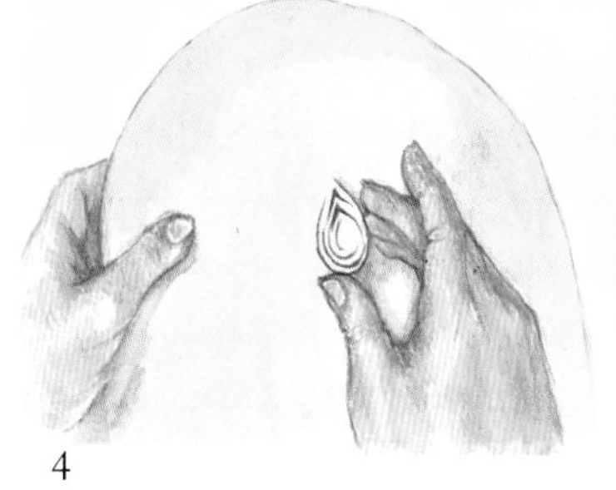
4

5

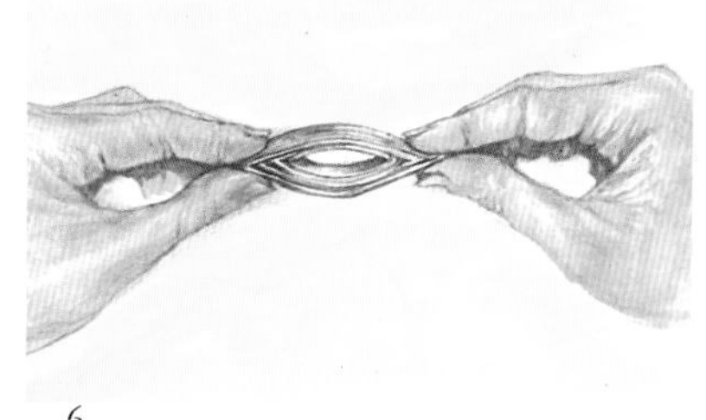
6

Materials

thick piece of cardboard, cut into an oval 8 in (20 cm) long and 6 in (15 cm) wide
piece of plain or glazed cotton cut larger than the cardboard oval, leaving a 1 in (2.5 cm) margin all round
sharp scissors
selection of coloured papers of similar thickness to writing paper
tweezers
quick-drying paper adhesive
cocktail sticks
ruler
large tapestry or wool needle
watercolour paints
metallic spray paints (optional)

Method

1. Make the background of the picture by covering the cardboard oval with the cotton fabric, wrapping the surplus material around the edges. Glue firmly into place on the back of the card.
2. Sketch the design lightly on the fabric. This will help to position the individual paper coils.
3. Measure and cut a sheet of coloured paper (or white paper which can be painted later) into thin, uniform strips 8 in (20 cm) long and $\frac{1}{8}$–$\frac{1}{4}$ in (3.5–5 mm) wide. Use the thin strips to make the branches by pulling each length over the edge of the ruler to create a curved effect.
4. Arrange these on the background, according to the sketch. Once assembled they can be glued on one edge and gently placed into position using the tweezers.

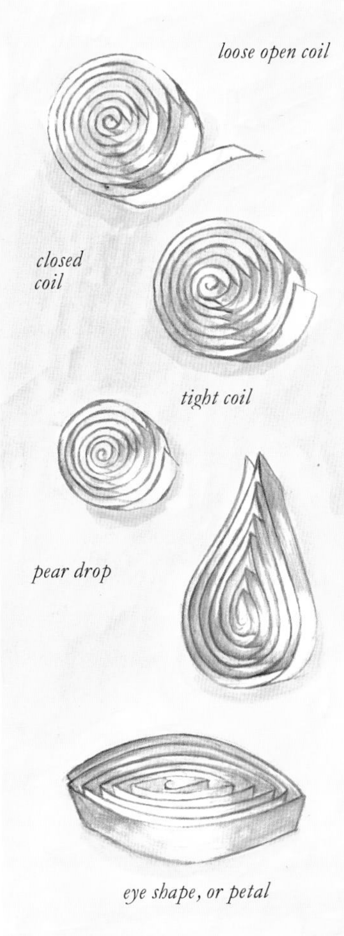

5. To make the leaves, take another strip of paper and wind it slowly and evenly round the needle or cocktail stick, wrapping it around tightly six or seven times to form a tight coil. Squeeze the coil gently to ensure that it is secure. Snip off any of the remaining paper strip and gently take the coil off the needle or cocktail stick. The loose end can be glued down to make a 'closed coil'.
6. Once the adhesive has dried, pinch the coil into a pointed 'leaf' shape. Altogether, around eighteen leaf shapes will be needed, which can be coloured afterwards either with watercolour paints using a damp brush (too much water may distort the paper), or with spray paint. Apply glue to the centre of the underside of each and press gently into place.

For the flowers, make fifteen large 'open coils' and arrange them in groups of two, three or four to form the petals. As above, apply glue to the centre of the underside of each and press onto the surface.

For the fly, make two large 'closed coils' to form the wings, pinching them into pointed 'pear' shapes for a more realistic effect. A smaller 'pear' shape will be required for the body and a 'tight coil' for the head. The legs can be made from two short lengths of paper.

The finished piece can be framed and glazed as a picture or used to decorate a greeting card.

SILHOUETTES

Clarissa draws her scissors from the case
to draw the line of poor Dan Jackson's face
One sloping line cut forehead nose and chin.
A nick produced a mouth and made him grin.
Miscellanies, Jonathan Swift, 1731

The making of 'shadow portraits' was one of many creative endeavours to be taken up by ladies of accomplishment during the last quarter of the eighteenth and the early nineteenth century. The figures were invariably depicted in profile and appeared in a variety of forms, from full-length portraits and busts, to genre scenes in cosy domestic settings. Among the most popular silhouettes were those executed in paper, mounted on backgrounds of contrasting shade (characteristically, in black-on-white combination) – a method of cutwork which appealed greatly to those adept with scissors and paste. Alternatively, the subjects were drawn in outline and painted by hand in Indian ink and 'lamp-black' watercolour onto paper or other surfaces such

36, 37. Details from silhouette cutouts, *above* and *below left*, of a woman dancing, 1837 and a woman seated at a piano, 1839. *(Ornamenta, London)*

as vellum, ivory or glass. Whichever technique was selected, an eye for accuracy was demanded of the worker in order to capture the true likeness and character of the sitter.

The term 'silhouette' was derived from the name of Louis XV's unpopular Controller General of Finance, Etienne de Silhouette (1709–69), whose tax reforms caused considerable uproar during the late 1750s. His hobby of cutting paper profiles was considered petty and unfashionable at a time when the finest portraits were executed in oils. Thus, what was regarded once as an unworthy pastime came to be known by the derogatory description 'silhouette' – a somewhat ironic course of events, since the 'art' was shortly to receive the patronage of both royalty and the genteel classes.

By the late eighteenth century, this unique form of portraiture was practised by professionals and novices alike. It should be borne in mind, however, that the work of gifted amateurs was often indistinguishable from that produced by trained experts (who were often paid handsomely for their efforts).

38. Traditional print-room decoration displaying silhouette pictures, with contemporary trompe-l'oeil medallions and tassled braids, inspired by nineteenth-century interior designs. *(Ornamenta, London)*

Indeed, in talented hands, the making of shadow portraits was elevated from a drawing-room amusement to that of an artistic medium, and was subscribed to with enthusiasm by many accomplished gentlewomen (and men) of the period. For Mary Delany (1700–88), for example, whose mastery in the field of paper 'mosaicks' was renowned in fashionable circles, the creation of silhouettes provided yet another opportunity to explore the intricacies of cutwork. She executed a small series of portraits of her friends and family, of which the majority appeared in reverse style. The subjects were cut out from a sheet of white paper leaving profile-shaped holes, and the sheet was then mounted on a black background so that the underlying colour could be seen through the pierced silhouettes above. These confident compositions were undoubtedly cut freehand, for in view of Mrs Delany's considerable abilities, it is unlikely that she would have resorted to any of the 'profile machines' which had become popular at the time. One novel contraption for tracing facial outlines was illustrated in the Dutch edition of Johann Casper Lavater's celebrated volume *Essays on Physiognomy* (1775–8). The sitter was placed in a special chair with his face against a translucent screen which, when lit from the front, cast a shadow. This could then be traced on the other side of the screen by the artist. The book enjoyed widespread success, and with its concise instructions and advice on shadow portraiture, it was considered an invaluable introduction to the art. Betsy Sheridan, sister of the playwright, was one of many to applaud its merits, as she described in a letter of 1788, '... I have been reading Lavater and intend becoming wise in my judgements on the cut of people's faces'.[1]

One of the most distinguished amateur silhouet-

39. Silhouette group of the Parminter family painted in 1783 by the French artist Francis Torond. Jane Parminter is seen watering plants, behind her sister, Elizabeth, who is seated. Both were exponents of the art of cut-paper and fancy work.
(A la Ronde, Exmouth)

tists was Princess Elizabeth (1770–1840), third daughter of George III. In an album of her work (in the Royal Collection, Windsor Castle), paper cutouts and drawings in Indian ink depicting the Royal Family, genre scenes and allegorical subjects recall the elegance of the pastime. Other gifted enthusiasts were Amelia Alderson (1769–1853), wife of the artist John Opie; and Mrs Leigh Hunt, who created a series of light-hearted silhouettes during the early nineteenth century, including an informal portrait of Byron, cut in white paper.[2]

In America, the gentlewoman Eleanor Custis, step-granddaughter of George Washington, created silhouette cutouts of the then elderly President and his wife, Martha, at their Mount Vernon residence.[3] It is likely that girls of similar background received some degree of training in the fashionable technique at the exclusive private schools established for instruction in the ornamental arts.

The vogue for shadow portraiture was by no means confined to the drawing rooms of the genteel classes, however, and it is interesting to note that several women turned to the commercial aspects of the art and became professional silhouettists – braving both the scorn of 'Society', and of their male colleagues. One of the first to show such initiative was Mrs Isabella Beetham, who opened her Fleet Street studio in 1782, where she created silhouettes in both cut paper and paint. She also devised miniature shadow portraits to adorn memorial jewellery. The acclaimed profiler Mrs Sarah Harrington was another to establish her own business during the late eighteenth century, and her delicate portrayals in cut paper and silk were highly regarded at the time. Josiah Wedgwood's jasper-ware medallion of the author Maria Edgworth was reproduced from the profile executed by her hand.

With the advent of photography by the mid-nineteenth century, the decorative art of shadow work lost its momentum. The technique, however, did not disappear entirely from the array of interior 'elegancies' to which Victorian ladies were devoted – and found a new place among the mementos of the scrap album and visitor's book.

40. Silhouette family group cut from black paper, mounted on a contrasting white background. English, *c.*1820.
(Mrs Monro, London)

SILHOUETTE GREETING CARD

For those skilled in drawing, silhouettes can be executed freehand on paper or card using Indian ink or black paint. Once complete, the image can be cut and mounted onto a background of contrasting colour. Alternatively, Lavater's method for tracing profiles can be used to obtain an exact image, which can then be reduced and mounted to make a picture or greeting card. Decorative border designs may be added to frame the image, using gold ink or paint.

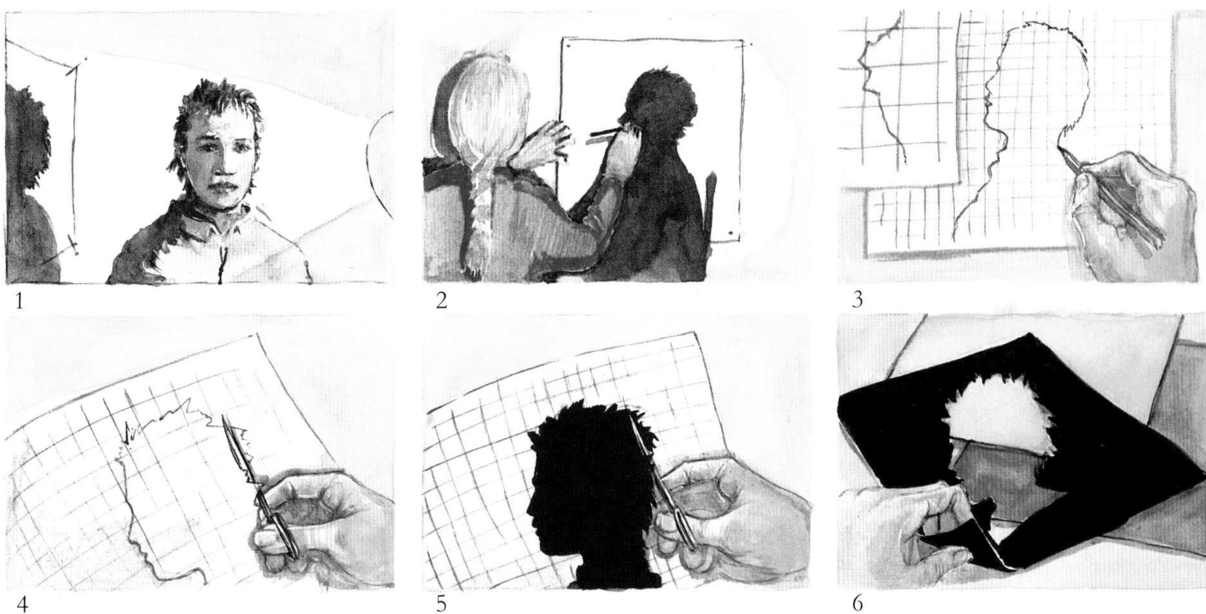

Materials
sheet of white cartridge paper 10 × 12 in (25 × 30 cm)
masking tape
adjustable desk lamp with 100 watt bulb
sharp pencil
stiff card 5 × 6 in (12.5 × 15 cm)
sharp scissors
sheet of white paper 5 × 6 in (12.5 × 15 cm)
Indian ink or black paint
paper adhesive
fine paint brush
black card 6 × 7 in (15 × 17.5 cm)
gold paint or ink (optional)

Method
1. Choose a room with a wall space free of pictures or fitments and draw the curtains so that it is reasonably dark. Place the subject in profile against the blank wall and shine the light on the face, so that a shadow is cast on the wall behind.
2. Attach the paper to the wall with the tape so that it catches the shadow, moving the subject, the light or both backwards and forwards until a full profile fits on the sheet. Trace the outline of the profile carefully onto the paper.
3. To reduce the profile to half size, draw a grid of thirty 2 in (5 cm) squares over the sheet. On the piece of card, draw a grid of thirty 1 in (2.5 cm) squares. Transfer the profile to the smaller sheet by copying the outline square by square.
4. Cut out very carefully and use this profile as a template. Draw round it on the small piece of cartridge paper, cut out and mount on black card.
5. Alternatively, a more traditional silhouette can be made by painting the profile black, cutting it out and mounting it on white card.
6. Hollow cutouts can be made by cutting out the inner portion of the profile, making sure the border remains intact. The border can then be glued to a card of contrasting colour.

PAPER CUTOUTS AND PINPRICKING

The little poppets are very well cut, but you must take more pains about the trees and shrubs . . . and the leaves must be shaped and cut distinctly . . . most of the paper I have cut has cost me much pains. . . .

From a letter written by Mary Delany to her sister, Anne, *c.*1733[1]

Few genteel occupations attracted a lady's attention more than her fancy work with coloured paper, sharp scissors and a pot of gum. These simple materials were all that were required to create a striking series of decorative pictures, imitation bouquets and exquisite valentine cards, which found their place in the home and among the cherished lacework patterns of the scrap album.

The fashion for paper cutouts emerged in Europe and America during the second half of the eighteenth century, and over the course of the next one hundred years, the pictorial character of the craft was displayed in lively genre scenes, allegorical subjects and still lifes. Blossoming shrubs set in urns, baskets of wild flowers and foliage wreaths and swags were conveyed in considerable detail, with their finely pierced outlines full of the minutest areas of patterning – from the sharp serrated edges of leaves to the elegant formations of petals. Marie Antoinette was one of several distinguished gentlewomen to subscribe to the 'art' (which she described as *découpure*) and her flair for design is evidenced in the delicate tracery of flowers and birds which she cut in white paper during the 1780s (in the Cooper-Hewitt Museum, New York).

41, 42. Two paper 'mosaicks' by Mary Delany (1700–88): *Æsculus Hippocastanum, Horse Chestnut, left*, and *Tamus communis, Black Briony, above*, which incorporates a real leaf, *lower centre*.
(By courtesy of the Trustees of the British Museum, London)

Precision in cutting necessitated the use of tiny scissors, such as the pair still preserved at *A la Ronde* in Exmouth, Devon, home of Jane Parminter and her young cousin, Mary, who created many splendid interior decorations in paper, shells and feathers (see plates 105, 106). A fine example of their cutwork is the allegorical picture, *The Shepherd and the Philosopher*, inspired by Alexander Pope's *A Fable Gay* (1742). The woodland scene and characters appear as crisp cutwork reliefs, set above a decorative frieze of interlaced and pinpricked paper and pierced calligraphy.

The technique of pinpricking occurred frequently in conjunction with cutwork. Other popular objects for this decoration were fashion plates, such as those issued in ladies' magazines of the period. The punctured designs were executed by means of variously sized steel needles, fixed onto handles to facilitate working. The paper was pierced at intervals, in an orderly manner, to produce a myriad of tiny stippled patterns. On fashion prints, pinpricking was employed to emphasize details of costume, and to convey embossed and other textured effects. The largest holes were reserved for bold outlines such as the pleats and folds of drapery, while plain surface areas were filled with hundreds of dot-like perforations, which were sometimes so minute that they were almost invisible.

Instructions for pinpricking were included in *The Young Ladies' Book; a Manual of Elegant Recreations, Exercises and Pursuits* (1829) by 'A. Lady', for decorating '. . . Turkish and other figures in Oriental costume'. The text recommended the use of '. . . watercolour painting for the features, with a series of small punctures made with needles of various sizes for the dresses . . . the folds of drapery are marked with a tracing needle'.

Pinpricked pictures and prints were often mounted on paper backgrounds of contrasting colour, to highlight the multi-patterned surfaces. In England, the finest examples of the combined effects of cutwork and pinpricking were achieved during the early nineteenth century by the gifted invalid Amelia Blackburn. Her flamboyant compositions of exotic birds, serpents, fish and foliage appeared in bold monochrome style (see plate 44).

In America, both cutwork and pinpricking flouri-

43. Paper picture depicting a flowering tree, parrots and winged cherubs, dated 1748.
(The Trustees, Cecil Higgins Art Gallery, Bedford)

shed as a 'parlour art' during the late eighteenth and early nineteenth centuries. Paper valentine cards pierced with scrolling hearts and flowers, saw-tooth patterned wheels and other stylized motifs were favoured designs in the Pennsylvania-German taste. Nationalistic emblems such as the eagle and American flag, and 'Liberty' slogans, were also popular decorations for small greeting cards and pictures, and recalled the folk art traditions of contemporary patchwork, hooked rugs and stencils. Many examples were signed and dated by their makers, and their charming naivety suggests that they were the work of young girls.

Apart from narrative scenes and still-life compositions, paper cutouts of coats of arms and other heraldic devices enjoyed a brief vogue in England during the second half of the eighteenth century. Several appeared of miniature size, no more than one or two inches (two and a half or five centimetres)

44. Cut and pinpricked paper picture by Amelia Blackburn, probably executed during the 1830s.
(By courtesy of the Trustees of the British Museum, London)

high, and were executed by professional 'herald painters' such as Nathaniel Bermingham, who advertised his skills as an '... improver of the curious art of cutting ... with the points of a pen knife'.[2] This style of cutwork was soon subscribed to by amateurs, and in keeping with the trend, the *New Lady's Magazine* for 1786 provided a series of pattern sheets and instructions for beginners.

In the talented hands of the ever-industrious Mary Delany, cutwork was transformed from a scissor craft to that of a 'painterly' art form of breathtaking originality. She embarked upon her invention of 'paper mosaicks' at the age of seventy-two, combining her skills as an artist and keen observer of nature to portray nearly 1,000 flowers of both common and exotic variety. These floral compositions, which she referred to affectionately as 'Flora Delanica', were created from tiny snippets of cut paper, each tinted its natural shade and assembled delicately onto black-inked backgrounds in overlapping layers. The painstaking methods to which she subscribed reflected an unwavering accuracy for botanical detail, and an '... unerring instinct for perfect grouping' – culminating in what one critic described as their 'radiant vitality'.[3] Mrs Delany's efforts continued, virtually uninterrupted, over the course of ten years, until failing eyesight could no longer sustain the precision required for this unique form of cutwork. Towards the end of her life, she composed a verse of 'Farewell' to her beloved flowers:

> The time has come! I can no more
> The vegetable world explore ...
> No more with admiration see
> Its beauteous form and symmetry ...
> Farewell! to all those friendly powers
> That blest my solitary hours ...[4]

The collected albums of her works are now housed in the British Museum, London (see plates 41, 42).

PAPER FLOWER COLLAGE

This delicate paper mosaic is inspired by Mrs Delany's 'Flora Delanica', whose flower collages each comprised hundreds of meticulously cut and coloured pieces of paper. Although considerably more simple than those of Mrs Delany, the project outlined here uses the same principles: not only the basic shapes but also the colour variations within each petal or leaf are made from separate paper pieces.

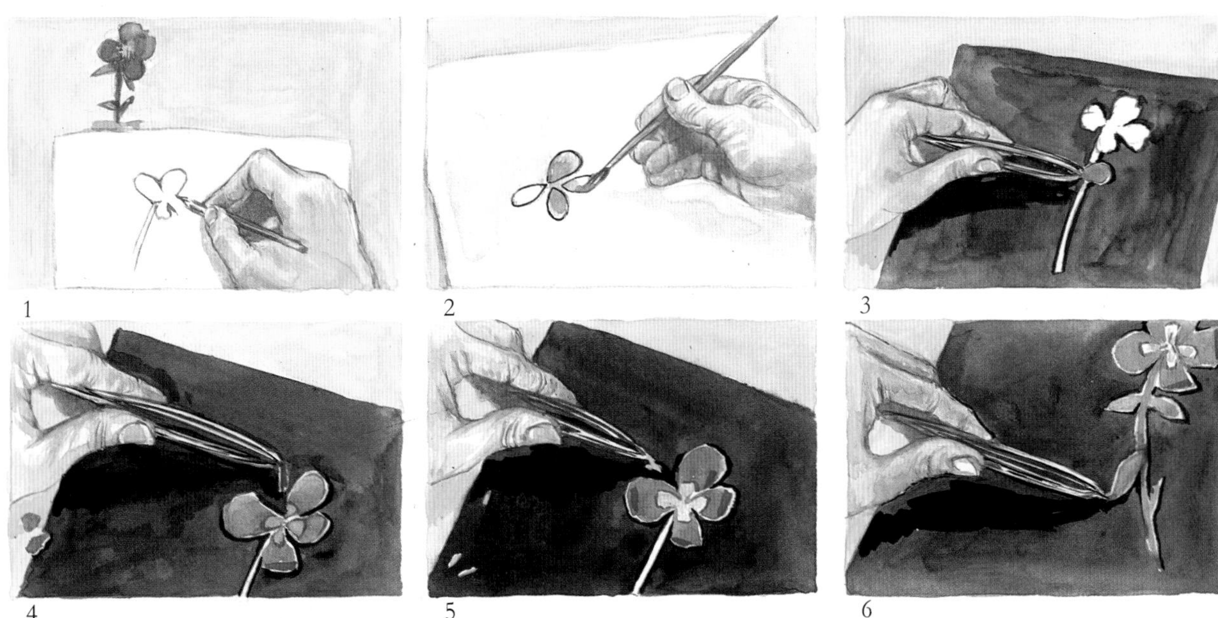

Materials
one freshly cut flower
several sheets of white cartridge paper
sheet of black paper 8 × 10 in (20 × 25 cm)
sharp pencil
fine watercolour paintbrushes
watercolour paints
small, sharp scissors or craft knife
tweezers
paper adhesive

Method
1. Place the flower in a vase so that its head and leaves fall naturally. Ignoring the individual petal and leaf shapes for the moment, draw the outline of the whole flower on a sheet of white paper. Cut it out carefully and glue it onto the black sheet.
2. Taking each of the flower's petals in turn, draw its outline on another sheet of white paper, leaving space between each so that it can be cut out easily. Mix some paint to match the predominant shade of each petal and, working in light brush strokes from the base of the petal to the tip, fill in each shape. Try to vary the depth of colour with each stroke to give a realistic effect.
3. Once the paint is dry, cut the petals out and glue them to the original outline, using the tweezers to place them accurately.
4. Following the natural shading within each petal, now draw, on a fresh piece of paper, the shapes formed by some of the shaded areas. Mix up some more paint according to the new shades and, using the same light brush strokes as above, fill in each sliver of paper. Cut out and glue into place, blending the tones of this new piece with those of the previous one as necessary. Build up every petal in this way – the number of pieces of paper used will depend on the degree of shading on the fresh flower, and your own enthusiasm.
5. Once the petals are in place, make the flower's stamens and centre, applying the same techniques of drawing, painting, cutting and glueing. Further layers of petals can then be added, overlapping the centre of the flower to create a realistic, three-dimensional effect.
6. Finally, draw the shapes of the individual leaves, stems and veins on another piece of paper. Mix the paints to produce a range of green tints and paint as above. Cut out each piece carefully and glue onto the original outline. Once complete, the collage can be framed and glazed for protection.

DECOUPAGE

To those who before never attempted any thing of this nature, to whom tis a perfect Terra incognita, an undiscovered Province; for their sakes I shall willingly . . . shew . . . the way of working some Patterns in this Book . . . . Any part of these may be placed on the work, as the fancy and ingenuity of the undertaker shall direct . . .

John Stalker and George Parker, *A Treatise of Japanning and Varnishing*, 1688

45. Mid-nineteenth-century Dutch mixed-media collage using cut and painted paper and embroidery. Every piece of paper is pasted individually onto the background. Signed Nicholas Hambrouck.
(Ian G. Hastie Antiques, Salisbury)

Découpage was another 'scissor art' to which ladies of leisure turned their attention during the late seventeenth and eighteenth centuries, and it provided a suitably 'genteel' alternative to snipping away at silhouettes and lacy paper cutouts. Its step-by-step methods were simple and involved little more than cutting decorative paper scraps and prints, colouring them, and arranging them into pleasing patterns on the exteriors of furniture and small objects. The scraps were then glued in place and coated with numerous layers of varnish. Under these lustrous surfaces, the prints imitated the effects of freehand painting, as well as highly-prized lacquerware (with its lively pictorial scenes), imported into Europe from the Far East. Indeed, with the immense vogue for oriental lacquer (and the scarcity of pieces during the late 1600s due to disruptions in trade), European imitations *à la chinois* were all the rage. Découpage in the chinoiserie taste embraced the fashion for exotica, and became the chief inspiration for amateurs, who were supplied with no end of printed vignettes of pagodas, mandarins and flamboyant foliage.

In Italy, découpage was translated as *lacche povere*, or 'poor man's lacquer' (a somewhat misleading description since the prints were expensive, and the 'art' reserved for a wealthy elite), while in France it was called *découpure*. The latter term, for cut paperwork, appeared in numerous French accounts of the period, as on the floral ornament cut by Marie Antoinette in *c.*1780 inscribed with the words '*Découpure faite par la reine*' (in the Cooper Union Museum, New York). In England and America, the process known as japanning – using black and tinted varnishes to simulate oriental lacquer – went hand in hand with découpage as the chief source of decoration, and directions for it were seldom published without a selection of printed scraps for cutting out.

One of the first crafts manuals devoted to the subject was *A Treatise of Japanning and Varnishing* (1688) by John Stalker and George Parker. Its recipes for 'guilding, burnishing and lackering' were accompanied by more than one hundred 'distinct Patterns ... in Imitation of the Indians, for Tables, Stands, Frames, etc. ... Curiously Engraven on Twenty-four large Copper-Plates'. The black-and-white engravings of oriental landscapes, animals, figures and floral bouquets (all that was then perceived exotic, or 'Indian' – a term used indiscriminately to describe almost any foreign design, regardless of origin) were rendered in primitive fashion, in a jumble of both European and Chinese stylizations. Small printed motifs, for amateurs seeking a quick 'finish', were provided for pasting onto powder and patch boxes, combs, brushes, workboxes and jewellery caskets for 'Ingenious Ladies ... shall put them into practice'.

Stalker and Parker's *Treatise* was aimed at an audience of 'Nobility and Gentry', and was an important source of reference for amateurs. Indeed, the writers emphasized that their instructions could be relied on with confidence '... and if any Gentlemen or Ladies, having met with disappointments in some of the Receipts, do question the truth and reality of them, they may for their satisfaction ... see them tried by the Auther'. As a pattern book, not only for découpage, but also for embroidery, painting and penwork decoration, Stalker and Parker's volume served as a worthy companion for the industrious gentlewoman of the late seventeenth century.

The fashion for japanning and découpage emerged in America during the early 1700s, when it was introduced as a refined recreation for well-bred young girls in New England. In Boston (which could boast of at least a dozen professional japanners during the years 1712–71), instruction in the art figured prominently in the ornamental syllabuses of ladies' seminaries. A Mrs Hiller offered tuition in japanning from 1725–48, as did numerous other instructresses who advertised their skills in the pages of the *Boston Gazette*. In 1739, Mr John Waghorne announced that he '... had lately received a fresh parcel of materials for the new method ... which was invented in France, for the amusement and benefit of the ladies, and is now practised by most of the Quality Gentry in Great Britain with the greatest satisfaction'. As was usually the case, American fashions depended on whatever was currently the rage in Europe, and advertisements were littered with phrases boasting of the very latest trend in 'civilized' living.

The taste for chinoiserie remained prevalent in Europe during the second half of the eighteenth century, only becoming more exuberant under the influence of Rococo and, later, Neoclassicism. For découpage enthusiasts, new sources of design could be found in the prints of the French artist Jean Pillement, whose picturesque vignettes *à la chinois* subscribed to the period elegance. His blend of

46. Detail from a panel of a Victorian scrap screen; once glued down, the coloured paper pieces were varnished for protection, *c.*1860. *(By courtesy of Loot, London)*

whimsical motifs, notably the *singeries* (or monkey characterizations) and other exotic devices, set a precedent for bolder and more exhilarated compositions. This style was also taken up by Antoine Watteau and Jacques Gabriel Hucquier, whose engraved designs made admirable cutouts.

Pillement's plates were published in London, 1757–64, as were the works of other European artists whose chinoiserie patterns were printed by Robert Sayer in his book, *The Ladies Amusement, or the whole art of Japanning Made Easy* (1762). Sayer compiled over 1,500 hand-coloured designs for his readers to cut out 'for joining in groups or to be placed singly'. The motifs consisted of a fanciful selection of flowers, shells, rockwork landscapes, oriental pavilions, figurines and mythological beasts, which the publisher emphasized must be 'neatly cut round with sicsars or the sharp point of a knife ... (and) brushed on the back with strong gum water or thin paste'. For japanning, seven coats of 'seedlac' (varnish) were recommended, although 'twelve are better still'. Instructions and recipes for ornamenting any surface – from 'a superb cabinet to the smallest toilet article' – were followed by suggestions for compositional arrangement. Sayer advised that 'if the scene be European, in the body of your design ... (choose) no exotic or preposterous object ... we have seen a butterfly supporting an elephant and things equally absurd'. If the amateur was to show restraint in her choice of subjects, she was permitted some leeway in the creation of things 'grotesque', for which 'wild connections between beasts with flowers (and) shells with birds' were considered appropriate.

The vogue for eastern exotica declined by the early nineteenth century, and découpage was given new impetus under the guise of Victorian sentimentalism. Brightly coloured relief-embossed scraps were published in Europe and America from the 1830s onwards and provided amateurs with ready-made emblems to paste onto large folding screens, blanket chests or the pages of 'token' albums (see pp. 78–83). The pictorial images embraced all the Victorian favourites – storybook characters, enchanting children, pets, flowers and costume fashions – and could be purchased in sheet form, ranging from a dozen to many hundreds of cutouts per plate. Découpage scrap-screens for children's nurseries were a popular source of decoration, and were recommended by *Cassell's Household Guide* (1875) as

47. One of a pair of mid-eighteenth-century French gouache and découpage pictures, showing 'the nobility gardening'. *(Ian G. Hastie Antiques, Salisbury)*

'... something at once permanent and ornamental ... and (an) amusing occupation ... for long evenings'. The worker was advised to arrange her scraps 'pell-mell ... (or) in studied confusion', while comic effects could be achieved by cutting out '... an umbrella and placing it as if held by a duck; or transfix a pair of spectacles to the countenance of a lion'.

During the twentieth century, découpage has continued to capture a wide audience of craftsmen and novices alike. In America, Caroline Duer's furniture recalls the splendour of eighteenth-century chinoiserie and Rococo, featuring printed cutouts by Pillement and Boucher. The revival of découpage chinois was also subscribed to during the first half of the century by the artists Lovina Kenyon and Helen Hinchliffe, and in Europe, the decoration took new inspiration from the stylish and extravagant presentations of Art Deco. The richly lacquered furniture of Eileen Gray embraced the elegance of the period décor, while the French artist Jean Dunand experimented with novel materials – embedding crushed eggshells, for instance, into his lacquer surfaces in the spirit of découpage.

The Art of Paper Flowers

We forsee the time when paper flowers will, in abundance, adorn every home that has any pretensions to taste.

*The Englishwoman's Corvezzione, c.*1845[1]

The making of imitation floral bouquets and plants using sheets of coloured paper was one of several pastimes taken up by the Victorian gentlewoman, ever keen to display her accomplishments and industry in fancy work. In a period which gave rise to the lady floriculturist (who hitherto had not been permitted to take an active interest in gardening), the theme of flowers became the focal point for all her various artistic pursuits in painting, canvas work, wax-modelling and paper cutouts. 'Flowers teach the lessons of patient submission, meek endurance, and innocent cheerfulness' wrote one contemporary observer, and if these virtues were upheld by the majority, then what better means of aspiring to them than through the 'favourable influences' of the home crafts.

Encouraged by journals such as the American *Godey's Lady's Book*, whose motto, 'There can be no excellence without industry', promoted a great deal of amateur craftsmanship, women turned to the decoration of their homes with new enthusiasm. Among the over-stuffed Berlin-work cushions, shell-work boxes, wax fruits and gilt-leather picture frames – all diligently created by the lady of the house – artificial flowers and plants soon found a ready place in the parlour and conservatory. Paper varieties were also displayed at the ubiquitous charity bazaars, where the latest achievements in handicrafts were exhibited among the usual litter of pincushions, watchcase covers and ink wipers.[2] The imitation flowers did not go unnoticed, either, by the doyennes of fashion, who suggested that they be worn as hair wreaths, dress corsages or held in the hand as nosegays. These small cone- or mushroom-shaped bouquets (described by one critic as 'French vulgarities') were considered indispensable accompaniments for all social occasions.

Instructions for making paper flowers at home were included in Victorian magazines devoted to the 'minor arts'. In the article entitled *The Englishwoman's Corvezzione*, the imitation of plants was recommended as a means of ornamenting '... nooks and niches where, for the want of sufficient light, camelias, geraniums, fuchsias, etc., would refuse to flourish ... branches of ivy (one of the very best subjects for the student in flower making to begin upon) may be made to festoon ... the sides of bookshelves, brackets, vases, etc.' Interior schemes using abundant quantities of ivy were illustrated in numerous journals of the period, in keeping with the Victorian penchant for covering every conceivable surface with 'pretty fancies (and) felicities'.

The merits of paper-flower making were also extolled in *Cassell's Household Guide* (1875), in which the art was described as being 'capable of very high perfection ... unlike other accomplishments, the very earliest attempts of amateurs are at least pretty, even if unfit to decorate the drawing-room'. Beginners were urged to 'observe flowers well', since the success of artificial foliage depended on its 'imitation (of) nature'. Having selected a garden flower to serve as a model, the worker was then advised to 'pick it to pieces', so that its petals and other parts could be traced onto paper, which was then cut into the appropriate shapes. The paper petals were often crimped or ruffled to achieve a realistic effect, and afterwards hand-painted, glued and wired onto stems. For those unable to devise their own patterns, line drawings accompanied the text for making 'cabbage roses, half-blown rose buds, stamens and pistils, carnations, fuchsias, daisies and poppies'.

48. Basket of flowers cut from stiffened pieces of cream-coloured paper, the leaves and petals indented and ridged to achieve a realistic effect. Only the moths have been painted in muted colours. Probably English, *c.*1825.
(The Trustees, Cecil Higgins Art Gallery, Bedford)

BOUQUET OF PAPER DAISIES

The daisy was a favourite flower in the Victorian cottage garden and its cultivation was recommended by authorities such as Mrs Isabella Beeton in her popular volume *All About Gardening* (1861). The paper daisy is relatively simple to make, and several displayed together would make an attractive bouquet, either on their own or combined with other artificial varieties.

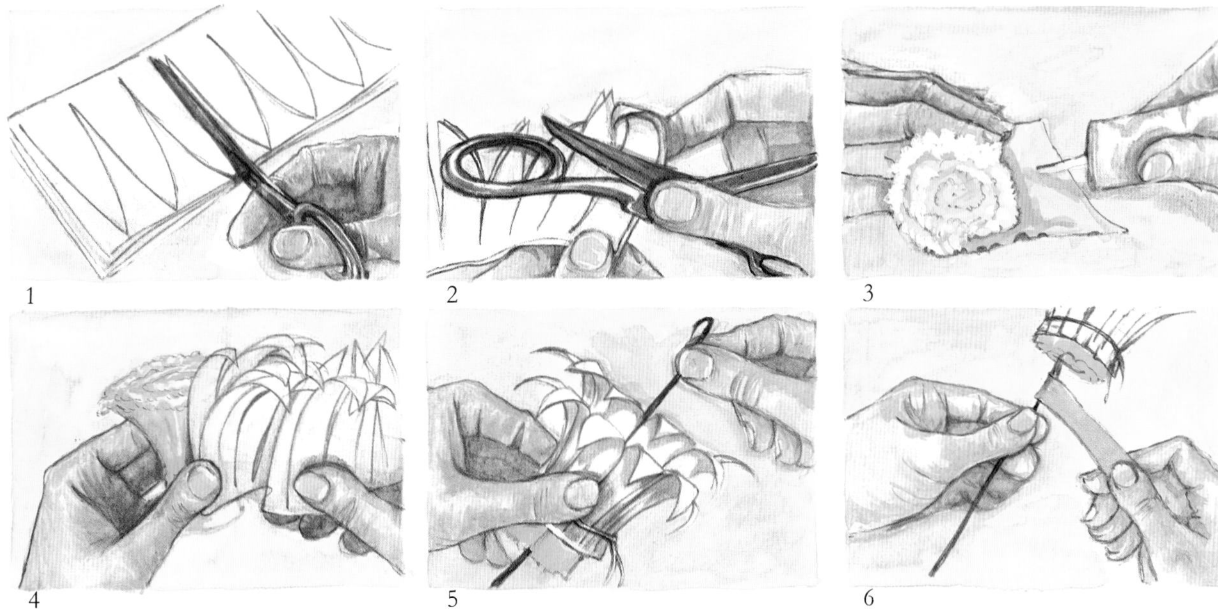

Materials

rolls of white, yellow and green crêpe paper

lengths of No. 1 and No. 3 wire (each daisy will need 10 in (25 cm) No. 1 and 6 in (15 cm) No. 3)

quick-drying, clear paper adhesive

sharp scissors

wire cutters or pliers

sharp pencil

Method

1. For the petals: from the roll of white crêpe paper cut a strip $3\frac{1}{2} \times 16$ in (8.5×40 cm). Fold it in half widthways and again lengthways, so that there are now four layers of paper. Draw ten petal shapes as shown above and cut around their edges, taking care not to cut into the longer of the two folds. Unfold the strip to reveal forty individual petals.

2. Shape the top edge of each petal into a curl by pulling it gently over the edge of a scissor blade.

3. For the centre: cut a piece of yellow crêpe paper 8×4 in (20×10 cm). Pull it gently to stretch it slightly. Fold it in half along its length and roll it tightly into a coil. Glue the end in place.

4. To make the head of the daisy, hold one end of the yellow coil and, with the curled edges facing outwards, fold the petal strip in even 'pleats' around it. Glue the strip in place and wrap a length of No. 3 wire tightly around the pleats to make sure they are secure.

5. For the stem: cut a 10 in (25 cm) length of No. 1 wire and bend one end over to form a small hook. Push the wire, straight end first, through the centre of the daisy head from front to back until the hook is lodged firmly in the yellow crêpe coil.

6. Cut a long strip of green crêpe paper $\frac{1}{2}$ in (1.2 cm) wide and glue one end to the white sepals. Wrap the strip around the base of the flower several times and then continue down the length of the wire. Snip off any excess paper and glue the end in place.

TINSEL AND FABRIC FASHION PLATES

... Gleaming with tinsel, they acquire something of the character of an ikon.

George Speaight, *Juvenile Drama: The History of the English Toy Theatre*

Tinsel pictures captured the imagination of adults and children alike during the first half of the nineteenth century, when prints could be purchased for 'a penny plain or tuppence coloured' and enriched with a selection of sparkling, coloured metallic foils. Many of the monochrome prints were issued by theatrical publishers and could be bought in conjunction with all the various tinselled accessories, which needed only to be cut and glued into place to highlight details of costume and other elements of the composition. For the most elaborate portraits, over one hundred separate pieces of tinsel would be incorporated as decorations – an ambitious and time-consuming effort when executed entirely by hand. For the less enterprising, however, ready-made foiled cutouts stamped by machine were available in kit form, along with other embellishments such as feathers, beads, stars, spangles and fabrics including velvet, satin and fake fur, to create textural, three-dimensional effects. The firm of J. Webb specialized in the manufacture of tinselled sheets, which were sold pre-cut and embossed with shallow relief patterns in shades of silver, gold, bronze, peacock blue, emerald green and red.

Tinsel pictures embraced a wide range of subjects, from allegorical themes to portraits of royalty such as Queen Victoria's eldest daughter, the Princess Royal. Theatrical figures were immensely popular and featured celebrated actors of the period, notably Mr Ellsgood and Mr Kemble, who posed dramatically in Shakespearean roles. Actresses appeared less commonly, although glittering tinsel prints of Madame Vestris in the part of Don Giovanni were produced, with the player disguised in a man's costume of fabric, foil and feathers. In the series of 'West's Theatrical Portraits', each plate was numbered and inscribed with the name of the actor, his role and the theatre in which the performance took place.

For ladies and girls, another popular diversion was the dressing-up of fashion plates, such as those issued in Regency and Victorian magazines, with brightly coloured fabrics. *The Young Ladies' Book* (1829) written by 'A. Lady', for instance, included instructions for decorating 'a Dressed Print'. Small pieces of material were cut out and arranged over the surface, and afterwards glued in place to convey stylish details of pleats and stiff ruffled flounces. High relief effects could be achieved by padding the underside of the fabric over which the material was then draped, recalling the stumpwork figurative embroideries of the late seventeenth century. The miniature gowns were frequently embellished by the addition of jewel-coloured sequins, beads, lace trimmings and tassled fringes. Matching accessories such as hats, hand muffs and parasols were adorned similarly, following the very latest styles. The picture was completed by filling in the monochrome backgrounds and details with watercolour paints, or with paper cutouts which were glued to the surface in the manner of collage (see plate 82).

49. *Mr Elton as Richard Coeur de Lion*, from a series of theatrical prints published in 1831. *(Museum of London)*

50. *Mr Osbaldiston as Grindoff*, the printed cutout coloured with paint and tinsel papers. English, early nineteenth century. *(Mrs Monro, London)*

Mr. OSBALDISTON as GRINDOFF.

VICTORIAN-STYLE TINSEL PORTRAIT

During the nineteenth century tinsel, glitter, fur, sequins and the like were used widely to decorate pre-printed portraits of famous actors, actresses and other notable figures. While such a pastime is no longer so common, the principles of 'dressing' an existing picture can be applied just as effectively to Christmas or birthday cards, particularly if the scene they depict is Victorian in style.

1

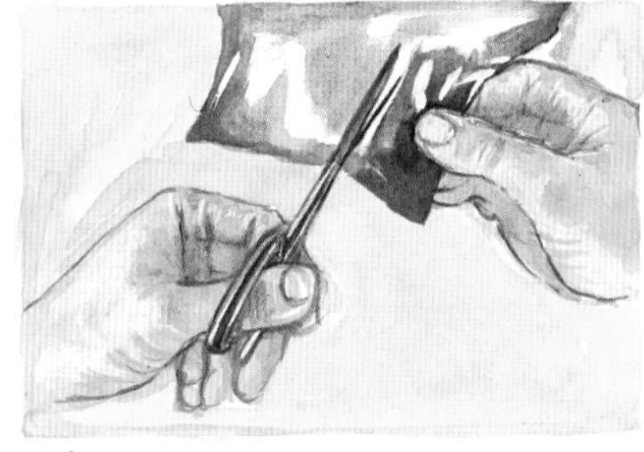

2

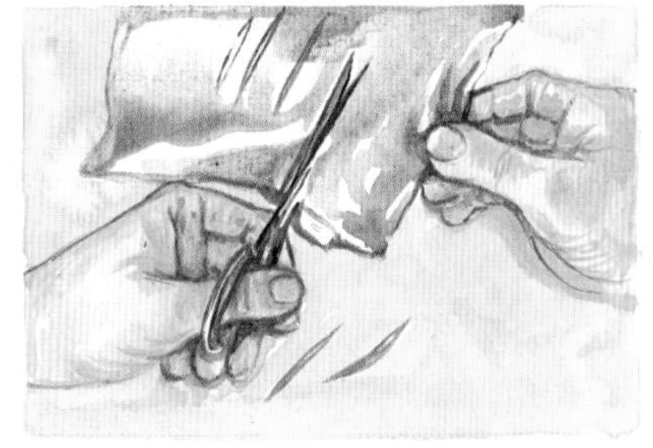

3

Materials

Victorian-style birthday or Christmas card
clear-drying adhesive
small, sharp scissors
multicoloured sequins
snippets of tinsel
silver and coloured metallic foils (such as those used for chocolate wrappings)
tweezers
tracing paper
sharp pencil

Method

1. Having selected the picture to be decorated, trace the outlines of the particular elements you wish to cover – a character's dress, for instance, or, if using a landscape scene, the branches of trees or windows of buildings.

2. Transfer the tracing to a piece of metallic paper, cut out carefully and stick down. Continue to build up the decoration in this way, simply cutting pieces of tinsel or fake fur to fit as required.

3. For a particularly rich effect, cover an area with one snippet of shiny paper: then cover again with a piece of contrasting colour, but before glueing down, cut razor-thin slivers out of this top piece, so that the first layer shines through. This method works particularly well on character's costumes, with the slits made along the folds of their dresses or jackets.

DECORATIVE PAPER SCRAPS

... Delightful old albums where perfumed valentines, hearts and darts, coloured scraps, and miniature landscapes were gummed down by our great-aunts and grand-mothers ... many a treasure may be found hidden between the leaves of the scrap-album.

Mrs E. Nevill Jackson, *Silhouettes*, *c.*1938

The vogue for collecting fancy paper scraps and applying them to various decorative schemes was subscribed to by ladies of leisure during the eighteenth century. Small monochrome prints and engravings could be purchased inexpensively and assembled into albums, interspersed perhaps with handwritten verses of poetry, watercolour sketches and pressed flowers and leaves. The fashion for pasting scraps onto furniture following the recommendations published in Robert Sayer's *The Ladies Amusement, or the whole art of Japanning Made Easy* (1762) was another popular diversion, in imitation of oriental lacquered designs (see pp. 66–9).

Commercially-printed, coloured and relief-embossed scrap sheets were issued from the 1820s onwards by firms such as Mamelok's in Germany, and William Cole in England. An immense range of pictorial subjects was portrayed, ensuring a wide audience of both adults and children alike. Cole's, for example, published an entertaining series of comic sheets entitled 'Humorous Scraps', as well as picturesque town and landscape 'Vignettes ... Beautifully Coloured, by Calvert, Eighteen-Pence each'.[1] The London manufacturer W. & H. Rock supplied complete album 'kits', made up of an imaginative selection of embossed scrap sheets for cutting out and inserting into attractive leather-tooled folders (its pages containing a variety of ready-made oval and rectangular frames). Devotees to the Victorian pastime enlarged their albums with hand-coloured paintings of floral bouquets and still lifes to adorn the frontispiece and decorative borders, and inscriptions executed in florid script, with words such as 'Scraps most thankfully received',[2] or similar sentiments. In spite of the fact that the printed decorative papers were commercially produced, the finished album was nevertheless regarded as a private collection of one's mementos, and a reflection of the personality and tastes of its own 'authoress'.

The fashion for ladies' albums flourished in America during the period *c.*1820–80. These dainty portfolios were sometimes referred to in contemporary accounts as 'Leaves of Affection' or 'Token' albums. They were assembled frequently under the guise of an amalgam of one's 'accomplishments', with their hand-painted compositions and rhyming couplets arranged between fancy lacework patterns of paper scraps and favourite prints.

This little Book, with all the prose,
Its varied page imparts,
I dedicate to gentle eyes,
And simpathising hearts.[3]

Such verses were popular and appeared with little variation in sentiment from album to album.

By the last quarter of the nineteenth century, these pastiches of paper scraps and rhymes declined in favour of autograph albums in which friends and

51. *Below*, Victorian scraps of children in national costume, published in sheet-form for cutting out and pasting into albums, or arranging as collages on screens and furniture. *(Christie's, London)*

52. *Right*, vase and lid decorated with potichomanie, created by pasting the interior glass walls with paper scraps, coated in white paint. English, *c.* 1820. *(Mallett at Bourdon House Ltd, London)*

acquaintances were asked to sign their names – affording them the opportunity to display their skills in ornate calligraphy. As before, a few lines of verse were expected of each contributor, but for the uninspired, one needed only to consult the journals devoted to etiquette and 'good breeding', in which appropriate 'Selections for the Autograph Album' were included.

The Victorian lady, ever fond of cutting and pasting paper scraps, found new inspiration by arranging them decoratively onto large folding screens – one of many 'elegancies' subscribed to by the housewife for '... embellishing and beautifying her humble home'.[4] Scrap screens adorned with endearing cutouts of fairytale characters and alphabet panels were created commonly for children's

53. Detail from a Victorian scrap album, its linen pages pasted with hundreds of paper cutouts depicting genre scenes and animals.
(Christie's, London)

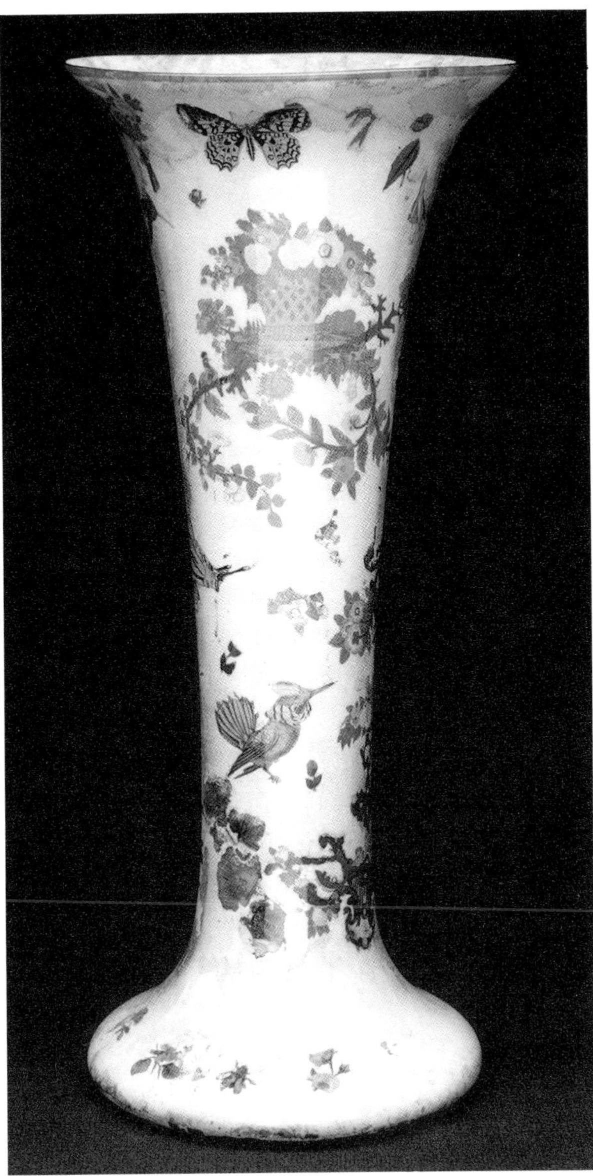

54. Potichomanie vase displaying paper birds, butterflies and flowers, over-painted in pale green to imitate porcelain, 1880. *(Mallett at Bourdon House Ltd, London)*

nurseries. Exotic jungle animals, the Queen's Guard, racing-red fire engines and figures of Little Miss Muffett, Dick Whittington and others were published in brilliant colours by firms such as Raphael Tuck and Sons. For older children, characters from Dickens and Shakespeare, complete with dialogue captions, were considered both decorative and educational. Fashion-plate scrap screens and floral compositions appealed to more sophisticated tastes, and the Berlin publisher Albrecht and Meister (with branches in London, Paris and New York) specialized in 'fine chromolithographic pictures in full sheets (of) Saints, fancy pictures of ladies ... busts and figures ... flowers, bouquets, etc., in all sizes from eight to 2,500 pictures per sheet'.[5]

Instructions for making scrap screens appeared frequently in ladies' journals in Europe and America. In *Cassell's Household Guide* (1875), for example, the pursuit was recommended as '... an employment that fills up a good deal of spare time, entails no mental exertion, and may be done at small expense, beyond that for the mere frame of the screen with a simple covering of black paper'. The procedure for cutting scraps and glueing them to the surface was summarized only briefly in the text, since '... it would be useless to lay down any very accurate rules where so much must be left to taste'.

Among the repertoire of paper scrap albums and screens, a final flowering of the 'art' appeared in France, England and America during the third quarter of the nineteenth century with the advent of *potichomanie* (derived from the French *potiche* for vase, and *manie* for craze). This novel technique of porcelain imitation, in the exuberant styles of Sèvres, Dresden and Chinese export wares, was achieved by pasting printed scrap motifs on the interior walls of a hollow glass vessel. These were then backed with a coat of paint to impart an overall surface colour such as the grey-green celadon fashionable at the time. The *Elegant Arts for Ladies* (*c.*1856) applauded its 'most elegant and beautiful' effects, and encouraged its practice 'amongst a circle of intimate friends ... and ... as on those occasions gentlemen always enliven the circle, (that) they assist the fair manufacturer, with their advice and aid ... although we doubt their ability in the niceties of cutting out ...'.[6] Chinoiserie motifs of chinamen, dragons, dogs of fō and phoenixes were illustrated alongside the text for those wishing to draw their own scraps and 'paint the figures in the brightest colours possible ... the more grotesque the Chinese design is, the better'. Exotic variations in the 'Etruscan and Assyrian style' were also suggested, provided that the glass vase selected for the exercise was 'in accordance with the model from the *antique*'.

A simplified version of potichomanie, appealing to those less dexterous in the 'art', was executed by pasting paper scraps onto the exterior surface of a ceramic vessel, which was afterwards varnished for protection. Such pieces were described in contemporary accounts as 'Dolly Varden' jars, and the ease with which they could be assembled made them a suitable 'kindergarten craft' for children.

POTICHOMANIE LAMP BASE
In the chinoiserie style

Adapted from the oriental imitations popular during the period *c.*1850–80, this lamp base requires a variety of Chinese- or Japanese-style paper cutouts, taken from magazines or museum and art gallery postcards.

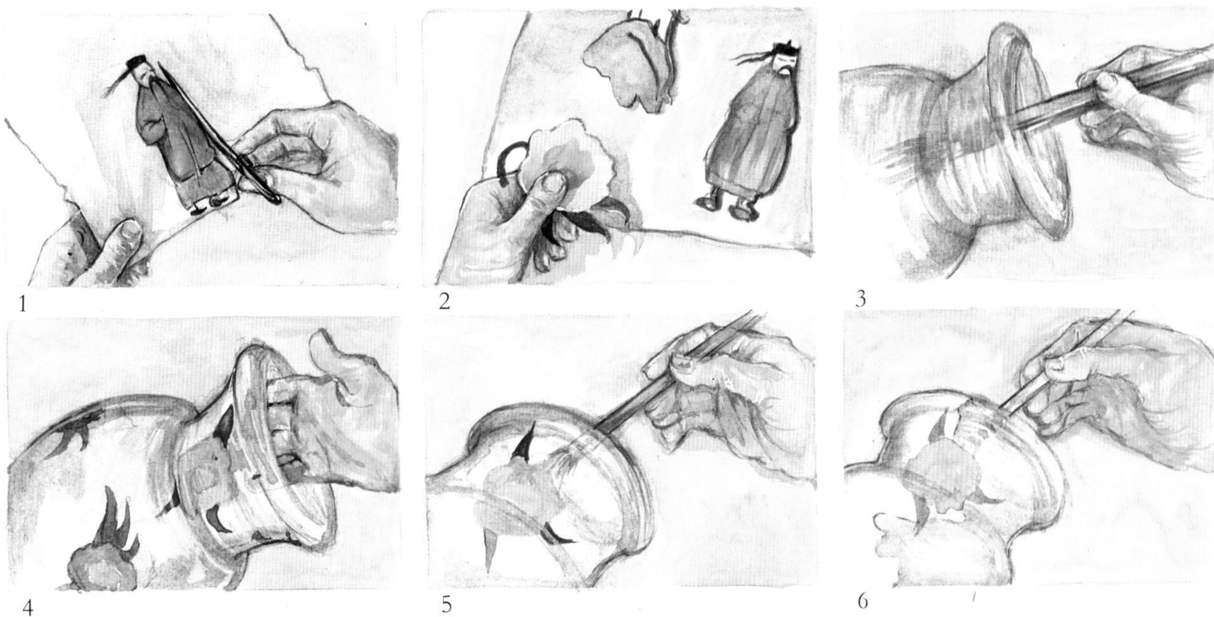

Materials
clear glass lamp base having a diameter large enough to insert your hand
selection of paper or thin card cutouts
small, sharp scissors or craft knife
tweezers
tin of clear gloss varnish
clear-drying paper adhesive
sable paintbrush fine enough to reach into the bottom of the base
narrow, flat bristle brush
semi-gloss oil paint in a shade to complement the colours of the cutouts
white spirit for cleaning brushes

Method
1. Cut out the motifs carefully from their backgrounds. The number of pieces needed will depend on the size of the lamp base and the design intended. Bear in mind that since they are to be glued to a curved surface, the cutouts must be of pliable paper or card.
2. With the cylindrical shape of the base in mind, arrange the motifs on a flat surface until a suitable pattern is found.
3. Making sure the inside surface of the base is free from dust and grease, apply a coat of varnish. Starting at the bottom, and using the fine brush to reach into the tight angles, work round and up the inside in a spiral, applying as even and smooth a coat as possible. Leave to dry.
4. Following the pattern already devised, glue and stick the cutouts face outwards around the inside of the base, using the tweezers to position them if necessary.
5. Once the cutouts are firmly in position, apply the paint, covering both the backs of the cutouts and the surrounding interior walls. Again, use the fine brush to reach into any corners and work round in a spiral until the whole area is covered. Leave to dry and then apply a second coat to give an even, dense finish.

BEST CROCHET

THE
LADY'S
WORKBOX
NEEDLES, THREADS
AND YARNS
ARDERN'S BEST

INTRODUCTION

... A woman who spent her days in sitting nicely dressed on a sofa,
doing some long piece of needlework, of little use and no beauty, thinking more
of her Pug than her children ... Lady Bertrum sunk back in one corner
of the sofa, the picture of health, wealth, ease and tranquility.

Jane Austen, *Mansfield Park*, 1814

If the pampered Regency gentlewoman devoted her leisure hours to ornamental needlework, she was no less the product of circumstance than her fashionable Elizabethan ancestress, whose prescribed daily activities consisted largely of fancy sewing and a host of other sedentary pursuits. For centuries, the 'accomplished' female was viewed as little more than a decorative appendage to her husband. Although she needed to be practical in managing his estates and army of servants, she was otherwise preoccupied with the creation of pretty showpieces for her home and master's pleasure. With considerable skill, she frequently embroidered her own gowns and aprons in keeping with the latest styles illustrated in ladies' magazines, and sewed her husband's shirts, handkerchiefs and waistcoats using silk and metallic threads. Lady Carlow wrote to her sister Lady Louisa Stuart in 1781 that 'My chief amusement since I came from town has been making myself a white polonaise, in which I have succeeded to a miracle', and Queen Charlotte's daughter, the Princess Royal, worked her own wedding dress as an example of her ability in fine stitchery. Even Jane Austen's highly critical view of female aspirations acknowledged the superiority of domestic needlework, and she described in a letter dated 1796 that she was 'very busy making Edward's [her brother's] shirts, and I am proud to say that I am the neatest worker of the party'. That women filled their houses with crewelwork bed hangings and needlepoint cushions, and their wardrobes with silk-embroidered finery, was ample (and deliberate) proof of their leisured existence.

While decorative needlework remained the gentlewoman's prerogative, her subordinates also relied on plain and fancy sewing as an often essential source of income. Local women proficient in pattern-drawing, lace-making and other techniques were indispensable to the amateur embroiderer, who depended on their services to help execute a complicated design or particular effect, and who paid them for their efforts. Servants, too, were delegated tasks – from mending household linens to assisting with the creation of new furnishings and accessories. A maid's ability to sew well ensured a higher status in the servants' hierarchy, and her handiwork was regularly scrutinized by the mistress of the house.

Well-bred schoolgirls in Europe and America were instructed in ornamental needlework from the age of about six or seven onwards. Most began their

56. *The Embroidery Lesson* by Jules Trayer. *(The Mansell Collection, London)*

55. *Opposite*, penwork Regency sewing box and tools. *(Antique Collector Magazine)*

tuition with samplers, and then proceeded to other techniques and decorative styles under the guidance of their teachers or governesses. Whereas the child embroiderer of the seventeenth century turned to stump- and beadwork, the eighteenth-century schoolgirl learned to sew silk pictorial scenes for the drawing-room pole-screen and mantelpiece. Only with the vogue for Berlin wool work did the Victorian pupil escape the rigours of a sound needlework education, as creativity was suppressed by ready-made canvases and simple stitchery, requiring little expertise or previous knowledge.

However, the last quarter of the nineteenth century saw the emergence of 'art needlework' – a return to traditional methods and high standards of workmanship instigated by William Morris and his followers. Berlin work gave way to crewel embroidery and appliqué, and the revival of outmoded techniques was soon taken up as a cause célèbre by the Royal School of Art Needlework, founded in 1872. Its noble aims included the education and employment of poor gentlewomen, while at the same time, the patronage of its distinguished President, the Princess Christian of Schleswig-Holstein, as well as a host of titled lady governesses, pronounced needlework an eminently fashionable pursuit.

SAMPLERS

Patty Polk did this and she hated every stitch she did in it. She loves to read much more.

Embroidered on a sampler by a ten-year-old American schoolgirl, 1800[1]

Patty Polk's lively words recall some of the drudgery of sampler-making as a schoolroom exercise during the eighteenth and early nineteenth centuries, when girls progressed from one piece to the next to demonstrate their proficiency in needlework. In the elite seminaries established for well-to-do young ladies in England and America, the sampler represented both the beginning and end of a girl's education in fancy stitchery. Her first attempts as a child might consist of plain panels of simple sewing and darning. Having mastered the repertoire of basic stitches, she moved on during her early teens to more complex samplers and pictorial scenes – eventually to triumph in a graduation showpiece, the pinnacle of her achievements.

Samplers embraced the theories and techniques behind most forms of domestic and decorative needlework, without which no girl of good breeding was considered accomplished. When the Boston schoolgirl, Anna Winslow, wrote to her mother during the 1770s that she could 'drive the goose quill a bit, (but) cannot manage the needle',[2] her confessed inability must have caused her parents and teachers considerable consternation. Learning to 'manage the needle' was regarded of fundamental importance to female education, as the schoolgirl's competence in executing samplers of a reasonable standard ensured her success later as a dexterous needlewoman and virtuous housewife.

57. The earliest known signed and dated English sampler, made by Jane Bostocke in 1598 for the two-year-old Alice Lee. *(By courtesy of the Trustees of the Victoria and Albert Museum, London)*

The term sampler is derived from the Latin *exemplum*, meaning 'an example or model to be followed'. Dr Samuel Johnson's definition appeared in his eighteenth-century *Dictionary* as '. . . a piece worked by young girls for improvement', which is perhaps a more accurate description, for the series of schoolroom samplers produced during that period displayed all the naivety characteristic of a children's exercise. This was not the case, however, during the sixteenth and early seventeenth centuries, when examples were worked by accomplished needlewomen as a means by which to explore a particular technique, motif or colour scheme. The scarcity of published pattern books meant that women had to rely on their own resources, and every design that caught their fancy (whether of their own invention, or copied from a popular print) was incorporated in a sampler as a point of reference. On the evidence of household inventories which listed samplers among the family treasures, the embroidered panels were highly valued. Women were advised to 'keep cleane your samplers (and) sleep not as you sit'[3] and, above all else, to maintain high standards of workmanship since materials were too precious to waste.

Few sixteenth-century samplers have survived. The earliest known signed and dated example (see plate 57) was created in 1598 by Jane Bostocke, and made as a present for the two-year-old Alice Lee. Sewn in coloured silk threads on a square of unbleached linen, the piece was enriched with pearl beads and metallic threads, recalling the lavishness of Tudor embroidery. Exotic beasts, animals and fruit-bearing trees are scattered over the top panel, above an alphabet frieze. The bulk of the panel consists of over twenty separate styles of stitching and patterning, all of which would have served the growing Alice well as a comprehensive store of designs.

As pattern books became more widely available during the seventeenth century, so the sampler's function gradually changed: originally a source of reference, it now simply provided an opportunity to *display* the diverse skills of the worker. One of the most important handbooks for the amateur needlewoman of the time was James Boler's *The Needle's Excellency*, which was issued in 1631. Its illustrations provided a rich selection of pictorial devices which could be traced and translated into embroidery, and its flamboyant imagery of unfamiliar plants and beasts catered to mass-market tastes for exotica.

The majority of seventeenth-century samplers conformed to one of two basic formats: the first was divided into segments or bands, each highlighted by a different method of stitchery; and the second featured numerous decorative motifs scattered haphazardly over the entire surface. The latter are sometimes described as 'spot' or 'random' samplers, as the embroiderer filled every available space with a liberal sprinkling of emblems and designs, stitched in multicoloured silks and glittering metallic threads. Unicorns rubbed shoulders with mermaids, and spiders' webs loomed larger than rabbits, in what became a playful jumble of real and fantastic forms. Fleurs-de-lys, diamonds and other geometric shapes were frequently crammed between beasts and flowers to demonstrate the full spectrum of stitches, which included, *inter alia*, cross, tent, Florentine, Hungarian, chain, rococo, eyelet, and the arduous raised, plaited braid. A few seventeenth-century samplers displayed both banded and 'spot' patterns, which were usually executed on long panels to contain the wealth of stitches and fanciful images.

By the late 1600s, samplers made by young children displayed alphabet panels and rows of numerals sewn in bright colours, ensuring that each pupil was as well versed in reading and arithmetic as she was competent in the skills of simple stitchery. Religious verses, moral inscriptions and crowded passages alluding to filial obligation were all commonplace – and became standard clauses for samplers during the course of the eighteenth and nineteenth centuries.

58. Multicoloured band sampler, sewn in wool, the centre panel displaying Florentine (or flame) stitch distinctive for its bold, zigzag patterning, early eighteenth century. *(Royal Museum of Scotland, Edinburgh)*

Hannah Taylor 1774
Virtue alone Can Never die. but Lives to imortality
from haughty Looks Ill turn aside. & mortifie my Pride
Hannah Taylor
Born December 17
1763 and made
this August 18 1774
at NewPort
RhodIsland
1774

American samplers made prior to the eighteenth century followed the stylistic formats of their counterparts in England. The earliest known dated example was made by Loara Standish (daughter of a sea captain of Plymouth Colony) in 1656, and was executed as a long, narrow panel measuring 36 × 7 inches (90 × 17.5 centimetres). During the early 1700s, simple alphabet and numerical samplers were worked by young children, supervised by their mothers or teachers at the local 'dame' school. For those girls fortunate enough to be sent, from the age of eleven or twelve, to one of the exclusive academies devoted to deportment and the 'pretty arts', however, sampler-making was transformed into an exercise of decorative embroidery. The majority of pieces were signed, dated and framed as pictures, and for proud parents offered ample proof of their daughters' dexterity (and consolation for the exorbitant school fees incurred).

60. Berlin-work sampler made by Sarah Ann Evans, 'Aged 15 Years', in 1876, sewn on canvas in the brilliant colours fashionable at the time.
(Phillips, London)

Colonial samplers soon charted an independent course from their English prototypes, a departure which occurred before the middle of the eighteenth century and blossomed into a variety of fresh interpretations. American sampler shapes became shorter and squatter, and compositions featured decorative border surrounds of stylized geometric patterns and foliage. Lively pictorial scenes of pastoral landscapes, pretty gardens and elegant figures in period costume became regular accompaniments for the alphabet friezes and inscriptions. Their primitive rendering – complete with spelling mistakes, crooked lines and other childish mishaps – contrasted greatly with the faultless workmanship expected from the strict British schoolma'am or governess. If American tutors appeared to turn a blind eye to their pupils' imperfections, their leniency nevertheless resulted in the creation of samplers which demonstrated '... a delightful freedom of form and a refreshing naiveté'.[4]

American samplers were generally worked in multicoloured silk threads on backgrounds of natural or bleached linen. Occasionally, tiffany gauze (a thin glazed cotton) and tammy (a fine wool tannery cloth) were employed as foundations, the latter being favoured in England after *c.*1750. Sampler designs were derived from published patterns imported from abroad, although several would appear to have been invented and drawn freehand by the school instructress herself, for her students to copy. Apart from pictorial scenes, alphabets and inscriptions, map samplers showing countries and continents made attractive subjects on both sides of the Atlantic – and provided an additional lesson in geography.

Sampler-making continued with little interruption in the schoolrooms of England and America during the nineteenth century. With the growing craze for Berlin wool work by the 1830s, long sampler panels in coloured wools on double canvas provided new sources of design. Such pieces demonstrated the Victorian taste for dazzling and florid patterning, but were met with severe criticism by the proponents of 'art needlework' during the latter half of the century. In the Fine Art Society's exhibition catalogue of 1900, for example, Berlin-style samplers were rated as 'degraded objects... of decayed needlework'.

59. American sampler made by eleven-year-old Hannah Taylor in 1774, worked in traditional style with alphabet panels, moralizing verses and pictorial motifs.
(The American Museum in Britain, Bath)

STUMPWORK & ENCRUSTED EMBROIDERY

Flowers, Plants and Fishes, Beasts, Birds Flys and Bees
Hils, Dales, Plaines, Pastures, Skies, Seas, Rivers, Trees,
Theres nothing neere at hand or furthest sought
But with the Needle may be shaped and wrought

John Taylor, *The Prayse of the Needle, c.*1636

The natural world provided a rich source for decorative needlework designs during the late sixteenth and seventeenth centuries, and numerous patterns were devised using an imaginative selection of plants, animals and insects. Some of the liveliest interpretations were executed by the technique of raised embroidery or stumpwork, where small sections of the needlework composition were padded and raised from the surface in a manner which imitated the three-dimensional qualities of low-relief sculpture. This method of embroidery allowed for areas of accent and emphasis, enabling the central figures or motifs to achieve greater prominence as they emerged from the surface. The technique was particularly well suited to narrative scenes which were favoured at the time, because it imparted to the characters in relief an aura of importance and a heightened sense of drama.

61. Stumpwork casket embroidered by Hannah Smith in 1657. *(Whitworth Art Gallery, University of Manchester)*

Stumpwork was one of several needlework exercises to be taken up by accomplished young girls during the period *c.*1650–1700. It was usually attempted after other more elementary techniques such as samplers and whitework had been mastered, to form the basis of a sound repertoire in decorative embroidery. The term, however, does not appear in contemporary accounts, and was probably not employed before the mid-eighteenth century, when the method was described in *A New and Complete Dictionary of Arts and Sciences* as 'embroidery on the stamp'.[1] This referred to the stamped outline of the design, which was printed or drawn in ink onto the satin background to indicate the position of the various parts to be attached. It is likely that the majority of examples were created from ready-to-assemble stumpwork kits, consisting of a professionally drawn outline and all the materials necessary to follow the delineated pattern. Heavy silver and gold threads and beads imported from Italy were used in conjunction with dyed silks, wools and cottons, worked with variously-sized steel needles to compensate for the differences in texture. Spangles (composed of flat beaten discs of silver wire) were also used for decoration, as found, for example, on the earliest known American stumpwork, created in 1644 by Rebeker Wheeler. Satin ribbons, brocade tassels, silk-covered wire coils or 'purls', seed pearls, semiprecious stones and sheets of talc and mica were added as finishing touches. Small, carved pieces of boxwood overlaid with satin, ivory and wax were employed for areas such as faces, hands and feet, and were probably included as accessories in the stumpwork kits.

Ivory satin, backed with linen or calico, was often selected for the background upon which the padded cutwork designs were sewn, and its soft lustrous tones provided an effective contrast to the rich surface stitchery. The satin ground was seldom overlaid in its entirety and,

62. Mid-seventeenth-century English stumpwork panel of courtly figures in a fantasy landscape, the background scattered with over-sized flowers, birds and beasts.
(Stair and Company Ltd, London)

indeed, became a pervasive feature of raised embroidery during the late seventeenth century. Once complete, the stumpwork – frequently made up of a series of pieces, as in the case of long narrative compositions – was sent to a cabinet maker or specialist craftsman for mounting onto the exterior of a workbox or jewellery casket. Small pictorial scenes were glazed and framed for hanging on a wall, or were arranged as decorative surrounds for mirrors.

An early stationary casket embroidered by Hannah Smith (see plate 61) was rendered in narrative style as a series of panels, and worked in a variety of stitches in coloured silks, metallic threads, spangles and 'purls'. A letter written by the fourteen-year-old girl was discovered in one of its drawers, in which she describes '... if ever I have any thoughts about the time when I went to Oxford ... my being there near two yers ... and I was almost twelve yers of age when I went; and I made an end of my cabinete at Oxford ... and my cabinet was mad up in the yere of 1656 at London'. This remarkably well-preserved example, coloured in shades of cream, gold and blue, depicts the Four Seasons and scenes from the Old Testament. Small areas of stumpwork appear on the figure of Joseph (who is surrounded on the lid by encrusted metallic threads and seed pearls) and on the lion and leopard motifs flanking the central lock.

Apart from cabinets, pictures and mirror frames, stumpwork was also employed for the decoration of pillowcases, cushions, book covers (such as those designed to contain bibles), baskets and small purses.

Biblical subjects, as well as mythological and allegorical scenes, were inspired by popular 'Old Master' engravings by artists such as Albrecht Dürer and Gerard de Jode. The latter's illustrations were published in 1585 in the volume, *Thesaurus Sacrarum Historiarum Veteris Testamenti*, and were easily transposed into embroidery compositions. Portraits of contemporary figures such as Charles I and Henrietta Maria and, later, Charles II and Catherine of Braganza, were also depited in the fashionable dress of the time. Costumes and jewelled accessories appeared in exquisite detail and features miniature panels of lace

63. Elaborate mirror frame displaying stumpwork figurines, heraldic beasts, buildings, flowers and insects, the surface made more glittering by the addition of mica, metallic sequins and seed pearls.
(Mallett and Son (Antiques) Ltd, London)

for collars and cuffs, sequinned trimmings, tiny seed pearls and tassles of gold thread. For greater realism, the stumpwork figures were enhanced further by the addition of real hair for their cascading locks and beards. Portraits of Charles I, for example, appeared in this style, and it is possible that the king's actual hair was granted for the purpose as 'true relics of Charles the Martyr'.[2]

The stumpwork figures were placed frequently in sumptuous landscape and garden settings, with only occasional architectural references to a house, fortress or distant town. Male characters were sometimes depicted in tents between open (and movable) curtains, such as Charles I, who was '... almost always seated... thereby concealing his short stature'.[3] Ladies appeared as full-length portraits, either individually or in small conversant groups arranged under graceful canopies of garlands of fruits and flowers. Scattered profusely around the figures, with little reference to scale or perspective, were numerous insects, animals and flowers, their bright colours and larger-than-life dimensions contributing to the effect of gaiety and playful fantasy.

In spite of such expansive decorative schemes, individual designs recurred with marked regularity, inspired no doubt by the publication of numerous pattern books at the time. An early source for cutwork was Conrad Gesner's *Icones Animalium*, published in four volumes from 1551 to 1558, followed by the *Historie of Four-Footed Beasts* (1607) by Edward Topsell. Richard Shorleyker's *Scholehouse for the Needle* (1624) provided '... certaine patterns of cut-workes; newly invented and never published before. Also sundry sorts of spots as Flowers, Birds, and fishe etc. and will fitly serve to be wrought, some with Gould, some with Silke, and some with Crewell in coullers; or other wise at your pleasure'.[4] The Londoner Peter Stent produced a number of design source books from *c.*1650, which were advertised widely for their '... Drafts of Men, Birds, Beasts, Flowers, Fruits, Flyes and Fishes'.[5] He also devised paper patterns covering a vast range of subjects, from allegorical themes to maps of the continents.

In comparison with other forms of ornamental needlework, stumpwork was a relatively expensive exercise, not only in its selection of choice materials, but also in terms of its construction into workboxes, jewllery caskets and mirror frames. As a result, the technique was practised by wealthy young ladies who could afford to embellish pieces with the surface glitter fashionable at the time.

The vogue for stumpwork declined by the early eighteenth century and what once had been considered a worthy pursuit for the privileged classes in 'an age of luxury and intolerable expense'[6] soon gave way to other decorative techniques.

64. Silk embroidered stumpwork box, the top panel depicting Sheba's meeting with Solomon. English, *c.*1670. *(Weidenfeld and Nicolson Archive)*

BEADWORK

(This) graceful and pretty employment for the fingers . . . calls for a certain degree of taste and imagination, and is very suggestive . . . it will amuse and interest.

Elegant Arts for Ladies, c.1856

Although the technique of beadwork can be traced back to ancient times, its emergence as a minor decorative art was not established before the mid-seventeenth century in Europe. Prior to this, beads were employed chiefly as adornment for costume accessories and ecclesiastical furnishings, and appeared in jewel-like colours enriched with gold threads to imitate precious and semiprecious stones.

During the seventeenth century, beadwork was promoted along with other forms of needlework as a fashionable exercise, embarked upon by young ladies accomplished in fine stitchery techniques. The child embroiderer Martha Edlin, for example, progressed to beadwork at the age of thirteen as one of her advanced 'projects', in keeping with other well-bred girls of her generation who '... tripped in dainty slippers down the ornamental paths of their education'.[1] Her beadwork jewellery casket was completed in 1673 – undoubtedly regarded at the time as one of the higher achievements in her tuition – and was preceded by instruction in the art of samplers, whitework and raised embroidery.

Beadwork and stumpwork (see pp. 92–5) were combined frequently to create lively pictorial compositions, with the padded motifs highlighted by contrasting decorations of brightly coloured beads. Like other forms of contemporary needlework, a wide range of subjects was depicted. Scenes of biblical and allegorical content and miniature portraits of lavishly dressed court figures were favoured, often derived from the popular designs published in pattern books of the period. Pastoral landscapes and exotic gardens full of plush greenery, flowering plants, beasts, birds and insects featured prominently in figural compositions. In many examples, such

65. Knitted baby's bonnets decorated with panels of lace and beaded flowers and leaves in bright colours. American, eighteenth century.
(Shelburne Museum, Shelburne, Vermont, USA)

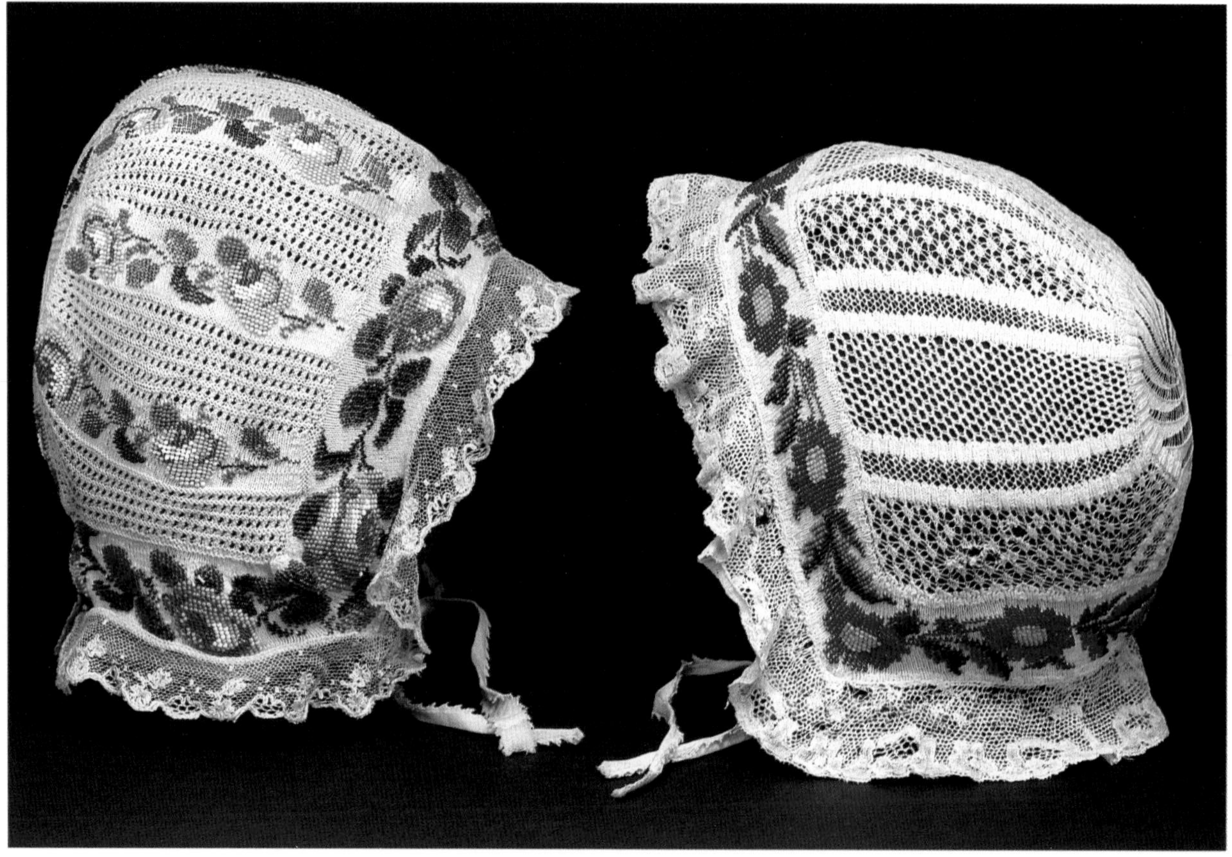

backgrounds became the central *tour de force*, with the characters relegated to mere ornamental roles.

A keen interest in nature was demonstrated throughout the needlework repertoire of the Restoration period, of which some of the most radiantly coloured interpretations were executed in beadwork. Unlike the flat stitchery of crewelwork and other forms of embroidery, the tightknit rows of glass beads appeared undulating and dynamic, partly as a result of their raised and reflective surfaces. Some dazzling visual effects were achieved in pieces executed entirely with beads, either sewn onto canvas or satin cloth backings, or supported by wire frameworks in the case of three-dimensional objects. Many embroidered examples were enhanced further by the characteristic dot-patterning of the background, consisting of hundreds of clear, colourless glass beads which were sewn individually onto the ivory satin cloth for additional sparkle.

Large numbers of beads were exported throughout Europe from places such as Italy, France and Germany, and appeared in a range of sizes and colours. Emerald and lime green, and royal and turquoise blue were used commonly, in pleasing combinations, whereas other shades appeared surprisingly garish, such as the excessively bright yellow-orange which was favoured at the time. Multicoloured, patterned beads were also produced in striped *latticino* styles. In all, several dozen shades could be incorporated into a single composition – an expansive colour spectrum which, perhaps, was only exceeded by the selection of dyed wools and silks available at the time.

66. English beadwork picture of a courting scene, worked characteristically in opaque shades of turquoise, emerald and lime-green, yellow, blue and brown, on a white satin ground. *(Mallett and Son (Antiques) Ltd, London)*

Due to the stable nature of the glass composition, the majority of antique beadwork specimens have retained their brilliance and freshness of tone, unlike their counterparts in silk and other materials, which have faded and deteriorated over the course of time. For this reason, beadwork provides a rare glimpse of the fashionable and authentic colour schemes of late seventeenth-century interior design.

The naively rendered beadwork of the Restoration period, showing little regard for scale or perspective, recalls what was essentially a children's art. These 'primitive' styles, however, soon gave way in the eighteenth century to greater refinement

67. 'King Solomon receiving the Queen of Sheba', a popular theme for embroidery composition during the late seventeenth century.
(Mallett and Son (Antiques) Ltd, London)

under the banner of Neoclassicism. Although the vogue for pictorial scenes continued, portraits of graceful shepherds and shepherdesses were preferred to the formal, artificially-posed courtly figures of previous years. Other alterations occurred in the treatment of the background, and elegant floral sprigs and bouquets, swags, ribbons and key-fret patterns conformed to a more sophisticated decorative order. The adherence to delicate, repetitive designs gained greater momentum during the second half of the eighteenth century with the introduction of much smaller beads in light, pastel shades. This style of beadwork required a certain technical expertise (and a great deal of patience) and as such, its appeal was limited to those of considerable experience and talent.

During the nineteenth century, the vogue for beadwork was fostered by the publication of numerous articles devoted to the subject, complete with designs and instructions for making up pieces. Ladies' magazines praised the technique as a 'graceful occupation and inexhaustible source of laudable and innocent amusement', while enthusiasts such as Mrs A.H. Christie recommended it as a '... fascinating material ... all kinds of pretty things can be done'. From about 1845, beadwork decorations were applied to an immense variety of interior furnishings such as cushions, upholstered furniture, fire screens, table tops, boxes, trays, wine coasters, tea cosies, napkin rings, bell pulls and tie-backs for curtains. Footstools and prie-dieu chairs were covered with panels of Berlin work and beads, the latter applied in muted tones to the richly coloured wool patterns. Personal accessories were ornamented similarly, and finely beaded smoking caps, lounging slippers, spectacle cases, buttons, jewellery and purses were popular.

During the Victorian era, the majority of beads were imported into England from Germany, and could be purchased in a range of shapes, sizes and colours. Jewel-like shades of opal, ruby, turquoise, coral, amber and emerald were employed singly, or in combination with white and metallic hues of silver, bronze, gold and steel. For mourning dress, 'grisaille' beaded accessories in 'black, white or gray bugles (which) make up very prettily' were recommended by the writers of the *Elegant Arts for Ladies*. The tiniest beads were reserved for small purses and items of jewellery, while larger varieties could be sewn more easily onto canvas backings for cushions and upholstery. Bugles of cylindrical form made striking dress corsages, such as the jet-coloured medallions with long fringed tassels which were often worn during periods of bereavement. Other bugles, known as 'Bohemians', ranged from three-eighths to one and a quarter inches (one and a quarter to three centimetres) long, and were used to adorn lampshades, vase covers, lambrequins, table mats and hanging baskets for plants. Both beads and bugles could be purchased from outlets such as Gotto's Berlin Repository in Regent Street, London (where patterns and wools for the popular Berlin work were also stocked).

Several ambitious beadwork projects were described in *Cassell's Household Guide* (1875), highlighted by a massive sideboard ornamented with a series of mosaic bead panels depicting scenes of rural life. The designs were first traced onto the flat wooden surface, and then overlaid with coloured beads which were fixed with cement. Also included were instructions for 'beadwork on wire', to create freestanding objects and a 'variety of decorative articles, either for personal use, or the mantelshelf, or the toilette table'.[2]

68. Beadwork box decorated with flowers and leaves in brilliant colours, on a black ground. English, *c.*1670–80. *(Mallett and Son (Antiques) Ltd, London)*

CREWEL EMBROIDERY

I do no other work but read my psalter, work in gold, silk or cruells, play a tune on my harp, checkmate someone at chess or feed the hawk on my wrist.

From a medieval manuscript, written by a Lady[1]

This colourful form of embroidery took its name from the lightly-twisted, two-ply worsted yarns or 'cruells'. These were worked in a variety of surface stitches, over grounds of woven linen, to adorn a range of household furnishings, wall hangings and small personal accessories. The soft crewel wools were rendered into bold pictorial designs of, commonly, scrolling foilage, birds, animals and exotic beasts, demonstrating a lively blend of both European and Eastern influences. The preference for naturalistic motifs persisted for centuries, differing only in the manner of its presentation to conform to contemporary taste. The rich, repetitive patterning characteristic of seventeenth-century Jacobean embroidery, for example, gave way in the eighteenth century to greater refinement under the banner of Rococo and Neoclassical ideals. Later, in the nineteenth century, the renewal of interest in medieval-style interpretations, as encouraged by William Morris, resulted in a revival of crewelwork in the free-flowing designs and vivid shades of previous generations.

Few wool embroideries prior to the early 1600s have survived, although one important exception is the Bayeux Tapestry, which was commissioned by William the Conqueror's half-brother Bishop Odo during the eleventh century. The narrative designs were executed throughout in eight colours on strips

69. English crewelwork carpet decorated with flowers, foliage and exotic birds, demonstrating the blend of both European and Eastern stylizations fashionable at the time, *c.* 1680. *(Mayorcas, London)*

70. The popular 'tree of life' pattern, worked in rococo stitch on a ground of silk diaper stitch. English, *c.*1720. *(Mallett and Son (Antiques) Ltd, London)*

of coarse linen, which were afterwards sewn together to form one vast composition, some 230 yards (207 metres) in length. The impressive scale was complemented by the use of powerful imagery, with the sailors, soldiers and marching troops portrayed in the chaos of warfare in gruesome detail, assembled between borders of heraldic beasts and inscriptions. Each of the figures was crisply delineated: their contours were edged in stem- and outline-stitch, and filled in subsequently with laid and couched wools. This graphic style combined a heightened sense of realism with a directness of approach, thereby fulfilling a vital role in a largely illiterate society.

In spite of the conspicuous absence of wool-embroidered designs over the next 600 years, references to 'cruell' yarns in medieval accounts suggest, nevertheless, that the medium played some part in the repertoire of early domestic needlework. By the beginning of the seventeenth century, however, the technique was taken up with enthusiasm by amateur embroiderers, who were keen to furnish their homes with sumptuously decorated textiles, in imitation of the expensive woven silks and chintzes imported from China and India. Bed hangings of linen and cotton twill made ideal backgrounds for the all-over furling motifs of large flowers, entwined leaves and stems, which were worked in rich, vegetable-dyed crewel wools. Delicate geometric 'fillings' of parallel lines, dots and areas of crosshatching were used between the outlines of petals, as well as to ornament plain areas of the fabric ground.

The flamboyant 'tree of life' design, as displayed on the hand-painted cotton hangings or palampores from India, was adapted to suit western tastes and became one of the most prominent decorations for crewelwork during the late seventeenth and early eighteenth centuries. With their profusion of exotic eastern devices, interspersed among the bold scrolling foliage so favoured since Elizabethan times, the colourful 'tree of life' embroideries captured something of the richness of their costlier counterparts in woven silk.

The fine crewelwork hangings made in 1675 by the accomplished embroiderer Abigail Pett (in the Victoria and Albert Museum, London) are further evidence of the fashion for 'fantasy' elements and oriental stylizations. Her ambitious series of bed

curtains and valances displays a striking selection of chinoiserie forms – mythological beasts, dragons and strangely unfamiliar birds – all scattered in close proximity across the surface. Her natural flair for spatial arrangement and patterning (where every element of the composition is individual) recalls the high standard of design and workmanship to which amateur needlewomen of the period aspired.

For those seeking assistance in their choice of subjects, numerous pattern books were published from which a wide selection of motifs could be traced and adapted for use as crewelwork decorations. In addition, the employment of specialist 'pattern-drawers' to reproduce popular designs – by means of painting or drawing them directly onto the linen grounds – was another ready source (particularly in the case of large-scale compositions, which were otherwise difficult to embroider). The amateur's unquestionable reliance on both publications and professional services is evidenced by the appearance of nearly identical forms which, with marked regularity, are seen to recur on examples of seventeenth- and eighteenth-century crewelwork.

The graceful Rococo designs of the early eighteenth century were reflected in crewelwork furnishings. The large and prominent foliage of Jacobean embroidery was passed over in favour of small and elegant floral bouquets in bright pastel shades. The exotic forms of previous years were also transformed into naturalistic displays of roses, daffodils, tulips, carnations and other common, garden varieties – all instantly recognizable. Later in the century, Neo-classical interpretations were more ordered and subdued, highlighted by the inclusion of floral swags and ribboned motifs to offset the larger expanses of underlying fabric.

The early nineteenth-century craze for Berlin canvas work (see pp. 134–9) led to the decline of embroidery in coloured wools and silks. Under the influence of William Morris, however, fine crewelwork was revived during the 1860s as a means of restoring the virtues of hand-craftsmanship and of artistic design in an age of mass-industrialization. The lurid, aniline-dyed wools of Berlin work were discarded by Morris and his followers in a return to the natural, 'earthy' shades of vegetable-dyed yarns.

The firm of Morris and Co., which was founded in 1875, produced an exquisite range of crewel embroideries based on traditional methods of working, but freshly interpreted in the spirit of Arts and Crafts ideals. Many were sold in kit form, complete with previously drawn, linen backgrounds and a range of vegetable-dyed wools. The aim was both to re-educate and encourage the amateur embroiderer in the worthwhile pursuit of 'art' needlework.

The revival of crewel embroidery was, indeed, supported by the Royal School of Art Needlework. Methods of stitchery and crewelwork designs were taught to students as part of their basic training. Numerous progressive institutions devoted to the arts and crafts followed their lead, including the Glasgow School of Art, where instruction in crewelwork (as well as in other outmoded techniques such as appliqué and needleweaving) was given by the talented Jessie Newbury. In her book, *Educational Needlecraft* (1911), co-written with her assistant Margaret Swanson, stitchery using brightly coloured wools was recommended as an exercise for children, not only as a means of encouraging traditional embroidery skills at an early age, but also to provide an aesthetic yardstick by which standards of quality could be discerned.

71. *Left*, one of a pair of English crewelwork bed hangings, worked on linen, in the 'tree of life' pattern, *c.* 1710. *(Mallett and Son (Antiques) Ltd, London)*

72. *Below*, American crewel embroidered bedspread, executed in white on a tan-coloured cotton ground. Signed and dated 'Susan T. Bartlett August 2nd 1827'. *(Shelburne Museum, Shelburne, Vermont, USA)*

BLACKWORK

Fair was the yonge wyf, and therwithal

As eny wesil hir body gent and smal . . .
Whit was hir smok and browdid al byfore
And eek bygyade on hir coler aboute

Of cole-blak silk, withinne and eeke withoute.

Chaucer, *Canterbury Tales*, *c.*1390–1400

The white smock adorned with 'coal-black' threads, referred to by Chaucer in the *Mylleres Tale*, suggests that this distinctive style of monochrome embroidery had already gained a degree of popularity during the late fourteenth century in England. However, it was not before the arrival at court in 1501 of Catherine of Aragon that 'blackwork' – by which is meant black stitchery on a white or cream background – achieved its greatest following.

It is believed that Catherine was an accomplished needlewoman, having learned fine embroidery techniques from her mother, Queen Isabella,[1] and included in the trousseau she brought with her from Spain were ivory-coloured silk and linen costume accessories worked decoratively in black threads. The style soon became *de rigueur* in fashionable circles, where it was known as 'Spanish work', although after *c.*1530 the term appears to have been superseded by the more appropriate description, 'blackwork'.

It is not known whether Catherine executed any blackwork herself, but according to John Taylor's preface in *The Needle's Excellency* (1636 edition) '. . . her dayes did paffe, in working the Needle curioufly . . . (and) for her paines, here her reward is just, Her workes proclaime her prayfe, though fhe be duft'.[2] Professional embroiderers were employed by the court to adorn formal items of dress in sumptuous styles, for which their efforts were highly rewarded. Gowns and doublets encrusted lavishly with precious stones and gold embroidery were complemented by elegant ruffed collars, frilled cuffs and sleeved undergarments in finely stitched blackwork. For everyday wear, it is likely that less extravagant pieces were adorned by ladies accomplished in fine needlework. The 'coifs', or undercaps, fashionable during the period, were rendered frequently in blackwork, and were presented and exchanged as New Year's gifts among royalty and the wealthy. Handkerchiefs, purses and nightcaps for men were also ornamented similarly with leaves and foliage in black embroidery, and their 'delightful air of the home'[3] would suggest that such pieces were created by amateurs. Bold, strapwork designs of Moorish inspiration were executed in black silk threads to decorate both costume accessories and domestic furnishings such as cushions, coverlets and bed hangings. These striking compositions were sometimes enriched by the addition of metallic cords

73. Seventeenth-century blackwork nightcap decorated with scrolling foliage. *(By courtesy of the Trustees of the Victoria and Albert Museum, London)*

74. Portrait of Mary Cornwallis by George Gower, her costume sumptuously decorated with blackwork panels of strapwork, flowers and leaves, *c.*1580–5.
(Manchester City Art Galleries)

and spangles to enhance the stark, monochrome surfaces.

Flowers and fruits were favoured subjects for blackwork during the sixteenth and seventeenth centuries, with individual patterns drawn from contemporary publications such as William Turner's *The New Herball* (1568). Catherine of Aragon selected pomegranates as a personal emblem,[4] and other motifs such as roses, carnations, pears and cherries were integrated profusely into the curvilinear or fretwork designs of the background. These exquisite black-on-white compositions – always clearly delineated and precise in detail – recall the formal splendour of court furnishings and costumes of the time.

Portraits of fashionable 'society' figures in blackwork costume were depicted meticulously by artists such as Hans Holbein, who executed numerous paintings of King Henry VIII, his wives and ministers during the period *c.*1532–43. In later works by George Gower, the textures and patterns of costume were rendered as lavishly, as in the portrait of Lady Kitson, painted in 1573 (in the Tate Gallery, London). She appears in an elaborate chemise adorned on the neckline and undersleeves with a lively flowing pattern of black-stitched blossoms and leaves. In more regal style, Gower's portrait of Mary Cornwallis, Lady Kitson's sister (see plate 74), shows the figure dressed in a sumptuous gown adorned with contrasting, intricate panels of blackwork. The sleeves, covered by a thin layer of transparent silk gauze, are ornamented boldly with giant-sized oak leaves and flowers, while her underskirt is highlighted by an impressive strapwork design.

While these formal costumes were undoubtedly created by professionals (such as those belonging to The Broderer's Company, re-established by Queen Elizabeth I in 1561), simpler versions of blackwork were devised by gentlewomen accomplished in fancy needlework techniques. Bess of Hardwick, for example, considered to be one of the most creative and industrious needlewomen of the Elizabethan period, was thought to have executed several fine domestic furnishings in blackwork for her new residence, Hardwick Hall, in Derbyshire. '... Three Curtins wrought with black silk nedlework uppon fine Holland Cloth with buttons and lowpes on black silk ...' were mentioned in the household inventories of 1601.[5] It is likely that Bess worked on some

75. Seventeenth-century blackwork panel embroidered with leaves and berries, each motif filled in with dense geometric patterning.
(By courtesy of the Trustees of the Victoria and Albert Museum, London)

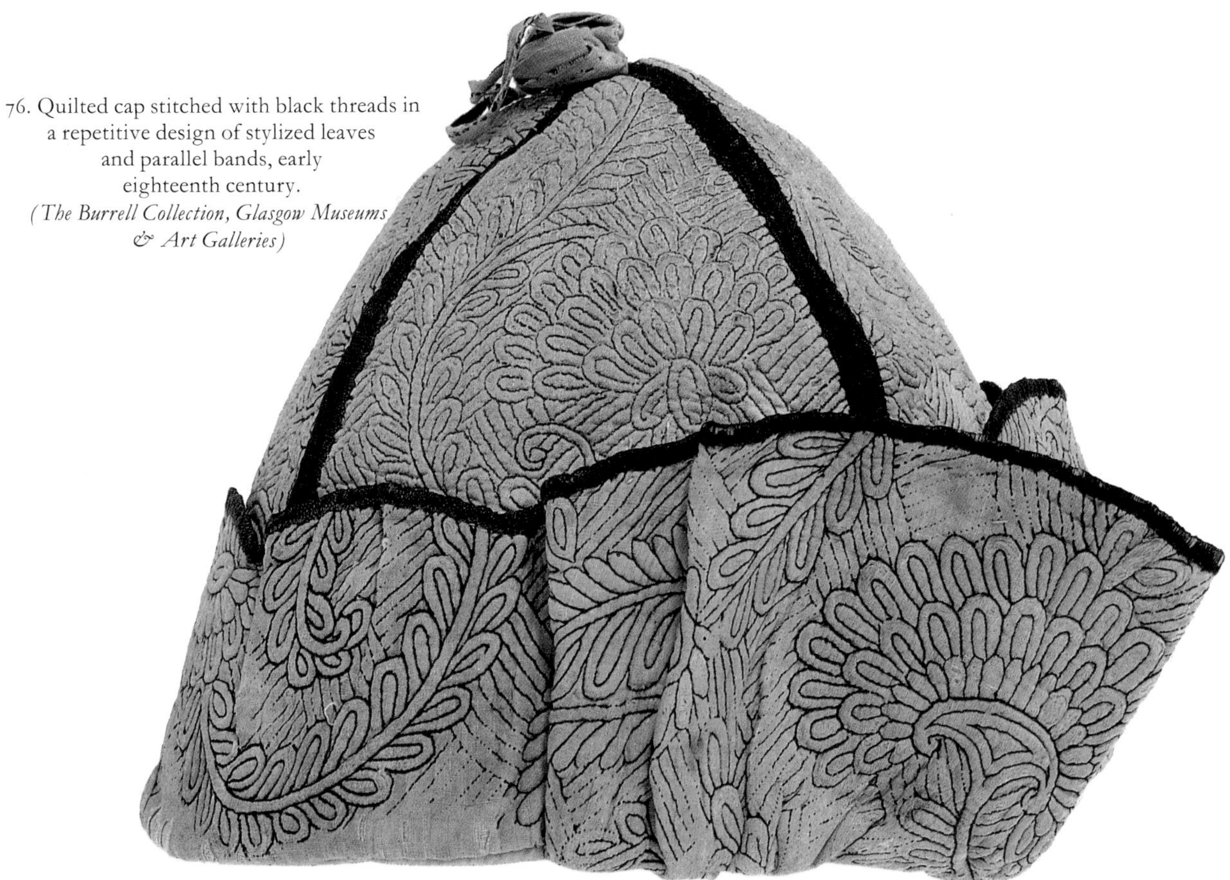

76. Quilted cap stitched with black threads in a repetitive design of stylized leaves and parallel bands, early eighteenth century.
(The Burrell Collection, Glasgow Museums & Art Galleries)

of these panels, possibly in collaboration with Mary, Queen of Scots who, during her lengthy term of imprisonment under the supervision of Bess's fourth husband, the Earl of Shrewsbury, found great comfort in practising her embroidery skills.

The demand for coloured embroidery during the eighteenth century saw the rapid decline of blackwork as a fashionable prerequisite. During the period *c.*1780–1820, however, embroidered pictures executed in black silk on cream backgrounds enjoyed a brief vogue (see also silk embroidery, pp. 114–17). The scenes, chiefly of cottages and rural landscapes, were copied directly from popular contemporary engravings and, indeed, their finely stitched outlines achieved more than a passing resemblance to their counterparts in black ink.

In America, a few samplers in monochrome wools were worked during the late eighteenth and nineteenth centuries by young girls as an exercise in domestic embroidery. The majority were created in blue-on-white combinations, as opposed to black, possibly inspired by the tin-glazed Delft tiles which were imported in large numbers during the period. The style was adopted later by the 'Deerfield Society of Blue and White Needlework', founded in Massachusetts in 1896 by two lady enthusiasts, Margaret Whiting and Ellen Miller. The term 'Deerfield work' is used today to describe these distinctive blue-on-white linens.

After a period of some two hundred years, the fashion for blackwork was revived in England with the advent at the turn of the century of the popular Arts and Crafts movement and the return to 'traditional' handicrafts. Many fine embroidered linens were created in monochrome style (characteristically in brown-on-white combinations) by Mrs Arthur Newall, whose small workshops at Fisherton-de-la-Mere were devoted to the virtues of '... perseverance, concentration, honesty ... patience'[6] and exquisite handworkmanship. Although the extravagant costume accessories of previous generations remained firmly rooted in the past, the vogue for 'art' embroidery looked to the technique of blackwork as a source of inspiration and design.

BLACKWORK EVENING SCARF

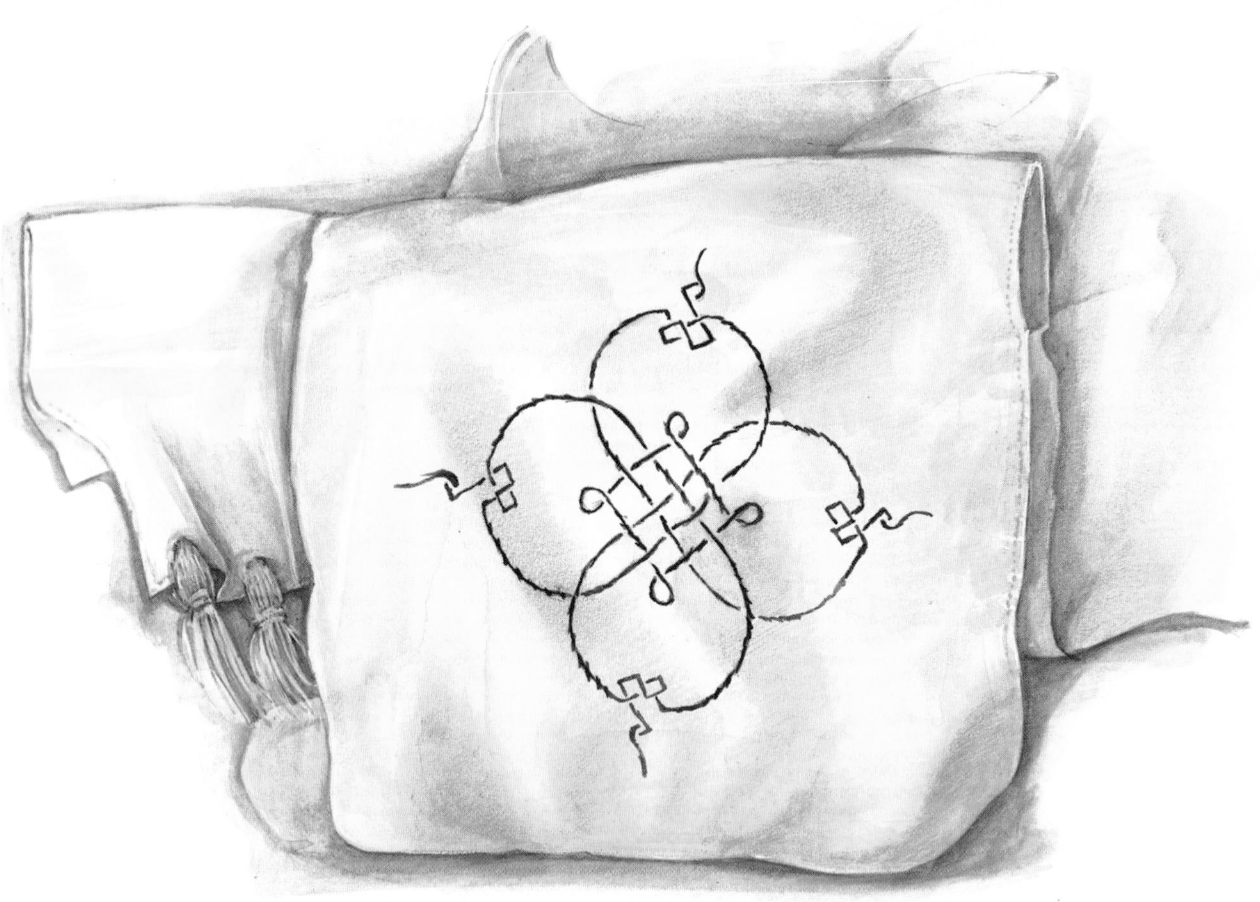

When it first became popular in sixteenth-century England, intricate blackwork patterns decorated nightcaps, cuffs, collars, sleeves and the fronts of skirts. Its effects are one of the most dramatic of all embroidery techniques – the black stitches contrasting sharply with the white or cream background. Yet the stitches commonly employed are very simple – Holbein (double running), single running or back stitch. All that is required is patience to follow the design.

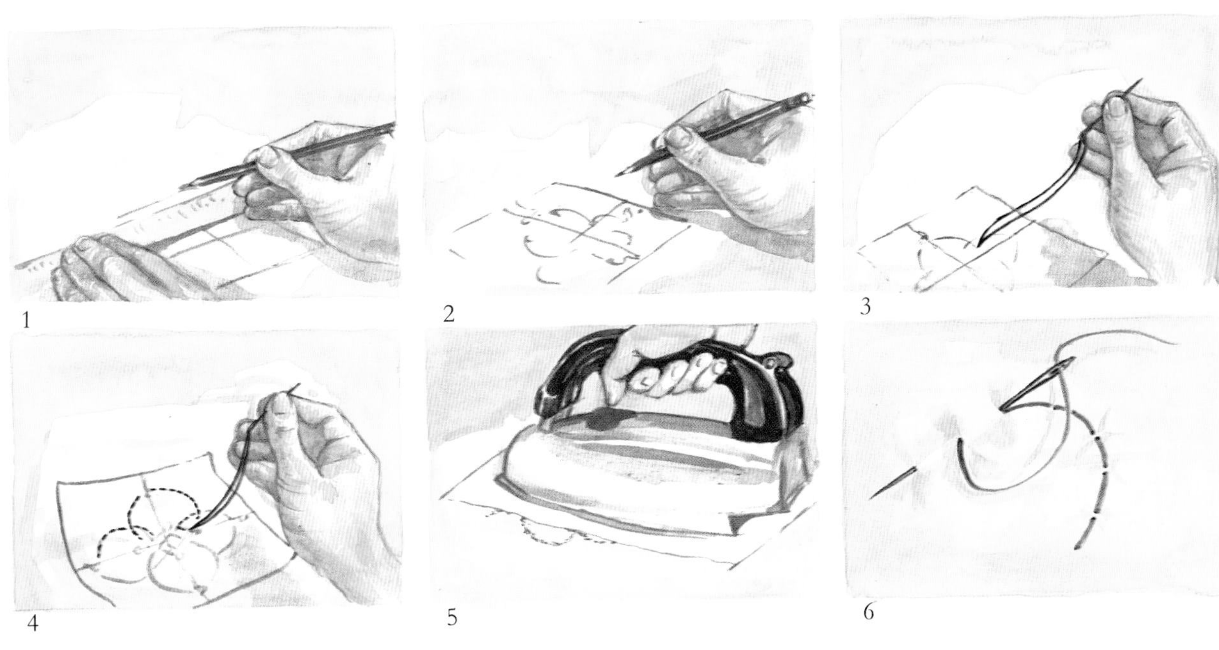
1 2 3 4 5 6

Materials
long white or cream washable evening scarf
skein of black silk embroidery thread
tapestry needle size 22
embroidery scissors
water-soluble pen
ruler

Method
1. With ruler and water-soluble pen measure and draw a 4 in (10 cm) square in the centre of each end of the scarf, 2 in (5 cm) from both bottom edges. Divide the square into quarters.
2. Following the design shown, copy the motif square by square onto the grid.
3. Sewing with two strands of thread at a time, embroider over the design using small, even backstitch – i.e. take the needle back over and forward under by the same distance.
4. Begin sewing at one of the corners and work methodically down and round the design. Do not jump from one line of the design to another leaving a large, loose stitch behind, but finish off and start the new line afresh.
5. When both motifs are complete, wash the scarf carefully to rinse out the soluble ink, dry and press gently using a damp cloth.

WHITEWORK

Fine whitework is perhaps the most artistic pursuit
in the world, and you must realise this and be glad it is so.

From the writings of Lady Evelyn Murray (1868–1940)

Of the many forms of needlework subscribed to by ladies and young girls through the centuries, whitework – by which is meant white stitchery on a white background – presented one of the greatest challenges. While the technique itself could be adapted readily to suit the skills of the worker, since a wide choice of both materials and stitches could be used, its successful rendering depended ultimately on the structure and precision of the design. Having none of the benefits of colour with which to enliven the surface, whitework, by its very nature, focused almost entirely on compositional elements to achieve a range of effects – from crisp, geometric cutwork motifs and 'fillings' of needlepoint lace, to boldly embroidered floral swags and bouquets set in urns. Texture played a vital role in distinguishing the whitework patterns from their plain fabric grounds: the most distinctive decorations therefore comprised

77. All-white Danish sampler displaying various styles of drawn and pulled work on a muslin ground, dated 1758.
(By courtesy of the Trustees of the Victoria and Albert Museum, London)

simple contrasts, which included juxtaposing solid areas with cutwork, and executing the surface stitchery to contrast with the grain of the underlying cloth (therefore delineating the designs clearly throughout). The subtleties of the style were evidenced by the wealth of fine accessories created for both the home and personal adornment by accomplished needlewomen from the early seventeenth century onwards. Indeed, the immense delicacy of these pieces was such that the term 'frost-worke'[1] was used in contemporary accounts to describe their shimmering whiteness and purity of form.

Whitework could be executed with threads of silk, cotton or wool (or any mixture of these) on coarse, opaque fabrics such as linen or wool, or on sheer materials including muslin, lawn, organdie, cambric and net. The choice of textile was determined by the function the piece was to serve, and the type of effect desired. Hand-woven linens and twill cottons were suitable for lightweight bedcovers and whitework quilts, while ivory-coloured silks made exquisite additions to men's waistcoats, caps and a host of costume trimmings.

Prior to working, a whitework sampler was often made both as a practice piece for the stitches employed, and as an important store of designs. During the late seventeenth century, young girls of eight or nine would produce such a sampler, usually

78. All-white coverlet made from three pieces of home-woven cotton twill joined together, embroidered with couched candlewicking and raised cross-stitch for the border of grapes. Initialled and dated 'V B 1818', Pennsylvania.
(The American Museum in Britain, Bath)

79. Candlewick bedspread made by Laura Collins of Goshen, Connecticut in 1825.
(Shelburne Museum, Shelburne, Vermont, USA)

after other more elementary needlework using coloured silks and wools. Surviving samplers of the period display a comprehensive selection of whitework patterns based on *reticella* (needlepoint lace), drawn work, cutwork, buttonholing and numerous forms of flat stitchery.

The sheer variety of sewing techniques, as featured on long sampler panels, provided important points of reference for the seventeenth-century embroiderer. Other sources of design could be found in pattern books which were published at the time such as the well-known *The Needle's Excellency* (1631), and the earlier volume, *New and Singular Patternes and Workes of Linnen Serving for Patternes to make all Sorts of Lace Edgings and Cut Workes*, which appeared in England in 1591.

The vogue for fine cotton fabrics and imported Madras muslins during the eighteenth century led to a new refinement in whitework designs, in imitation of the costlier bobbin laces produced in France and Belgium. The delicate stitchery, combining drawn and pulled work, was usually executed in cotton threads on a cotton or linen ground. Known as Dresden work, the style was characterized by the use of elegant floral motifs interspersed with densely patterned 'fillings' of minute geometric forms. The free-flowing designs were soon copied in England (and elsewhere in Europe and America) to adorn costume accessories such as elaborate aprons, neckerchiefs, lappets, sleeve ruffs and fichu borders.

Towards the end of the century, under the influence of Neoclassicism, the fashion for high-waisted muslin and gauze dresses adorned with whitework panels was patronized with much enthusiasm. Women favoured the 'look' of youthful innocence, which was also one of considerable daring by virtue of the sheerness of the lightweight fabrics employed.

With the increasing demand for fine cotton and muslin fabrics, which had hitherto been imported into Europe from America and India, a cotton- and linen-weaving industry was established in Scotland by the early 1800s. The 'sewed muslin' produced here (and later in Ireland) became known as Ayrshire work, characterized by its use of very fine cotton threads.

By the second half of the nineteenth century, however, the introduction of machine embroidery from France and Switzerland, as well as disruptions in the cotton trade resulting from the American Civil War, soon led to the decline of whitework produced by hand.

In America, whitework samplers were executed by girls as part of their tuition in decorative embroidery techniques. Dresden-work panels were especially popular during the second half of the eighteenth century, and the style was recommended as a pursuit worthy of well-bred young ladies by the many elite schools established in the New England area. Floral motifs were most prevalent, as in England, although pieces produced in Philadelphia were distinctive for their ornamental ribboned borders.

During the 1790s, the fashion for all-white rooms and furnishings captured the imagination of American women and whitework, therefore, became very popular. This distinctive style was described by a lady of Salem, Massachusetts, when visiting her aunt's home: 'The room was furnished in white painted furniture, the dimity drapery of windows and bed were white, the straw matting on the floor was white...the great white bed stood like a snowdrift ...'.[2] White-on-white bedcovers enjoyed an enormous vogue during the period *c.*1790–1845, and were created by many accomplished needlewomen in a lively range of styles. Quilted and embroidered pieces were favoured, as were candlewick spreads with their soft roundels of yarn in low relief, depicting animals, birds, fruits and flowers. A fine example, in French-knot candlewick embroidery, was created by Laura Collins of Connecticut in 1825 (see plate 79) and portrays a large weeping willow tree (symbol of mourning) and two doves (for love), surrounded by borders of grape vines and scrolling flowers. The sentiments expressed in the design reflect the personality of the maker, and her sadness at having never married.

Whitework accessories for personal use were also produced with great flair by American ladies during the first half of the nineteenth century. Pockets, which were worn around the waist underneath the skirt, and 'reticules' (small drawstring bags) were created in the most dainty styles with tassled borders, ruffled frills and trimmings. Towards the end of the 1840s, however, the Victorian fondness for brilliant colour (as embraced, for example, by Berlin work; see pp. 134–9) led to the demise of whitework as a fashionable pastime.

In recent years, whitework has again become popular in keeping with the current interest in traditional embroidery – a revival which has been fostered by both sewing enthusiasts (including today's leading *haute couturiers*) and collectors of antique textiles.

80. Detail from a cotton twill bedspread decorated with baskets of flowers and posies, in a variety of stitches, early nineteenth-century.
(Shelburne Museum, Shelburne, Vermont, USA)

SILK EMBROIDERED PICTURES

> Female accomplishments consisted largely of embroidering mourning pieces, with a family monument in the centre, a green ground worked in chenille and floss silk, an exuberant willow tree, and a number of weeping mourners . . .
>
> Harriet Beecher Stowe, *Oldtown Folks* 1889

Pictures embroidered on silk were immensely popular during the late eighteenth and early nineteenth centuries, and instruction in the 'art' was included at the numerous finishing schools established for fashionable young women in Europe and America. Ornamental needlework was considered one of the most important aspects of a well-bred girl's education, and while a few institutions offered some degree of academic training in 'Reading, Writing, Arithemetic . . . and the Use of the Globes . . .',[1] others concentrated on the genteel pastimes of music, dancing and fancy work. Silk embroidery, with its lustrous threads and shimmering fabrics, represented one of the highest achievements in fine stitchery, and as such its practice was reserved for accomplished students between the ages of about fourteen and twenty.

81. 'Needlepainted' picture sewn in silk on a wool-canvas ground. The figures are sewn in satin stitch over paper padding, reminiscent of stumpwork. Signed and dated M. A. Ryder, 1819. *(The Crane Gallery, London)*

82. Continental, mid-eighteenth-century collage picture, with the figure embroidered in silk, overlaid with contrasting fabrics.
(Halcyon Days, London)

The embroidered compositions were worked invariably in flat stitch, using coloured silks on silk or satin grounds. Other materials such as wool, chenille yarns, fine metallic cords and glittering spangles were added occasionally for contrast. It was usual for certain areas of the design to be hand-painted in watercolours or washes of ink, as found commonly on the faces and hands of figures which, by virtue of their small size, were difficult to embroider. Landscape backgrounds and areas of sky were also rendered similarly, to achieve an effect of greater delicacy.

Prior to stitching, the outlines of the scene were first sketched onto the silk cloth. This task was usually performed by either the school instructress, or by a professional designer, who would also paint freehand designated parts of the composition. Miniaturists such as T. C. Bell Jr of Baltimore, Maryland, advertised his services in 1814 as a colourist of 'Faces, etc., of Needlework',[2] while in Boston, the craftsman James M'Gibbon could 'design, draw and Paint Embroidery in a superior style'.[3] Glaziers and picture framers also offered their skills as needlework 'artists', although the naively rendered paintings of several period embroideries would suggest that the girls themselves were responsible for the decoration.

83. Silk embroidered panel inscribed 'The Lord is my shepherd', recalling the vogue for elegant pastoral scenes during the late eighteenth century, *c.*1815. *(Weidenfeld and Nicolson Archive)*

A wide range of subjects was depicted, from biblical and allegorical themes to scenes of graceful shepherdesses in pastoral landscapes. Portraits of Regency ladies in garden and woodland settings were popular, with the figures dressed in the high-waisted, sheer muslin gowns fashionable at the time, and women anglers in ribboned bonnets made exquisite additions to the series. These scenes of refinement reflected the ideals of beauty and 'civilized' living among the genteel classes of the late eighteenth and early nineteenth centuries.

Most popular, however, were mourning embroideries, which enjoyed a considerable vogue on both sides of the Atlantic during the period *c.*1790–1820. Their lively, emotive content appealed greatly to the imaginations of young girls. The grieving figures were arranged invariably around a central tomb, set under a large weeping willow tree with its branches bent sorrowfully, like giant teardrops. In England, prints and paintings on the theme of death, such as Angelica Kauffmann's *Fame Adorning Shakespeare's Tomb*, were transcribed readily into silk embroideries, of which nearly-identical pieces worked in silks and watercolours have survived. Literary sources provided further inspiration, and Goethe's novel, *The Sorrows of Werther*, for example, gave rise to numerous needlework pictures of the grief-stricken Charlotte at Werther's tomb.

In America, the fashion for mourning was given greater impetus following the death of George Washington in 1799, when there was a sudden profusion of dedicatory embroideries, based on contemporary engravings. Some featured painted miniatures of the late President, flanked by groups of silken angels and goddesses in the Neoclassical taste. Others focused on private moments of family mourning, with the name and dates of the departed relative stitched or inscribed on the tombstone. The majority of pieces were mounted sympathetically in black glass within richly gilded frames, and were intended as both wall pictures and chimney ornaments. Often, the name of the embroiderer (and,

84. English early eighteenth-century silk embroidered picture of Judith and the head of Holofernes.
(Alistair Sampson Antiques Ltd, London)

frequently, the school she attended) were written in gold calligraphy at the bottom of the frame.

Schoolgirl embroideries have survived in their dozens from the New England area, some of the finest examples of which were created under the supervision of inspired tutors at institutions such as Miss Mary Balch's Academy in Providence, Rhode Island; Mrs Susanna Rowson's Academy in Boston; and at the fashionable Mrs Saunders' and Miss Beaches' Academy, which opened in 1803 in Dorchester, Massachusetts. In Mississippi, where small finishing schools were established during the early 1800s, the fashion for silk memorials did not go unnoticed, and interpretations often included alluring and indolent southern 'belles'.

More delicate, perhaps, were the silk needlework pictures executed in black-on-white combinations, in which the pictorial scenes took on the appearance of etchings or stipple engravings. According to *The Young Ladies' Book* (1830), the pieces were worked on a white or ivory-coloured silk ground '... with a very fine needle in black silk, or in silk of different shades, from a jet black through all the gradations of a lead hue, to the palest slate-colour'. Schoolgirls exercised their skills in this challenging branch of monochrome embroidery – known as 'printwork' – using the tiniest stitches and needles to create charming rustic landscapes and elegant memorials. Occasionally, fine strands of hair were woven into the designs (see Hairwork, pp. 170–71). Sources for printwork were found in contemporary engravings after George Morland, John Hamilton ARA and other well-known artists. The scenes were copied by tracing their outlines in pencil or ink onto the silk grounds, which were then filled in by stitching.

The vogue for silk embroidery declined by the late 1820s, and with it the revival of Classical ideals. Painted compositions on backgrounds of velvet and silk (see Amateur Painting, pp. 14–17, and theorems, pp. 21–5) became the new fashion for the leisured classes – pursuits which, to some extent, had evolved from the watercolour and silk embroideries of previous years. The temporary lull in needlecrafts, however, did not endure for long, as the radiant Berlin wool work was soon to capture a vast female audience on both sides of the Atlantic.

QUILTING AND PATCHWORK

Hannah had queer ways. She was given to interior adornments, and the fruits of her needlework were thick in the house . . . (she) hoarded scraps of silk and cambric, and pieced them into pin-balls, chair-cushions and coverlets . . .

Description of a New England maid's 'Homely Handiwork', from a letter written in *c.*1850[1]

85. Nineteenth-century 'Christmas Bride' quilt, featuring feathered circles, running feather and floral designs, surrounded by an appliqué border. *(The American Museum in Britain, Bath)*

The techniques of quilting and patchwork were the mainstays of American domestic needlecraft during the eighteenth and nineteenth centuries, and most girls were expected to have sewn twelve or thirteen quilts by their late teens – the last of which, by tradition, was intended as a bride's showpiece. There was no limit to the invention of bold designs and brilliant colour schemes, as women progressed from one quilt to the next to produce hundreds of examples in a lifetime. As their skills sharpened, so their artistry appeared to blossom, and of the wealth of magnificent quilts passed down through the generations as family heirlooms, few have lost their vigour or appeal.

Quilting was first introduced into Europe via the Orient and Near East during the early medieval period. It was brought to America during the seventeenth century by the colonists, whose survival during the bitter winter months depended on the home-production of warm bedcovers and thickly padded clothes. Most quilts consisted of three layers sandwiched together, with a wool or cotton stuffing used as a lining between a top and bottom sheet. These were joined together by a series of running stitches, with the uppermost surface either left plain, or rendered decoratively by fancy stitchery, patchwork or appliqué. Patchwork designs were made up of numerous fabric remnants sewn or 'pieced' together (hence, the process was often referred to as 'piecework'), assembled frequently in geometric styles using a few basic shapes. Appliquéd examples featured cutouts of fabric (such as flowers or baskets of fruit) which were sewn onto a separate background cloth (or blocks of cloth) and afterwards stitched onto the surface of the bedcover. Appliqué served primarily for pictorial representations, and combined readily with patchwork or quilting. If the appliquéd piece itself was to be quilted, the running stitches were executed over the applied decorations last of all.

In some of the finest examples, the techniques merged into harmonious patterns: running stitches followed the outlines of the decorative motifs to surround and emphasize every shape. Alternatively, the stitchery might introduce an entirely novel design, independent of the surrounding cutouts or patches, to enliven the surface with new areas of dense patterning. The possibilities for compositional arrangement were infinite and, whether one, two or all of the methods – quilting, patchwork or appliqué – were used, the results could be astonishingly innovative.

American quilts made prior to the mid-eighteenth century were only seldom pieced or appliquéd. The majority were made from lengths of wool or linen which were sewn together (since early looms were unable to weave wide, single pieces). The materials were usually dyed a deep solid colour, notably dark blue, red, yellow, green or brown. Sheep's wool was favoured as a stuffing, over which a top cloth such as calamanco (a glazed worsted fabric imported from England) was sewn and, for added warmth, the backing was made from homespun linen or linsey-woolsey (a combination of linen and wool). The decoration of these 'whole-cloth' quilts, as they are described today, relied entirely on surface stitchery, which ranged from simple geometric designs of parallel bands, arcs and diamonds to intricate pictorial devices of, commonly, furling foliage and baskets of fruit. The patterns bore a close resem-

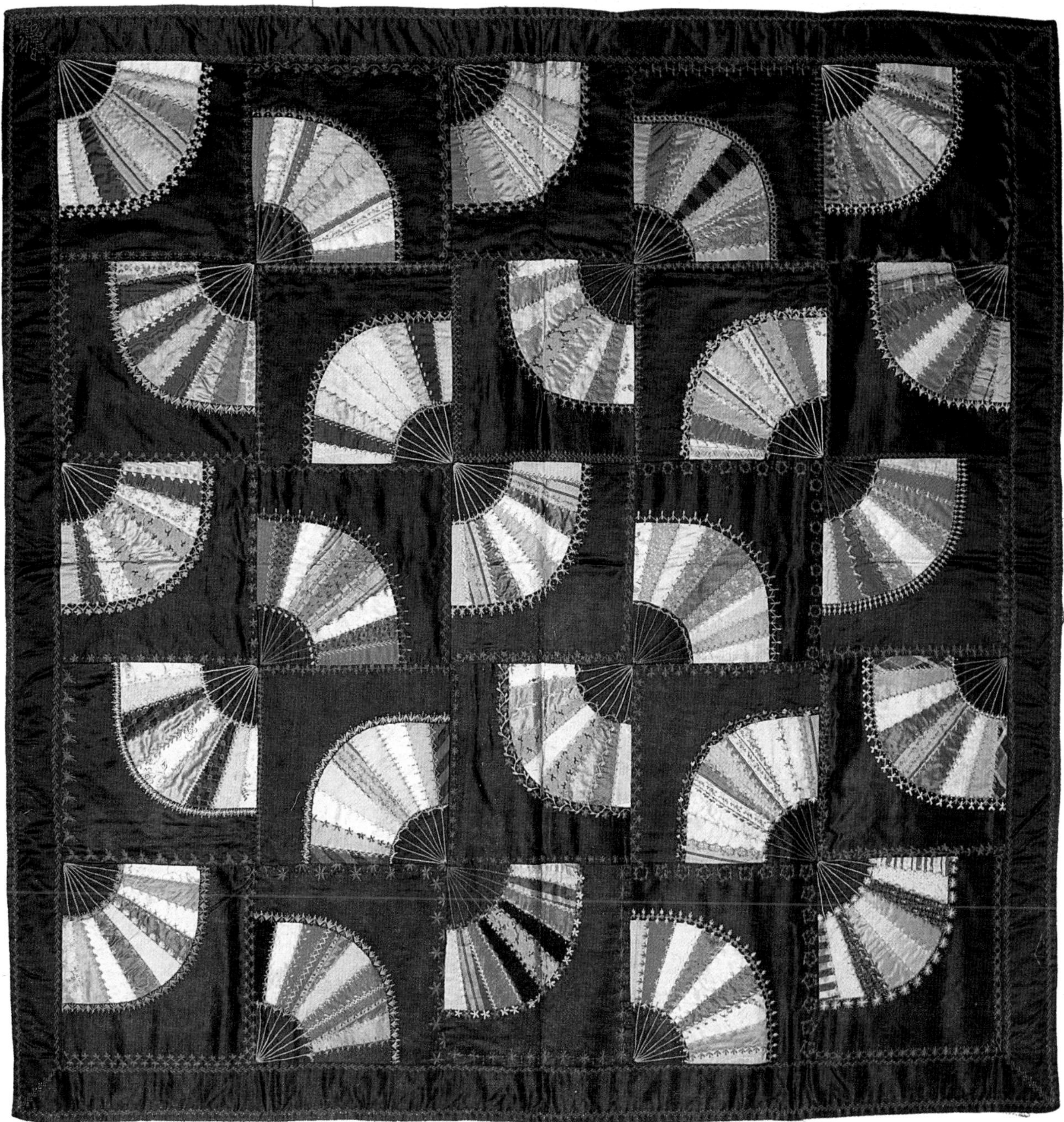

86. Fan-patterned quilt made in 1900 by Rachel Boone Wintersteen of Pennsylvania, for her dowry chest – she never married, however, and the cover was unused. *(The American Museum in Britain, Bath)*

blance to the calamanco quilted petticoats and aprons of the period. The stitchery was often executed in a medallion format, with the central ornamentation surrounded by broad borders of scattered or interconnected motifs.

American 'whole-cloth' quilts resembled those produced in rural districts of England (particularly in the north) and south Wales. British designs favoured solid colours and simple geometric configurations of diamonds, circles, waves and zigzags – one or more of which was stitched all over the surface. Specific patterns were indigenous to certain regions. Quilts from Carmarthen, for example, featured lively spiralling motifs, while those from Glamorgan showed a marked preference for stylized leaves. The American custom of filling a girl's dower chest with a dozen or so quilts, however, was not traditional in England, where just one was considered sufficient – made either by the mother or daughter. In Wales, six quilts and a 'carthen' (or woven coverlet) comprised the usual lot of bridal contributions.

Copperplate printing to ornament fabric was introduced after 1750 in Ireland, and during the

1780s London manufacturers turned to the technique as a novel means of decorating cloth, producing large repeat patterns in fine detail. Many of the subjects were inspired by the flamboyant chinoiserie styles fashionable at the time. The materials, however, were expensive to manufacture, and when exported to America, their appeal was limited to a wealthy elite for use as 'best' bedcovers and drawing-room furnishings. Elaborately printed Indian chintzes and calicoes were also imported into America and their profuse patterns made striking additions to coverlets and bed hangings. As a result of their high cost, chintzes were seldom selected for the expansive 'whole-cloth' quilts, but were employed, rather, in the form of small cutouts which were appliquéd onto white fabric grounds. Compositions for chintz appliqué were devised frequently in imitation of Persian embroidery *(broderie perse)* and the highly-prized Indian palampores with their hand-painted 'tree of life' patterns. Both styles reflected contemporary tastes for exotica, which remained prevalent on both sides of the Atlantic well into the nineteenth century.

Quilting parties or 'bees' were a popular source of diversion and entertainment for women in America (across the Atlantic, however, such social gatherings appear to have been confined to the area around Ulster). Mothers, daughters, grandmothers, aunts and neighbours met regularly to quilt and gossip, and their activities were only interrupted when the men came home for supper. Mary Warren wrote in a letter in 1800 that she was 'so engaged in frolicking, (that) there is nothing here among us but quiltings and weddings'.[2] Other contemporary accounts tell of the busy schedules of the village 'bees', which were seldom cancelled come blizzards or heatwaves.

Bridal quilts were a speciality at the gatherings. In some regions, it was considered unlucky for the prospective bride to complete her own wedding quilt, and symbolic decorations of hearts, interlocked circles (representing betrothal rings) and other finishing touches were sewn instead by the quilting party. Pennsylvanian superstitions were such that when the 'bee' had completed its task, the quilt was removed from the frame and its corners given to four unmarried women. A cat was placed in the centre and the cover '. . . vigorously shaken; the young woman nearest the cat when she jumped out would surely be married within the year'.[3]

Patchwork quilts became increasingly popular by the end of the eighteenth century, and for thrifty housewives the process of piecing together seemingly useless scraps of material (saved from worn clothing and furnishings) was a necessary exercise in household economy. Most women were not without their ragbags, and once enough remnants of chintz, calico, muslin, silk or velvet had been amassed, the children of the house were given the task of cutting and assembling them into groups. Young girls would usually sew the fabric squares together into blocks of, typically, four or nine patches, while older ones helped with the more difficult chore of quilting. Repetitive, all-over designs of rectangles and squares were attempted first, followed by triangles and diamonds, the latter often sewn together into lively 'lily' patterns.

88. *Right*, nineteenth-century 'Darts of Death' or 'Widow's Quilt', the pieced black darts alternating with quilted white blocks in a harp pattern.
(The American Museum in Britain, Bath)

87. *Below*, detail from an American, nineteenth-century 'Feathered Star' quilt, coloured in brilliant shades of orange and pink.
(The American Museum in Britain, Bath)

Although piecework was not technically as demanding as quilting, the exercise was nevertheless challenging and creative. The selection of colours and shapes, and their precise arrangement – all of which required careful planning – was fundamental to the success of the composition. While some women were limited in their choice of materials (depending on what they could find in the scrap bag), others exchanged patches or purchased new ones to complete a particular design.

Once a girl had mastered geometric piecework, she was taught to appliqué curvilinear shapes and pictorial emblems. The motifs were first drawn freehand onto cloth and then cut out. The edges of each were turned under, and the whole sewn carefully onto a plain ground using a fine hemming or buttonhole stitch. As chintz was expensive, cotton became the firm favourite after the 1830s, when it could be purchased cheaply and used for large decorations. During the early nineteenth century, appliqué was combined frequently with piecework, and appeared particularly on borders in the form of garlands, ribbons and bows.

89. Detail from a 'Rose Garden' quilt. The individual pieces were sewn onto the background of white, quilted cotton, and then they were oversewn with small running stitch. English, *c.* 1860. *(The Crane Gallery, London)*

American women relied on an expansive decorative repertoire of real and imaginary forms for both patchwork and appliqué. Fruits, flowers and everyday objects were familiar and recurrent themes, sometimes juxtaposed with abstract shapes – some purely ornamental, others symbolic. In the Widow's Quilt (see plate 88) for example, the black-and-white scheme is punctuated by sharp, dart-like devices sewn over the surface – a powerful imagery imbued with grief and torment. Happier sentiments were expressed by bright orange and yellow pineapples, a sign of welcome and hospitality, and tulips which, for the Pennsylvania-Germans, were reminders of a joyful afterlife in heaven. The well-known 'Log Cabin' pattern (inspired originally by timbered rooftops) was a pervasive theme, with its shaded diagonals and squares made from coloured fabric strips. The format lent itself well to a variety of interpretations, since the colours and shapes could be altered to produce subtle optical effects. Tumbling blocks of three-dimensional appearance, feathered swirls, oak leaves, star bursts, sailing boats, fences and saw-tooth wheels were just a few of the subjects explored. The motifs were sometimes passed down from mother to daughter, and adhered to faithfully, as if they were family crests.

The quilts created by the Amish community in particular demonstrate a pronounced flair for brilliant colour and composition. Vibrant combinations of emerald green, cerise, mauve, blue, navy and black were used in non-representational designs of pure colour and abstraction (rarely encountered again until the Op Art era of the 1960s). The geometric blocks were arranged as stripes and diamonds, often placed within a large central 'field' surrounded by borders and corner decorations. The quilting, in contrast, was often elaborate, and was executed in black threads to offset the solid areas of rainbow shades.

Victorian patchwork conformed to the novel, fancy-work styles fashionable at the time, for which ladies' journals of the period recommended the use of plush materials such as velvet, silk and satin. In *The Ladies' Hand Book of Fancy and Ornamental Work* (1859) by Miss Florence Hartley, 'silk sewed together for parlour ornaments' was applauded as *the* new piecework, as cotton patchwork was demoted

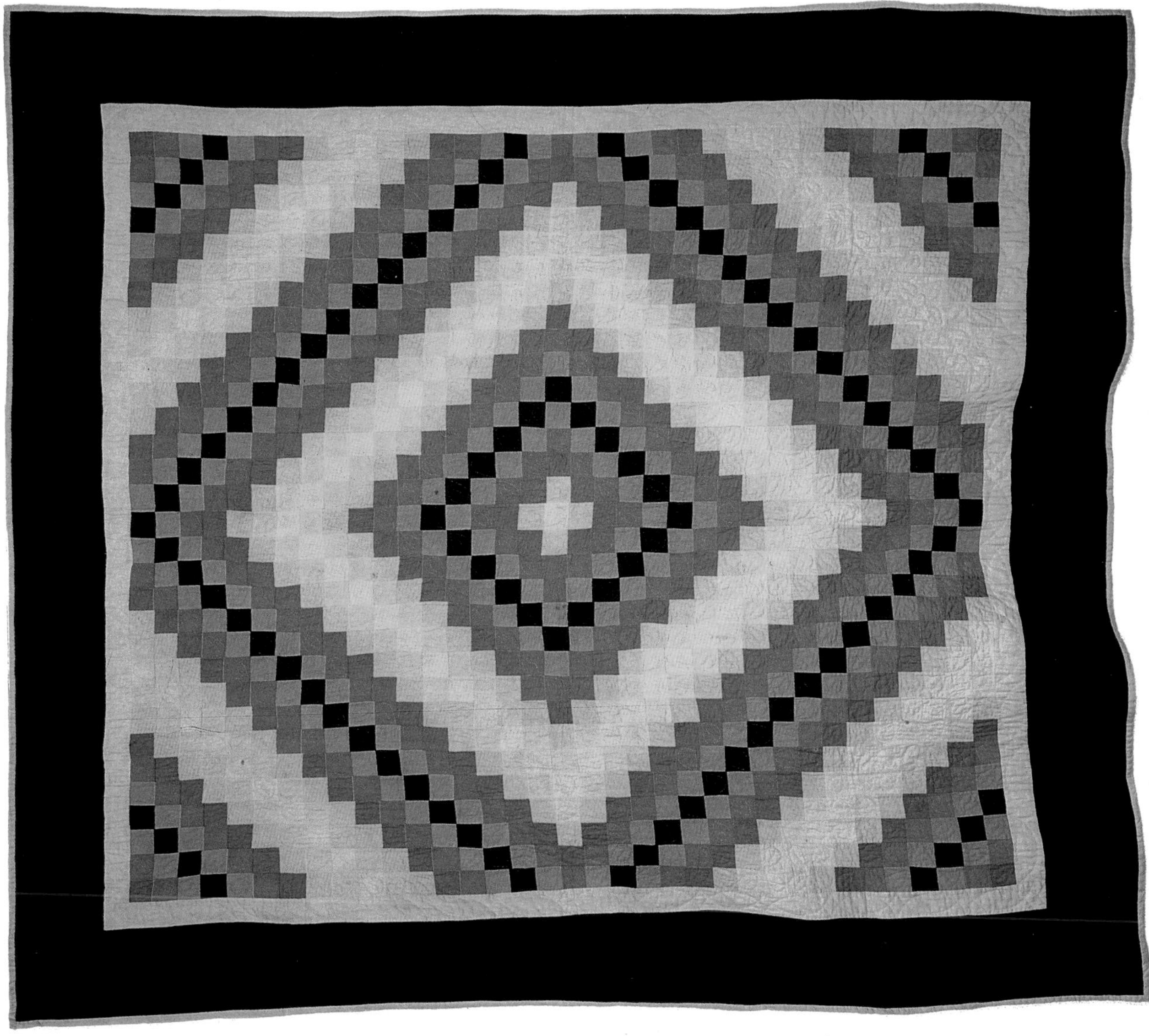

90. 'Sunshine and Shadow' American square patchwork quilt. Once the pieces were sewn together the entire surface was oversewn with running stitch to give a quilted effect. Ohio, 1910. *(The Crane Gallery, London)*

to the lowly status of a rustic and distinctly inelegant craft. Album and autograph quilts signed by each contributor enjoyed an immense following during the 1850s on both sides of the Atlantic, in keeping with the taste for precious, handwritten mementos and 'token albums' (see pp. 78–81). Silk patchwork in honeycomb and mosaic patterns was also popular, for which instructions were included ad infinitum in the American *Godey's Lady's Book* (1830–98) and its rival, *Petersen's Magazine* (1842–98).

'Crazy' patchwork was another Victorian invention, characterized by the use of irregularly-shaped pieces of velvet, satin and silk which were feather stitched together into haphazard patterns – the more random the effect the better, according to contemporary sources. All manner of household accessories were subjected to 'crazy' patchwork: from cushion- and bedcovers, to egg cosies and coffee pot warmers, there appeared no limit to the Victorian housewife's ability to cover her belongings with lavish quantities of these crudely cut patches.

Quilting and patchwork declined by the close of the nineteenth century; but there was only a temporary lull before the techniques were taken up again during the Depression years when, for reasons of economy (and perhaps consolation), women revived old styles and invented new ones.

PATCHWORK QUILT

Patchwork pieces can be made from a wide range of materials, and combined in an extraordinary number of eye-catching ways. This quilt uses simple diamond-shaped patches, hand-sewn into a traditional 'baby-block' pattern. The overall effect of the quilt depends entirely on the arrangement of dark and light shades within each block of diamonds – it can look strikingly three-dimensional, for instance, if dark-, medium- and pale-coloured fabrics are used.

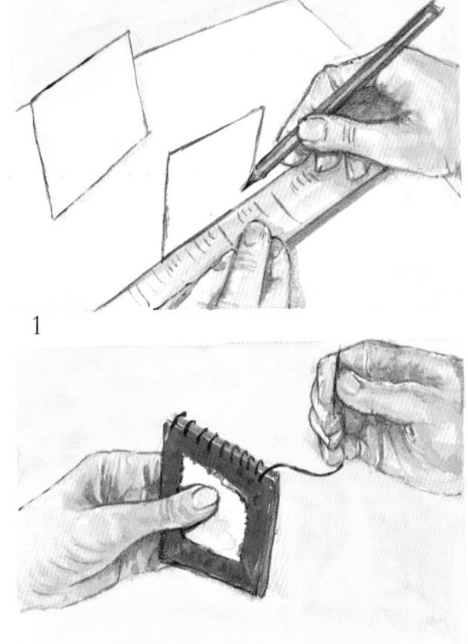

1

2

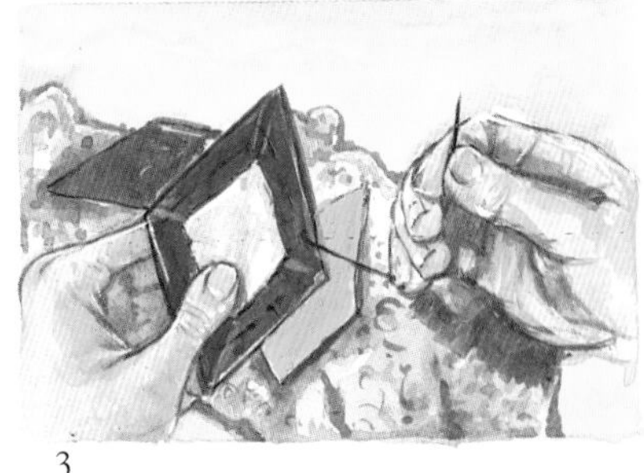

3

4

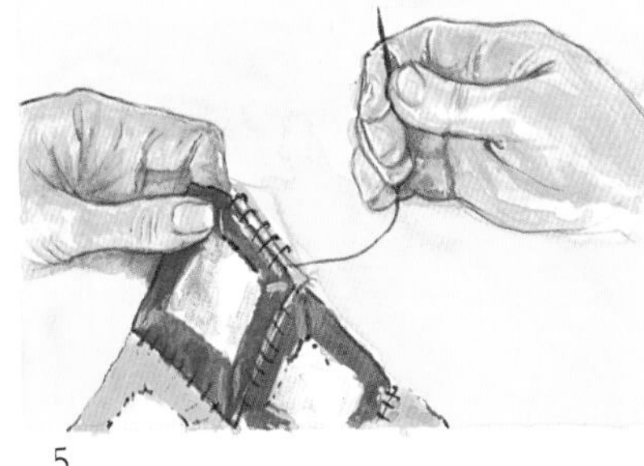

5

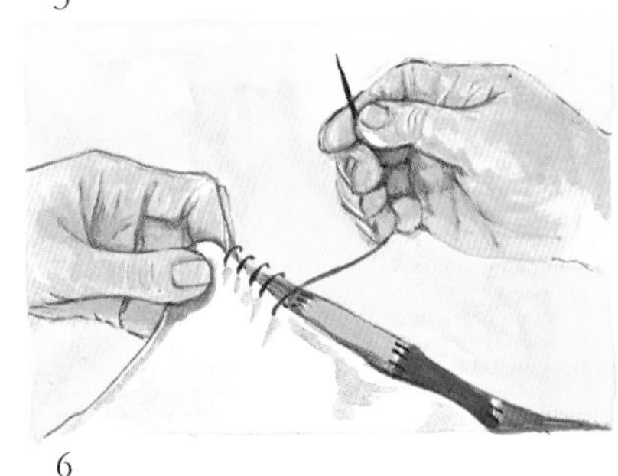

6

Materials
quantity of material in three contrasting shades. Medium-weight cotton is easy to sew; but any fabric can be used as long as all three types are of the same weight.
ruler
sharp pencil
stiff card
stiff paper such as cartridge or brown wrapping paper
craft knife
mercerised cotton. Use in preference to tacking thread for sewing the material to the paper patches, since it is stronger.
sharp needle
cotton thread in shades to match the materials. When sewing together patches of two different shades, match the thread to the darker colour.
large piece of cotton or calico to back the finished quilt.

Method
1. Make two templates by drawing and cutting diamonds carefully from the stiff card, one of which has sides each measuring 2 in (5 cm), the other $2\frac{1}{2}$ in (6 cm). Alternatively, metal templates can be bought in needlework shops, measured by the length of one side. They are longer-lasting than card templates and have the added advantage of being hollow – the internal shape to be used for cutting the paper patterns, the outer for the material.
2. Once the templates have been made, use the smaller of the two to cut identical diamonds from the paper. Rather than using scissors and cutting each individually, a more accurate and time-saving way is to place the template on top of three or four pieces of paper, cutting round the template with a craft knife. Use the larger template and sharp scissors to cut diamond-shaped pieces of material, drawing round the template lightly in pencil first.
3. Place one paper diamond on the wrong side of a piece of fabric and pin in place. Fold the material round the edges, catching the corners, and tack in place. Make two more patches, one from each of the other two shades of material.
4. To join the patches, hold two – right sides together and edge to edge – and oversew along one side, making sure not to catch either of the paper patterns underneath.
5. Then, matching the edges and with right sides together, sew the third patch to both of the first two. This three-diamond block forms the basic pattern, of which any number can be made until the quilt is the desired size. It is quicker, once one block has been made as a model, to make a number of patches – perhaps 30 or 60 – at one sitting before being sewn together.
6. When the quilt is complete, remove the tacking thread and paper and press on the right side with a cool iron. To back the quilt, take a large piece of cotton or calico, turn in and press a 1 in (2.5 cm) hem all round and, with wrong sides together, pin and oversew to the quilt edges.

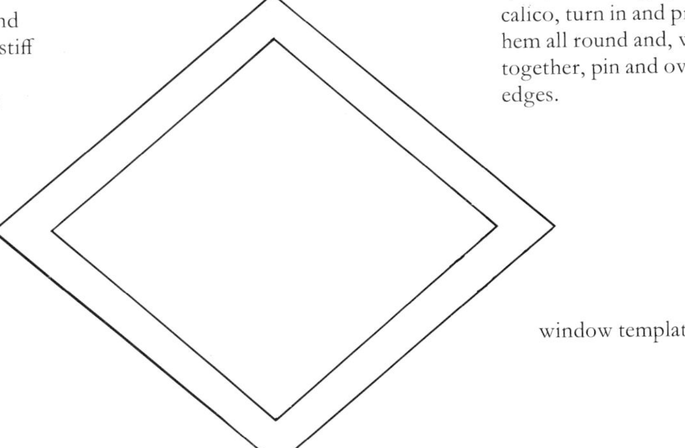

window template

KNITTING AND CROCHET

Home should always contain a grandmother . . . the lovely old lady
is a great treasure in a household, has often agreeable accomplishments in the way of
needlework and knitting, has . . . recipes for cakes and custards,
and knows the most delightful old-fashioned games of cards

Mary Elizabeth Sherwood, *Amenities of the Home*[1]

Prior to the nineteenth century, knitting was usually regarded as a form of plain needlework and in affluent households the task was delegated to servants, or local women who earned pin money for their efforts. Most school children practised the technique as part of their education in domesticity, while for girls of good breeding, the exercise – although hardly an 'accomplishment' – was considered good discipline (and fundamental to household management in future married life). At many of the elite women's seminaries established in America during the eighteenth century, for example, spinning, sewing and knitting came under the general category of 'Useful Needlework'. Although a cursory knowledge of these was required, the aim was to instruct pupils in its fashionable applications – notably in knitting fancy gloves, lacy stockings and all manner of decorative trimmings. When the newlywed Martha Washington arrived at Mount Vernon, accompanied by 150 slaves, she ensured as part of her wifely duties that her household staff maintained high standards of knitting. During the Revolutionary War, when knitting needles and pins were scarce, she set an example for other lady patriots and took to knitting in the army camps, helping the troops to combat the freezing winters ahead.

91. Crochet provided yet another 'sedentary occupation' for ladies of leisure, *c.*1883.
(The Mary Evans Picture Library, London)

With the advent of knitting machines during the early 1800s, cottage industries were established for the production of stockings and other basic apparel, thus relieving the mistress of the house (or her staff) of the monotonous chore of plain sewing. However, knitting in fancy styles was soon encouraged as a pleasing diversion to while away one's leisure hours by the fire. In an early handbook to knitting, published in the 1840s, the exercise was deemed suitably 'genteel' for '. . . passing the evening in one another's society, even when passing a morning visit, or after dinner at a dinner party, or while sipping coffee, or taking ices at the public garden . . . knitting needles (are) an indispensable accompaniment'.[2] The purely mechanical aspects of knitting made it an ideal therapy for 'idle hands', and since it required little observation, it served as a candlelight occupation (and one which combined readily with other sedentary activities). Girls frequently boasted of their ability to knit and read at the same time.

Ladies' magazines were quick to jump on the bandwagon, and provided their readers with knitting instructions and patterns with which to create the latest fashionable accessories. During the 1840s, *Godey's Lady's Book* in America published regular articles on knitting under the guidance of their resident needlework expert, 'Mlle DuFour'. Domestic ornaments such as doilies and freestanding imitations of flowers and fruits were immensely popular, while for costume finery there were knitted muffs and 'Victorines' (worn like giant collars around the neck). *Godey's* Editor wrote confidently of the magazine's contributions when she pronoun-

92. Crocheted needlework carpet decorated with panels of colourful floral bouquets between borders of pink roses and grape vines. English, *c.*1860.
(Mayorcas, London)

ced in the 1846 issue: 'We are sure of the thanks of all ladies, young as well as old, for calling their attention to this useful and elegant branch of female art. No other periodical attends to these things.' In spite of *Godey's* aspirations to be 'first and foremost in all things', other journals promoted knitting for amateurs at home (and published nearly identical patterns) – among them, *Petersen's*, the *Lady's Magazine*, *Harper's Bazar* and the *Atlantic*. Manuals such as *The Ladies' Work-Box Companion* (which advertised 'entirely new receipts') and the best seller, *Miss Lambert's Guide* (which appeared in numerous editions on both sides of the Atlantic), further ensured the widespread popularity of the pastime.

Victorian patterns stressed the practicality of knitwear for infants, children and husbands, and were firm evidence of a housewife's industry. The 'Gentleman's Bosom Friend', a warm double-knit garment designed with a turtleneck, was one of many home-produced accessories lovingly created by the mistress of the house for her husband's pleasure (in spite of the fact that the correspondence columns of contemporary journals were sometimes replete with complaints from gentlemen weary of their wives' unceasing knitting at all hours of the day and night). As regards women's attire, knitted shawls became *de rigueur* during the 1850s, for which hundreds of patterns were supplied, such as those included in Miss Lambert's *The Ladies Complete Guide to Needle-work and Embroidery* (1859). The writers of *Godey's* pronounced them indispensable and devoted numerous fashion plates to the stylish wearing of shawls.

Crochet, a fancy version of knitting using a small hook to create lace-like designs, became popular in England and America by the late 1830s. One of the first handbooks devoted to the technique was Miss Lambert's *My Crochet Sampler* (1840), in which the exercise was recommended '. . . over all other ornamental works'. Patterns for crochet often accompanied those for knitting. Both *Godey's* and *Petersen's* prided themselves in providing their readers with the newest styles from Europe, and included directions for making whimsical items such as a 'Jacket for a Greyhound', and a 'Handle for a Riding Whip' for fashion-conscious sportswomen. During the 1890s, *Weldon's Practical Crochet*[3] became the housewife's companion *par excellence*, with its profusion of articles devoted to every conceivable aspect of dress and interior furnishings. For children there were patterns for petticoats, hoods, jackets, 'Dorothy frocks', vests, muffs and gloves, while infants were well catered for with 'bootikins', rattles, soft toys, bonnets, mittens and cot blankets. Household necessities included crochet drapes for mantel borders and wall brackets; afghans and antimacassars 'to drape over an easy chair'; curtain tie-backs; bedspreads; 'toilet tidies . . . to hang upon the knob of a toilet glass', and all manner of decorative edgings for sewing onto bed and table linen.

93. German knitted wall hanging displaying traditional designs of scrolling foliage, flowers and birds, dated 1781.
(By courtesy of the Trustees of the Victoria and Albert Museum, London)

DECORATIVE RUGS

I had no yarn to knit, nothing to sew, not even patches . . .
One day Mrs. Parrish gave me a sack full of rags and I never received a present before nor since that I so highly appreciated as I did those rags.

C. Kurt Dewhurst and Betty and Marsha MacDowell, *Artists in Aprons*, 1979[1]

94. Rag rug hooked and braided on burlap. American, mid-nineteenth century.
(The American Museum in Britain, Bath)

The small decorative rugs made from remnants of old materials in the eighteenth and nineteenth centuries did not appear in the grand stately homes of the British aristocracy. Indeed, rug-making hardly featured among the graceful occupations taken up by young ladies of accomplishment, and the technique was seldom mentioned in European journals devoted to the female arts. The finest residences were furnished elegantly in keeping with fashionable period tastes. These formal schemes were enriched by the inclusion of oriental carpets imported from Turkey and the Near East, and during the eighteenth century many celebrated interior designers created wall-to-wall floor coverings to their clients' own specifications. Kidderminster or 'Scotch' rugs, as well as those of Brussels and Wilton manufacture, were popular alternatives. In view of the well-established textile industry, it is hardly surprising that the craft of rug-making formed little part of a well-bred girl's tuition in fancy needlework and the ornamental arts.

In America, however, the homely skills of rug-making were adopted by women for both functional and aesthetic reasons. Relatively few of the finely woven carpets from Europe and the East were imported into the country, and these could be afforded by only the wealthiest households for use in formal parlours. For the remaining population, there was little else to relieve the stark monotony of bare wooden floorboards, or the dirt and rush-matting which featured commonly in the majority of colonial dwellings. Little further encouragement was needed to stimulate the appearance of domestic rug-making, and by the nineteenth century, the cottage craft was elevated to that of an artistic medium, with its brilliant colours and designs worked to perfection. As a sign of its acceptance as a fashionable craft, the skills required for rug-making were expounded in contemporary journals such as *Godey's Lady's Book* and *Petersen's Magazine*, which were devoted to the usual female diversions.

The majority of domestic rugs were made from materials such as vegetable-dyed rags and other fabric remnants deemed too old or worn for making into patchwork. The scraps of cloth were collected from discarded household items and clothes, and saved religiously until enough pieces could be assembled and worked into small carpets and door mats. For parlours and bedrooms, 'area' rugs were placed in the centre of the room or by the fireplace. Wall-to-wall coverings were created by sewing numerous hand-stitched or woven segments together, sometimes with each strip adorned by a contrasting design. Bold rainbow-striped patterns worked on a loom made colourful embellishments for draughty and poorly lit corridors and staircases.

The finest pieces were executed by hand, either sewn with a needle or 'hooked' to achieve a variety of surface effects. Early nineteenth-century examples often combined the techniques of embroidery and appliqué to create pictorial scenes of, commonly, homesteads and gardens. Stylized floral patterns were also popular and bear a striking resemblance to the stencilled decorations of the period, with baskets of wild flowers, potted plants and fruits rendered in lively, naive fashion.

Hooked rugs achieved wide recognition during the 1840s, when they were executed with great flair and imagination by women in New England and Canada. The newly imported material known as burlap, a coarse loosely-woven jute used for making sacks, made an ideal background onto which the wide fabric strips could be looped in and out by means of a hooked implement. The designs were first

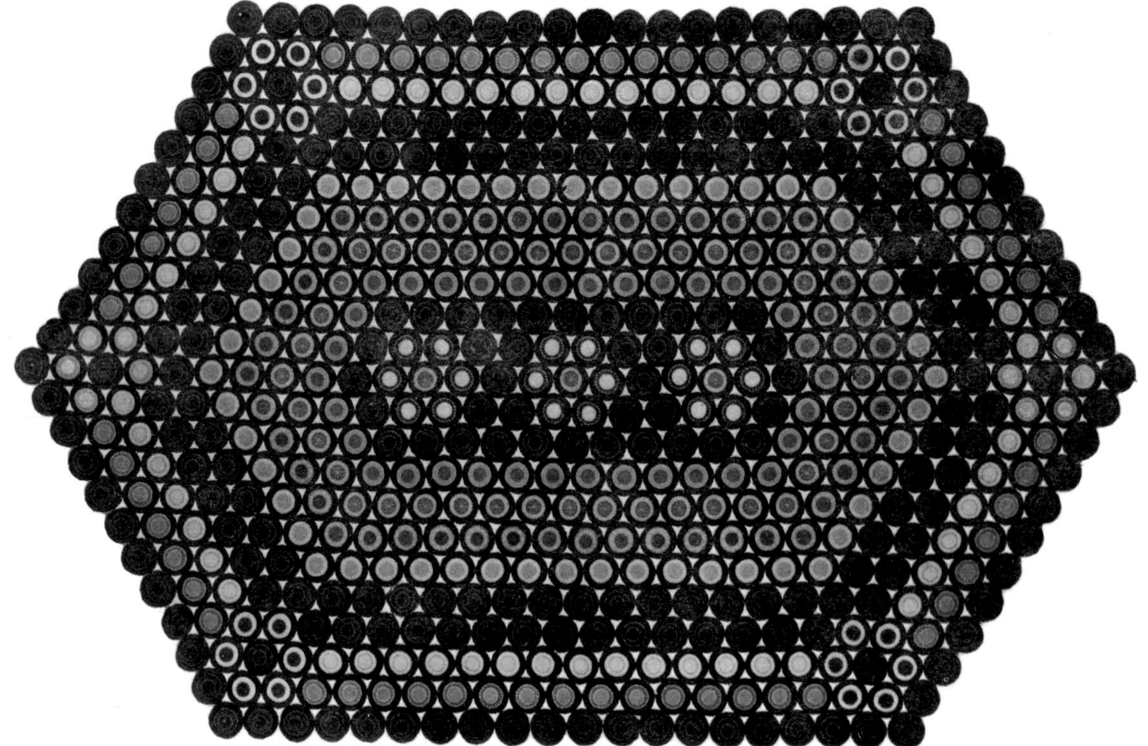

95. Nineteenth-century American 'dollar' rug, the roundels of fabric sewn layer upon layer in rich solid colours.
(The American Museum in Britain, Bath)

96. American hooked rug decorated with a spotted 'firehouse' dog, surrounded by budding flowers and leaves, and corner accents of red roses, nineteenth century.
(The American Museum in Britain, Bath)

drawn in charcoal or chalk onto the burlap to guide the position of the coloured rags. These were then hooked or punched through the holes of the canvas so that the patterns appeared on both sides. The loops could be drawn in tightly, left as loose coils or sheared to form a shaggy pile. During the 1860s pre-stencilled backgrounds were introduced for those less artistically inclined, and could be purchased from travelling salesmen such as Edward Sands Frost, who advertised his 'invention' so widely that he soon became known as 'Frost, the rug man'.[2] 'Primitive' scenes of farmyards and rural dwellings, brilliantly coloured flowers and bold geometric compositions were all favoured. Many of the designs were adapted from contemporary quilts and featured patterns such as the sophisticated 'Log Cabin', with its shaded blocks in contrasting tones, and the so-called 'Hit or Miss' style, with its randomly assembled shapes.

The immensely varied designs of small 'area' rugs were complemented by an almost unlimited colour repertoire. Rainbow stripes appeared on black, blue or scarlet backgrounds, while other interpretations incorporated over a dozen different shades to create an almost blinding effect of pure colour, in the Amish style. In contrast, geometric compositions were sometimes executed in muted tones throughout, and two or more distinctive patterns were worked into one, to achieve subtle optical effects. Carpet shapes were equally diverse and appeared crisply outlined, their hexagonal or octagonal form, for instance, reinforced by parallel lines of looped or entwined fabric.

Other popular variants included braided rugs, which comprised plaited strands of rags, and the so-called 'penny' or 'dollar' rugs, made from numerous felt roundels sewn one upon the other in three layers. The latter were often used to cover a table or chest.

In rural districts of England, the craft of rug-making was also practised skilfully in the traditions of folk art. Examples dating from the late nineteenth and early twentieth centuries were largely of geometric or abstract design, although a few featured pictorial scenes, recording the everyday lives of the women who made them. More recently, the simple technique of rug-hooking has been revived by enthusiasts wishing to create country-style furnishings in the spirit of the past.

A MINIATURE HOOKED RUG

Based on a nineteenth-century American stencil design

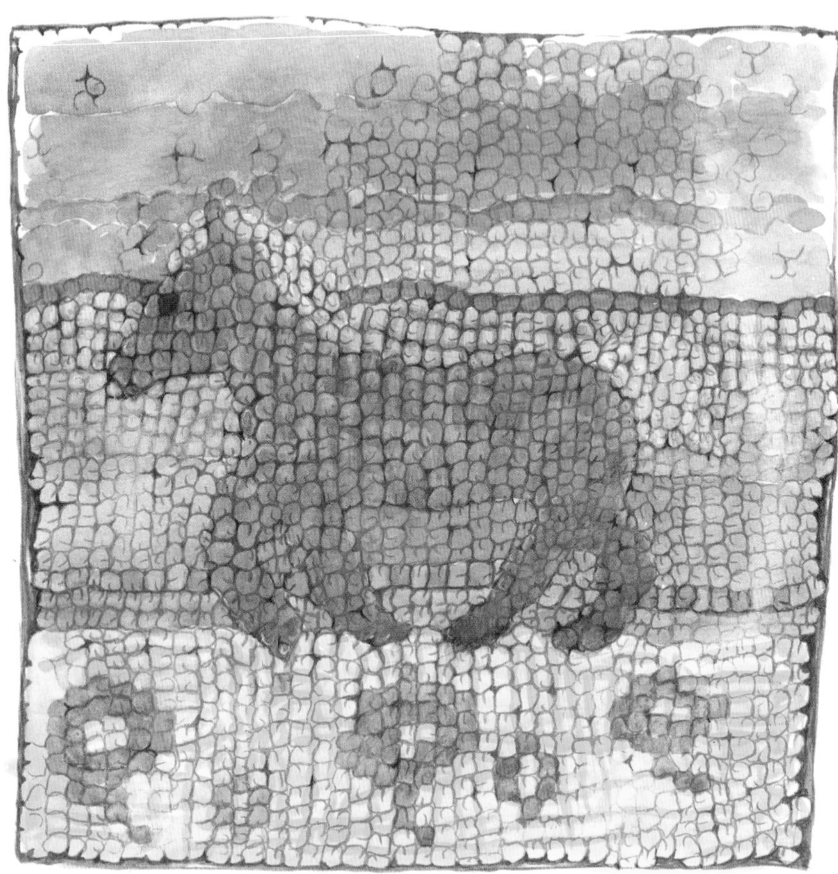

This decorative rug may be worked easily by beginners and, due to its small size, can be executed without a frame. When complete, it would make an attractive wall hanging or coverlet in a child's bedroom.

Different coloured rags can be used to create a wide range of effects – outlines can be picked out in a dark tone for dramatic effect, contrasting coloured strips can be used in eye-catching borders, subtle shades give a three-dimensional effect to large areas. It is well worth experimenting on a trial piece of canvas prior to starting the project, to explore a variety of colour combinations.

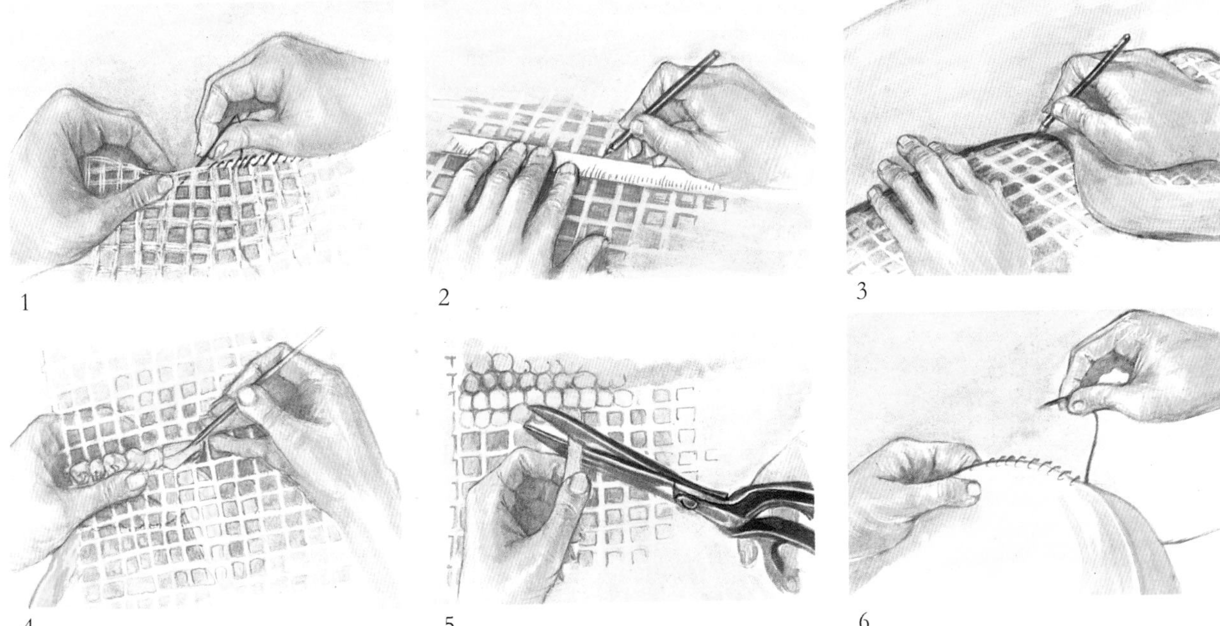

1 2 3 4 5 6

Materials
piece of No. 5 double canvas, 12 × 10½ in (30 × 26.25 cm)
crochet hook ⅛ in (3.5 mm)
large quantity of long cotton rag strips in different colours. Bear in mind that 3 in (7.5 cm) of cloth will be required for every 1 in (2.5 cm) of canvas. This rug will use the equivalent of sixty 24 in (60 cm) long strips.
large sharp scissors
felt tip pen
ruler
latex adhesive
stiff card 12 × 10½ in (30 × 26.25 cm)
piece of cotton cloth 12 × 10½ in (30 × 26.25 cm)

Method
1. Oversew the raw edges of the canvas to prevent them from fraying.
2. With ruler and pen mark a 1½ in (3.7 cm) margin around the sides of the canvas, followed by the centre point, 5¼ in (13 cm) from the shorter edge and 4 in (10 cm) from the longer.
3. Make a template of the horse from stiff card, cut out, place in the centre of the canvas and mark its outline.
4. Cut the cloth into long strips ½ in (1.2 cm) wide. Starting at the top left-hand corner of the canvas, take a rag strip and hold it flat underneath the canvas. Insert the crochet hook through a hole from the front of the canvas and pull up a small loop ½ in (1.2 cm) high. Insert the hook into the next hole and repeat the process along the row. Use all the rows and as many holes as possible to ensure a tight and neat finish.
5. Should you run out of rag strip while working, want to change direction or use a different colour, pull the strip being used to the front and cut to the height of the other loops. It will soon blend in with the surrounding 'pile'.
6. Once the hooking is complete, turn in the raw edges and sew firmly in place. The back of the canvas can be treated with adhesive to ensure that the loops remain secure. Finally, take the piece of cotton cloth, turn in and press a 1½ in (3.7 cm) hem, pin and oversew it to the back of the rug.

BERLIN WORK

Think of the many years which English women have spent over wickedly hideous Berlin wool pictures, working their bad drawing and vilely crude colours into those awful canvases . . . at the expense of (their) minds.

Chats on Needlework, 1908

Of all forms of needlecraft, no other captured a wider audience (and later met with harsher criticism) than Berlin wool work – the fashionable Victorian lady's steady companion over a period of some eighty or ninety years. Its easy step-by-step methods, brilliant palette and vast range of popular subjects ensured its enduring success as the new medium *par excellence*, and contemporary journals applauded the pastime as the 'most elegant of female accomplishments'.[1]

Berlin work was regarded as a creative sedentary occupation for gentlewomen, and when not worked at home was taken along in small leather pouches or pretty Tunbridge-ware boxes as an accompaniment deemed suitable for all social occasions. Tiny port-

97. Berlin-work screen whose pre-printed design is sewn in richly coloured wool threads, nineteenth century.
(By courtesy of the Trustees of the Victoria and Albert Museum, London)

able patterns were devised specifically for the purpose. M.T. Morrall remarked in his book, *A History of Needlemaking* (1852): 'If any lady comes to tea her bag is first surveyed, and if the pattern pleases her a copy there is made'. In making small trifles, the Victorian gentlewoman was in her element, and her Berlin-work pincushion covers and watch pockets all found a ready place at the charity bazaar.

Berlin work was first introduced in England during the first decade of the nineteenth century. It was executed on square-meshed canvas in plain tent or cross-stitch, following the desired pattern which was printed or painted on the surface in various shades. Each tiny square of the foundation was sewn with one stitch of wool, in accordance with the colour chart provided – rather like painting by numbers. The worker needed only to count the squares correctly to produce Berlin work of a reasonable standard (the exercise requiring little else in the way of experience or knowledge).

The majority of early patterns were issued by a handful of print sellers in Berlin (from which the term 'Berlin work' was derived) and were imported into England, initially in small, limited editions, and sold by outlets such as Ackermann's in London. By 1831, Mr Wilk's shop in Regent Street was one of several emporiums to import large quantities of the Berlin printed canvases and wools, which he advertised widely for 'the effective representation of flowers, birds and ornamental design'.[2] His so-called 'worked specimens' were exhibited at his Regent Street premises, where they could be admired for their 'beauty, simplicity and universal applicability', as well as providing a source of inspiration.

During the 1840s some 14,000 different patterns were available for purchase. The majority were created in workshops in Germany, France and England, where the printed monochrome designs were coloured by hand (until the advent of colour printing a few years later).[3] Large numbers of colourists, chiefly women, were employed by the manufacturers to paint over the patterns where required and, in some cases, to execute scenes in their entirety, often reproducing in immense detail the work of well-known artists. Their efforts, however, were poorly rewarded and despite the great success of the Berlin-work industry, the majority of labourers received little more than pin money according to the Countess of Wilton, whose observations of working conditions were published in her book, *The Art of Needlework* (1840).

98. Detail from a Victorian Berlin-work flower picture, stitched on canvas in coloured raised wool work, needlepoint and glass beads *en grisaille*. English, *c.*1850.
(Mrs Monro, London)

As the craze for Berlin work intensified, so the ease with which pieces could be worked was facilitated by an immense range of patterns to suit all levels and tastes. Simple floral motifs, worked in a few basic colours, appealed to amateurs, while more sophisticated 'painterly' compositions were reserved for those most accomplished in the art. For convenience, canvases could be purchased with areas of the design partially sewn, leaving the beginner with the straightforward task of completing the background and, perhaps, a few of the central motifs. Such pieces were undoubtedly favoured by those wishing to exert 'no physical or mental effort'[4]: Berlin work in its most elementary form fulfilled this requirement admirably.

During the early nineteenth century, Berlin patterns were executed frequently in coloured silks, as found on the pair of hand screens created by Queen Victoria, adorned with exotic birds (in the Museum of Costume, Bath). The use of silk, however, was soon superseded by vegetable-dyed wools imported from Germany and France, which were preferred for their extensive range of colours (over 4000 different shades) and fleecy texture. These, in turn, gave way to chemical, aniline-dyed wools during the late 1850s, which appeared in many new, brilliant and often garish tones. Magenta was one of several novel colours to be introduced at this time, and its fashionable potential was applauded in *The Ladies' Treasury* (1867), whose writers even suggested its suitability as writing ink. During the second half of the nineteenth century, large quantities of wool were spun and dyed in Yorkshire and Scotland for the home market, although materials from abroad continued to be imported and, in some instances, preferred for their radiant colours.

Other materials were also employed in conjunction with Berlin wools. Coloured silks, glass beads and bugles were reserved for areas of highlighting, and furry chenille threads permitted raised textural effects reminiscent of late seventeenth-century stumpwork. Their plush 'sculpted' surfaces were well-suited to animal and bird subjects, and made a striking contrast to the flat stitchery of the background.

Berlin samplers were worked by Victorian school children and featured the traditional design elements of an alphabet panel or verse, framed by a border of entwined flowers and leaves. Small pictorial scenes were created by young girls as part of their tuition in fancy needlework, under the supervision of a governess or teacher. Following these elementary exercises, more ambitious projects were attempted, including portraits of historical figures, who were considered of appropriate educational value. An American Berlin-work picture of Benjamin Franklin, for example, bears the inscription 'Presented by the pupils of the female department of Public School No. 2, Williamsburgh, N.Y. August 1, 1851'.[5]

After about 1850, the vogue for 'painterly' scenes appeared to dominate Berlin work, as countless reproductions of famous pictures were translated (and 'improved') in minute detail onto the square-meshed canvases. Romantic, religious and historical depictions were most popular, ranging from Leonardo da Vinci's *The Last Supper* (which was considered one of the most advanced exercises) to Sir Edwin Landseer's *The Monarch of the Glen*. Other themes were derived from literary sources, such as the heroic tales of Sir Walter Scott. The vast Berlin-work wall hanging of *Mary, Queen of Scots mourning over Black Douglas after the Battle of Langside* (in the Rochester Museum), for example, was inspired by Scott's novel *The Abbot* (1820), and was executed with astonishing determination by a fourteen-year-old girl in 1851, after the painting by Regent Murray.

99. Detail from a contemporary canvaswork carpet designed by Elizabeth Bradley, based on nineteenth-century Berlin styles, displaying the Victorian fondness for animals and pets. *(Elizabeth Bradley Designs, Beaumaris, Anglesey)*

Pictorial scenes were generally used to decorate cheval and banner fire screens, and occurred also on large 'tapestry' panels and carpets. When framed and glazed, examples were displayed like paintings in the drawing room or parlour, along with children's Berlin samplers and hand-stitched mottoes such as the ubiquitous 'Home Sweet Home'. Floral and geometric patterns were usually reserved for cushions and upholstery, where, on settees, stools and prie-dieu chairs, for instance, the Berlin panels were frequently highlighted by sections of beadwork. This combination of materials found its way onto the surfaces of innumerable household objects and accessories, and contemporary magazines provided patterns ad infinitum for the fashionable Victorian housewife.

By the last quarter of the nineteenth century, the vogue for Berlin work met with severe criticism from the proponents of 'art needlework', who frowned not only on the excesses of Victorian design, but also on its dismissal of creativity. As women looked towards greater emancipation – no longer content to play the role of submissive and 'loving wife (who) obeys her husband still, (to) lay aside her frame to meet his lordly will'[6] – so Berlin work was rejected as a symptom of a bygone age.

100. Carpet worked in multicoloured wools on canvas following the traditional counted thread methods of Berlin work.
(Elizabeth Bradley Designs, Beaumaris, Anglesey)

BERLIN-WORK CURTAIN TIEBACKS

Berlin work, extremely popular during the Victorian period, is one of the easiest embroidery techniques to learn since it uses wide-gauge canvas and simple stitches. Its applications are numerous and the results hard-wearing. Today, as in the nineteenth century, a range of vividly coloured tapestry wools is available and can be used for both pictorial and abstract designs – the zigzag pattern on these curtain tiebacks is most effective if executed in vibrant colours which complement the colour of the curtains themselves.

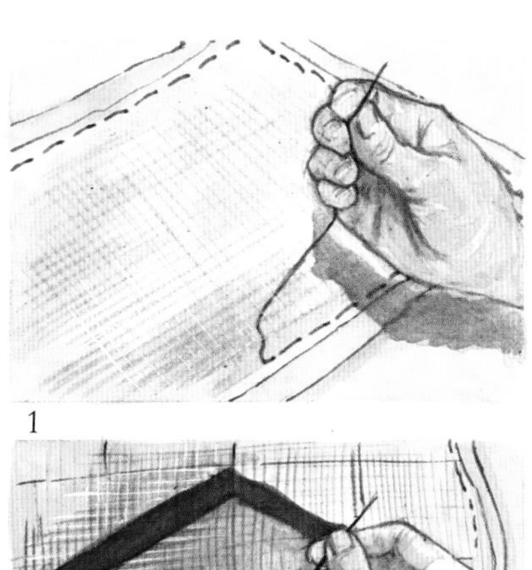
1

2

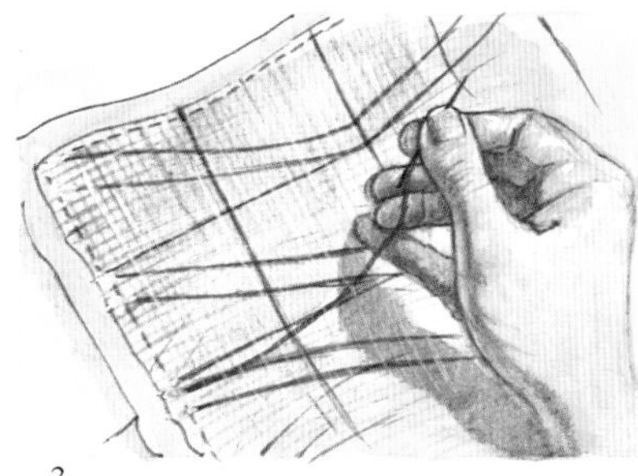
3

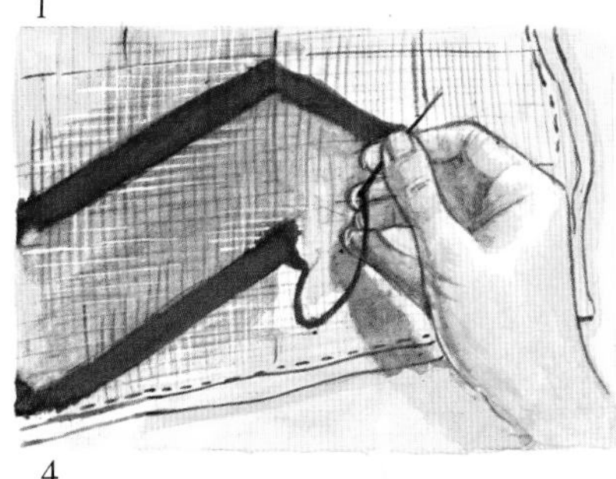
4

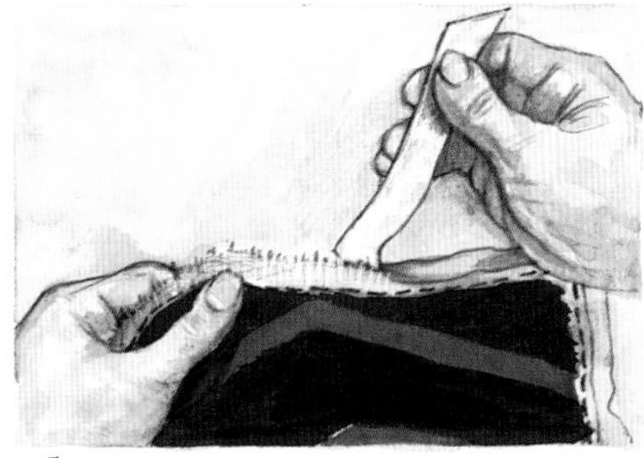
5

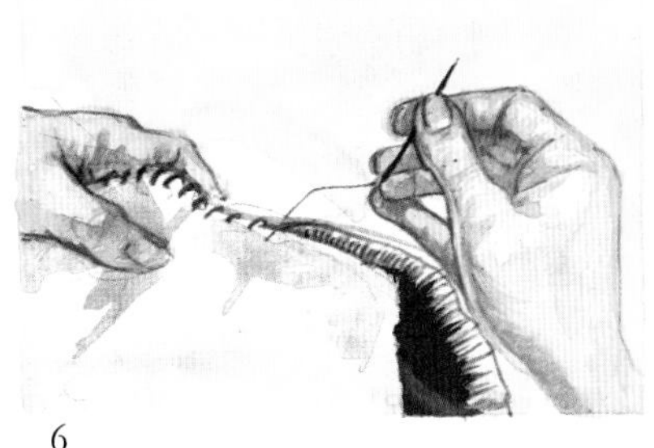
6

7 satin stitch

Materials (for 2 bands)
two pieces single thread, 14 gauge canvas
18 × 8 in (45 × 20 cm)
140 g tapestry wool – 80 g for
background, 60 g for zigzags
tapestry needle size 20
masking tape
waterproof pen
tacking thread
crewel needle
dressmaking scissors
two pieces medium-weight plain cotton
17 × 7 in (42.5 × 17.5 cm) in a shade which
complements those of the wools
four 2 in (5 cm) lengths of $\frac{1}{2}$ in (1.2 cm)
wide ribbon, again in matching shade
pins
ruler

Method

1. Bind the raw edges of the canvas with masking tape to prevent them from fraying. Tack round the edges of the canvas leaving a 2 in (5 cm) hem.
2. With ruler and pen draw a grid of twenty-four 2 in (5 cm) squares onto the canvas within the area marked by the tacking thread. Use the squares as a guide to draw three $\frac{1}{2}$ in (1.2 cm) deep zigzags over the canvas (ignoring the hem) following the design shown.
3. To begin sewing, bring the needle through the canvas from back to front, leaving a 1 in (2.5 cm) length of wool behind. When working the next six stitches, catch this loose end as you sew. Do not tie knots in the wool – they will either loosen or create a lump in the canvas. To finish sewing, weave the thread through the stitches on the wrong side.

There are no hard and fast rules about the order in which to sew but with a pattern such as this, which requires wool of several colours, it is easier to sew one whole block of colour at a time, starting with the darkest shade. When sewing, try if possible to take the needle up through an empty hole to avoid splitting threads in a hole that is partly filled. There will be occasions when this cannot be avoided, but with care two threads can fill one hole without fraying.

4. Work the first block of dark coloured area in satin stitch – a variation on tent stitch, which is sewn over two threads – pulling the thread firmly but not too tightly to leave an even finish on both sides of the canvas. Continue in this way over the entire pattern.
5. Once each band is complete, remove the masking tape and tacking thread, fold the hem over onto the wrong side and press lightly.
6. Take a piece of cotton backing and turn in and press a 1 in (2.5 cm) hem. Fold two of the pieces of ribbon in half. With wrong sides together, pin and oversew the canvas to the cotton, catching the ribbons in halfway along each of the tieback's shorter sides.

FANCY
WORK
FROM FISH SCALES
TO PORCUPINE QUILLS

> ... in works professedly published for feminine perusal, no attempt has been made to consult the intellectual capacity of women, or to advance in any way the cultivation of her mind. A series of frivolous articles ... meet with a grateful reception from the taste and discernment ... to whom they (are) offered.
>
> *The Lady's Newspaper and Pictorial Times*, 1847

While the pursuits recommended for Victorian ladies met with occasional criticism, the vast majority of women subscribed wholeheartedly to the views published by the doyennes of fashion and 'good taste'. Domestic management and creative industry in the home were encouraged relentlessly in contemporary journals. In America, *Petersen's Magazine* regularly reminded its female audience that its pages *alone* could be relied on for news of the latest trends in decoration and interior design, while in England, fierce competition among lady columnists resulted in several outlandish suggestions for 'felicitous handiwork'.

The Victorian fashion for fish-scale embroidery emerged out of this milieu of cloistered ambitions, and was one of several bizarre techniques to be taken up by lady amateurs at home. Its merits were highly praised by the writers of *Cassell's Household Guide* (1875) as an exemplary exercise in domestic economy, '... of how to utilise trifles which would otherwise be valueless ... enabling the housewife to render her home attractive'. The iridescent scales of common freshwater fish such as the carp or perch were scraped off and immersed in cold water. After soaking, the softened scales were each pierced with two holes at the base. The pieces could then be dyed and varnished and afterwards sewn onto background cloths of silk, satin or velvet. The scales were usually arranged in overlapping layers, to conceal the underlying threads, and used to form flowers, birds and insects, which were then embroidered with chenille threads, metallic cords, beads and spangles. Pincushions, purses and banner screens made suitable objects for the decoration, and their glittering surfaces served as reminders that 'out of nothing, something beautiful could be made'.

101. A nineteenth-century valentine card decorated with cutouts of embossed tinsel, paper, seaweed, ferns and shells, all assembled into an elaborate, 'fantasy' collage. *(Museum of London)*

102. *Pegwell Bay, Kent*, an oil painting by William Dyce, *c.*1859. The women gather shells and seaweed in wicker baskets, for decorating small objects at home. (*Tate Gallery, London*)

Whereas fish scales may have been readily to hand in the Victorian larder, the materials required for porcupine-quill work frequently necessitated diligent searching. 'Why do you give us directions for work we cannot do?', inquired a few perplexed readers of the *Elegant Arts for Ladies* (*c.*1856), whose authors replied, somewhat categorically, that 'Fashion rules the day' in spite of ensuing difficulties. Porcupine quills and other oddities could be purchased, however, from specialist crafts and 'curiosity' shops. Once assembled, the quills were split in half lengthways with the aid of a penknife, and arranged over the flat wooden surface of a workbox, tray or card case. They were then glued in place, weighted and afterwards varnished in a clear or coloured tint.

In her handiwork for charity bazaars, the Victorian woman was in her element, and her contributions of home-produced knick-knacks were met by her peers with unanimous approval. The Royal School of Art Needlework provided many of the materials required for furnishing a bazaar stall (apart from yarns and embroidery accessories) and could be relied upon to 'send out boxes of ready-made goods'.

Crafts manuals devoted to specific skills were published by the leading fancy-work repositories. J. Barnard's of Oxford Street, London, sold booklets for 2s 6d on all aspects of handiwork, from wax-modelling and potichomanie (or 'the art of decorating glass to imitate painted porcelain,' see p. 81) to leatherwork and diaphanie (in imitation of stained-glass windows). Other publications gave instructions *inter alia* for seaweed and sand collages, woven hairwork, imitation carved ivory (using a homemade rice paste) and buttonwork (for which many hundreds of buttons were torn off discarded clothes, and saved religiously, to ornament tea cosies, 'egg baskets' and place mats). Journals continued to stress the economic principles of 'waste not, want not' and if the parlour shelf began to sway under its heavy burden of wax fruits, paper ivy wreaths, hand-burnished plaster busts and shell-work festoons, here was ample evidence of the Victorian woman's industry.

FEATHERWORK

. . . the student of 'Elegant Arts' cannot well avoid
an acquaintance, amongst other things, with the
interesting histories of birds . . .
Elegant Arts for Ladies, *c.*1856

Among the variety of interior elegancies to which ladies of leisure turned their attention in the eighteenth and nineteenth centuries were the fanciful arrangements of bird feathers into decorative pictures, murals and imitation floral bouquets. Freestanding models of artificial birds were constructed by those dexterous in the 'art', and during the late Victorian period, Mrs Beeton's indispensable volume, *All About Everything*, also included instructions for taxidermy.

The vogue for bird pictures was stimulated in the eighteenth century by the publication of copperplate engravings such as the popular series *Song Birds*, executed by Eleazar Albin and his daughter in 1737. George Edward's lively illustrations for the *Gleanings of Natural History* (1756) provided further inspiration for those wishing to create their own compositions. Not surprisingly, one of the earliest exponents of featherwork was the gifted gentlewoman Mary Delany (see paper cutouts, pp. 60–65 and shellwork, pp. 147–51) and in 1727 she sent her sister Anne 'a tippet', or small cape, 'of her own making and invention', composed of brilliantly coloured macaw and canary feathers. Her great friend, the Duchess of Portland, kept an aviary of rare and exotic birds at her residence, Bulstrode (as was then fashionable), which undoubtedly provided Mrs Delany with a steady source of feathers of unusual shade and form.

Pictures of feathered birds perched on hand-painted boughs appeared in profusion during the Georgian and Regency periods, and achieved both an accuracy and realism which suggest that the ladies who created them had more than a passing knowledge of ornithology. In the *Ladies' School of Art* (1771) by Mrs Hannah Robertson, directions on how to 'Preserve Birds with their Elegant Plumage Unhurt' were set out for amateurs. Later, Mrs Kinglon devoted a chapter to feather decoration in her popular book, *The Wreath* (1835). The birds and details of foliage were first drawn very precisely by hand onto a plain coloured background. The 'body' of the bird was gummed, and the various coloured feathers laid down in orderly fashion, working from the tail to the neck to conceal the unsightly quill ends. The smallest feathers were reserved for the head, and for filling in bald patches around the neck, where they were arranged in overlapping patterns over the quills below. When complete, the feathers were pressed down with 'leaden weights' to secure them firmly in place. Finally, the foliage backgrounds were painted in watercolours or ink.

The fashion for featherwork did not go unnoticed in America, and its instruction was included among the many accomplishments required of girls of good breeding. In the *Boston Gazette* of 1755, the technique was listed in a school advertisement as an exercise worthy of '... young Ladies (who) may be taught Wax-work, Transparant and Filigree, Painting on glass, Quillwork and Featherwork, Japanning, (and) Embroidery with silver and gold'.[1]

Featherwork as an integral element of interior design enjoyed a brief vogue during the closing years of the eighteenth century. The enterprising cousins, Jane and Mary Parminter (see shellwork, p. 147) executed an elaborate series of bird murals for their house, *A la Ronde*, in Exmouth. The drawing-room cornice was highlighted by a frieze of coloured

103. *Left*, nineteenth-century featherwork composition of a peacock, a favourite subject for pictures and ornamental fans. *(By courtesy of Loot, London)*

104. *Above*, Victorian featherwork picture worked in both natural- and artificially-dyed feathers. *(Mrs Monro, London)*

feathers, while the upstairs gallery featured panels of birds interspersed with shellwork mosaics. They also composed freestanding models of birds assembled onto small frameworks, as well as more conventional wall pictures, with their feathered subjects perched on leafy boughs.

Other imaginative schemes were devised by Mrs Elizabeth Montague (1720–1800), who decorated her Portman Square town house with colourful 'feather hangings'. Indeed, so striking was their effect that the poet Cowper (one of many literary figures to attend Mrs Montague's soirées) was inspired to compose a verse on their 'splendour', opening with the lines:

> The birds put off their every hue,
> To dress a room for Montague
> The Peacock sends his heavenly dyes,
> His rainbows and his starry eyes . . .[2]

During the Victorian era, bouquets, wreaths and 'nosegays' consisting of clipped and curled feathers were considered elegant parlour displays. The most delicate examples were housed in glazed cases, or placed under glass domes for protection against dust and grime. Despite their novel appeal, however, examples were difficult to make and the instructions described at length in ladies' journals of the period must have deterred all but the most ambitious amateurs. The first step was to collect an appropriate number of feathers according to the design. Once assembled, they were washed in a solution of quicklime and water. After drying, the specimens were dyed a range of colours, following recipes such as those which appeared in the *Elegant Arts for Ladies* (*c.*1856), using the following ingredients: 'best indigo in powder' for blue; 'best tumeric' for yellow; 'cudbear' for lilac; and 'prepared cochineal (with) a few drops of moriate of tin' for red. Having completed this task, the next step involved the precise cutting of the feathers with the aid of a sharp knife and scissors to form the individual petals and leaves, and rendering them into curvilinear forms by means of curling tongs. Glue and lengths of wire were required to secure the flowers, and to create freestanding forms. Undoubtedly, a certain manual dexterity was necessary, and as such, this cumbersome 'art' was patronized by a relatively small number of enthusiasts.

By the late nineteenth century, the vogue for featherwork disappeared as the once-admired Victorian parlour – with its clutter of ornamental 'fancies' and 'loud patterns and gaudy colours'[3] – drifted into insignificance under the banner of Arts and Crafts ideals.

105. Detail of a late eighteenth-century featherwork frieze, from the dado of the drawing room at A la Ronde, created by Jane Parminter and her young cousin, Mary.
(A la Ronde, Exmouth)

SHELLWORK

There is no cruelty in the pursuit and subjects are so clean and ornamental to a Boudoir.
The Ladies' Magazine, early nineteenth century[1]

106. Detail of a late eighteenth-century shellwork frieze from a window frame in the shell gallery at A la Ronde, designed by the Parminter cousins.
(A la Ronde, Exmouth)

Decorating with shells was a favourite ladies' pastime during the eighteenth and nineteenth centuries, and the relative ease with which examples could be collected and applied to adorn objects and interiors ensured its widespread success. One of the earliest exponents of the art in England was Mary Delany, whose numerous accomplishments in the field of paper 'mosaicks' extended to the creation of imaginative shell displays for drawing rooms and grottoes. In a letter dated 1734, she described her enthusiasm as 'a new madness, I am running wild after shells' and she went on to amass a considerable collection, which she housed in a cabinet constructed especially for the purpose. Her great friend, the Duchess of Portland, was considered one of the foremost collectors of shells in Europe (indeed, so passionate was her interest that she was said to have killed one thousand snails for their shells).[2] Vast shell collections were mounted by numerous aristocratic patrons, and Lord Shaftesbury was recorded to have spent in the region of £10,000 to obtain rare specimens.

Shell grottoes featured commonly in the rustic landscape designs commissioned by the wealthy, in which elements of fantasy were conveyed by the inclusion of follies and other architectural novelties. In keeping with eighteenth-century trends, Louis XVI had a Shell Cottage built at Rambouillet for Marie Antoinette, the interior walls of which were covered with intricate shell mosaics, while in England, almost every fashionable residence devoted at least one room or garden focal point to this lavish form of 'marine art'. A superb example of eighteenth-century shellwork was created by the second Duchess of Richmond and her two daughters for their grotto at Goodwood House, near Chichester in Sussex. The walls and arched vaulted ceilings were decorated profusely with rich floral patterns of shells left in their natural colours of cream, yellow, pink, mauve and grey-blue. This arduous task took seven years to complete, and incorporated the use of many thousands of shells believed to have been presented to the Duchess by her numerous admirers.

Shell panels were executed in 1791 by the cousins Jane and Mary Parminter for their house *A la Ronde* (see plate 106). The flamboyant mosaic work, interspersed with feathered bird pictures and seaweed, was created from shells collected locally from Devon's beaches. In Ireland, Mary Delany amassed large numbers of shells during her frequent expeditions along the coastline near her home, and at Killala, where she was a guest of the resident Bishop. It was here that she completed her first grotto in shell work, commencing '... work at seven in the morning', while 'the men of the party did the fetching and carrying, and probably mixed the mortar for her'.[3]

Mrs Delany's passion for flowers (see also paper cutouts, p. 60) soon led to her preference for shell designs in the form of floral bouquets and swags to adorn ceiling cornices, window frames and mantelpieces in the manner of relief stucco work. For her home at Delville, in Ireland, she executed detailed shell compositions for the chapel, which she described in a letter as having consumed '... every hour of the day ... I make the flowers and other ornaments by candle-light, and by daylight when I don't paint, put together the festoons that are for the ceiling'. George Montagu remarked upon her astonishing efforts (which she took up from the age of fifty) in a letter to Horace Walpole, 'All fitted up and painted by her own hand the stucco composed of shells and ears of corn the prettily-est disposed imaginable'.[4]

Apart from their obvious uses in interior design, shells were also employed for the decoration of small boxes and picture frames, by gumming each piece onto the surface to form various pictorial or geometric compositions. Shell pictures, and freestanding objects with the pieces wired onto frameworks, achieved widespread recognition in the nineteenth century. The latter were assembled into massive floral bouquets and placed under glass domes for parlour display. This fashionable pastime was patronized by ladies in both Europe and America, using shells collected during seaside excursions (which could be coloured by hand later), as well as pre-painted samples from specialist shops.

In *Cassell's Household Guide* (1875), several projects were illustrated with instructions for 'tea caddies ... boxes and pin cushions' and '... for decking small wooden toys ... with the smallest kind of shells ... which will render them well suited to the drawing-room whatnot'.[5] In the *Elegant Arts for Ladies* (*c.*1856), the craft was recommended as 'an elegant drawing-room occupation, as well as one calculated to call forth the artistic taste and inventive powers of the worker'.[6] A chapter devoted to what was known as 'rice shell-work', using tiny shells 'resembling grains of rice' imported from the West Indies, described the technique for composing delicate hair ornaments, *tremblants* and dress corsages by piercing the shells and wiring them into decorative wreaths. Rice shells could also be employed effectively for making freestanding baskets and other table ornaments, as recommended in the popular manual, *Parlour Recreations for Ladies* (1854). Figurines and small animal subjects composed almost entirely of shells made attractive mantelpiece ornaments, and instructions for making these appeared in ladies' magazines on both sides of the Atlantic. A pair of shell-dressed dolls in early Victorian costume can be seen at the Shell Museum, Glandford, Norfolk. The majority of pieces were carved in wood and layered with hundreds of minute shells to convey textural details, pleats and drapery. Their lacquered, sharp-edged surfaces recall the hand-painted porcelain statuettes of the period.

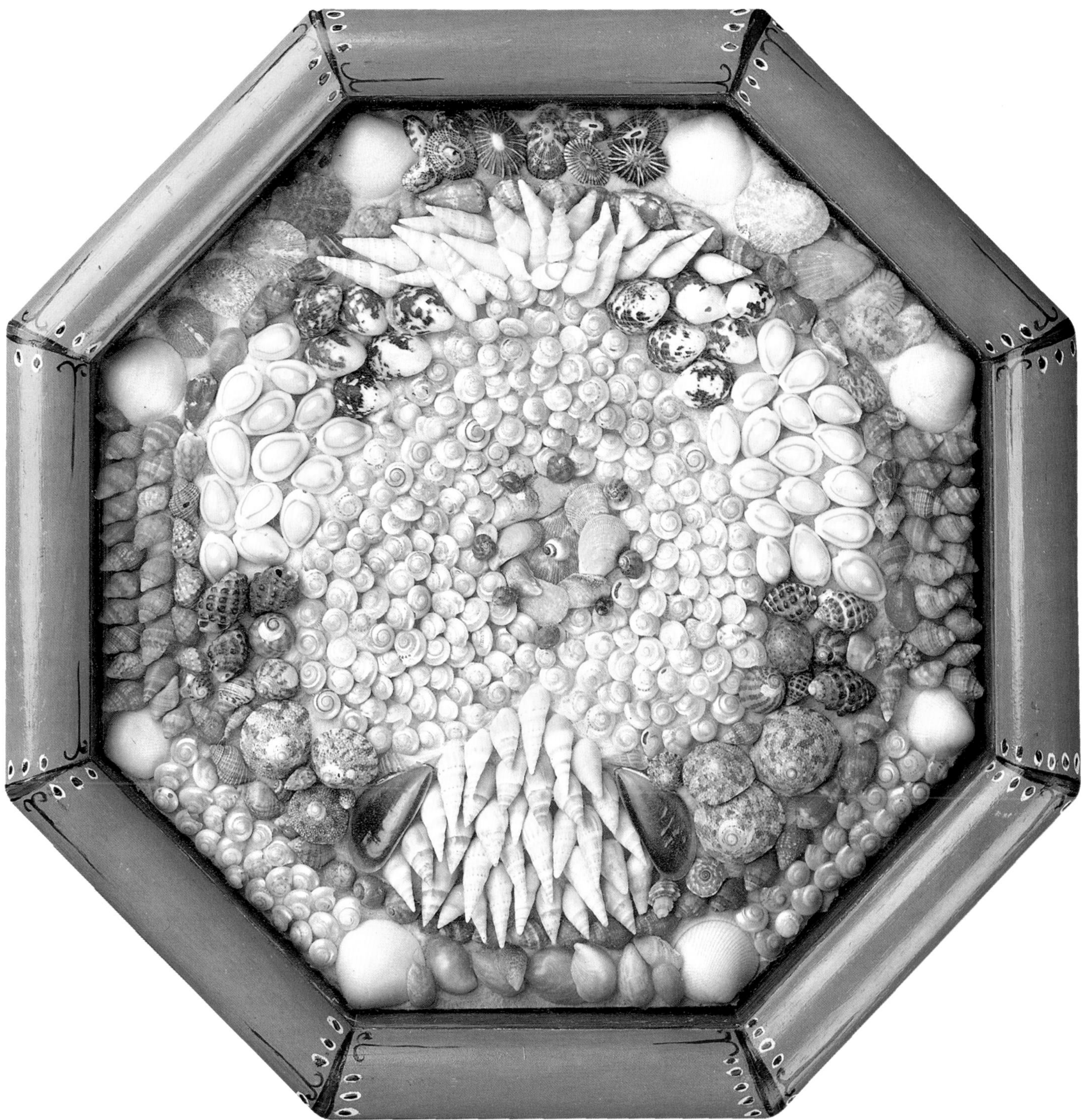

107. Contemporary shellwork decoration, housed in an octagonal faux-bamboo frame, inspired by the shell mosaics popular in England and America during the early 1800s.
(Mrs Monro, London)

SHELLWORK MINIATURE OF FLOWERS

Inspired by the delicate eighteenth- and nineteenth-century flower pictures which were glazed and hung decoratively, the shellwork 'miniature' described here makes an ideal starting point from which numerous floral compositions can be devised. Relatively few shells are needed for this project and examples can easily be found along any coastline. Multicoloured specimens can also be purchased from seaside tourist shops.

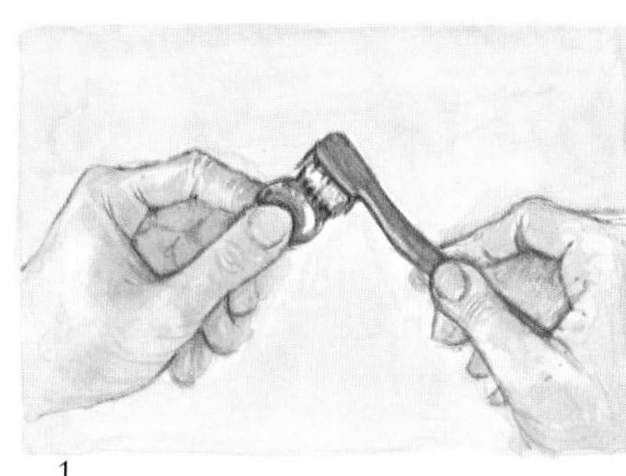
1

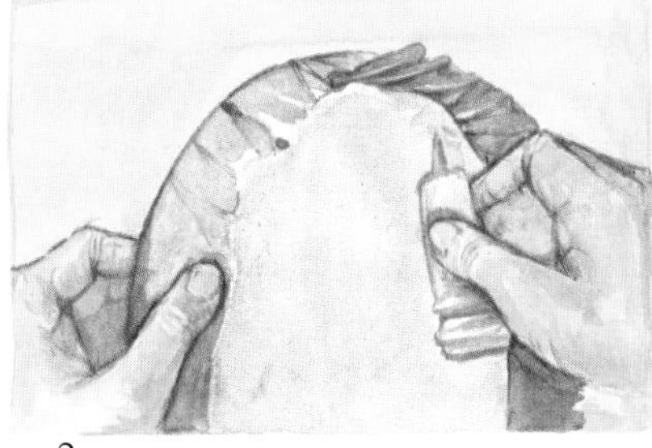
2

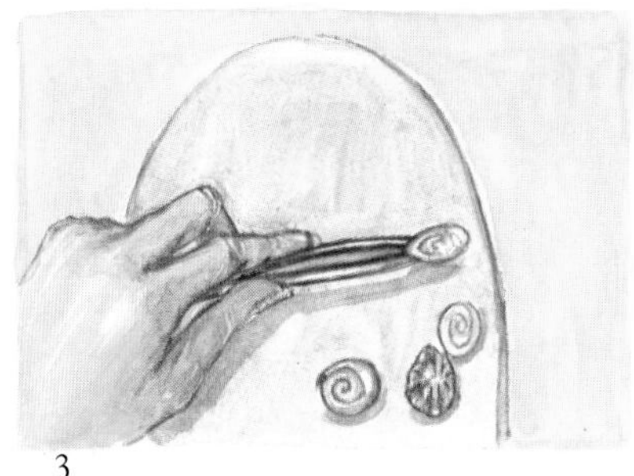
3

Materials
variety of tiny shells no bigger than ½ in (1.2 cm) long. Select about 35–40 in pale pastel shades – winkles, horn shells, scallops, rose petals and pieces of stem coral
variety of small buttons, beads or minute shells to form flower centres
old toothbrush
bleach
piece of stiff card cut into an oval 6 in (15 cm) high
piece of strong cotton, velvet or linen cut ½ in (1.2 cm) larger than the card
baby oil
cotton wool
cocktail sticks
tweezers
frame and glass oval cut to size
Bostik adhesive

Method
1. Clean the shells by soaking them in warm soapy water, removing surface dirt with a toothbrush. Badly stained shells can be cleaned in bleach solution – leave them to soak overnight and then wash thoroughly to remove all traces of the chemical. Once clean, place the shells open-side down on paper towels to dry.
2. Cover the card with the fabric, turning the overlap onto the back and glueing firmly into place.
3. Arrange the shells into a floral pattern. Use rounded shells for the petals and pieces of coral and elongated specimens for the stems and leaves. Do not use too many shells, since a cluttered design will spoil the delicacy of the subject. If the shells have lost some of their shine or appear dry, rub the tops (but not the undersides, which will be glued) with cotton wool dipped in a little baby oil. Using a cocktail stick, apply glue to the underside of each shell and press it gently onto the fabric. Tiny shells can be held in place with tweezers while glueing. Bostik dries in about ten minutes, leaving time to correct any mistakes or re-position the shells if necessary. Should the glue run onto the fabric, it can be removed easily before it sets using the end of a clean cocktail stick.
4. Once the design is finished and completely dry, it can be framed and glazed. Larger floral compositions look particularly attractive with simple shell borders arranged as decorative surrounds to frame the subject. These can be made from tiny spiral and petal shapes assembled into a repetitive, geometric pattern.

FELTWORK

What a delightful entertainment must it be to the fair sex . . . to pass their hours in imitating fruits and flowers . . .
The *Spectator*, 1714

Feltwork is usually associated with the amateur handicrafts of the Regency period, at a time when women – perhaps somewhat weary of the usual selection of silk embroideries and canvas work – looked for new and previously unexplored materials to use in interior design. Like its 'sister' art, theorem painting (see pp. 21–5), which enjoyed immense popularity during the early 1800s, feltwork relied on a limited decorative vocabulary of floral subjects and still lifes, which were mounted and glazed as pictures and hung from the wall. Felt-collage appeared as a natural extension of painting on velvet. While the two techniques were executed by very different means (the former, by cutting and sewing; the latter, by stencilling and brushwork) they shared a thematic content, rendered in rich colours and soft pliable fabrics.

Pieces of felt were stitched directly onto background cloth, or padded to create three-dimensional effects – not unlike the schoolgirl stumpwork (or raised embroidery) of the late seventeenth century (see pp. 92–5). Flowers and fruits were particularly well suited to relief presentations, and by projecting boldly from the surface, appeared almost lifelike. Many were rendered actual size, or larger. Strawberries, apples, grapes, plums, pears and pineapples were modelled from fabric stuffings, onto which the different coloured felts were appliquéd with silk embroidery. The exteriors were then over-stitched to create pronounced areas of light and shade, and to highlight their textures and markings (such as the speckled seed patterns of strawberries). An abundant selection of fruits was portrayed overflowing from imitation wickerwork baskets composed of criss-crossed strips of cream-tinted felt, silk or chenille. Velvet was sometimes employed together with felt, its plush surface pile capturing the soft furriness of peaches and summer fruits.

Vases and baskets of flowers were also popular subjects. The petals and leaves were only slightly padded, and half-sewn onto the felt background to create a random effect of flat and freestanding forms. Two or more felts of different colours were sometimes sewn together, with the edges of the top fabric

108. Feltwork picture of a basket of fruits and foliage. The pineapple, strawberries and grapes have been padded to create a three-dimensional effect, reminiscent of seventeenth-century stumpwork. English. *c.*1820.
(Alistair Sampson Antiques Ltd, London)

109. Feltwork picture of flowers in a basket, the pieces of felt embroidered in silk to convey subtle details and colour-shading. English, *c.*1820.
(Alistair Sampson Antiques Ltd, London)

serrated to reveal the underlying shades below. Over-stitching in silk threads was used to delineate the veins of leaves and other surface details, sometimes conveyed in a lively 'primitive' manner, but at other times executed with great artistry (and botanical accuracy).

Although the majority of feltwork pictures were unsigned, they were most likely to have been created by schoolgirls or lady amateurs at home. One important exception, however, was the series of naive genre scenes and portraits created by George Smart of Frant, near Tunbridge Wells, during the second quarter of the nineteenth century. A tailor by trade, he advertised his services as an 'Artist in Cloth and Velvet Pictures to H.R.H. The Duke of Sussex' (George III's sixth son), and was one of the very few commercial artists to work in the medium. Smart's collages were made from scraps of lace, linen, felt, buckram and kid – materials saved from the suits he made for the gentry. While he compared his talents to the artist Rubens, as indicated on the printed labels which he attached to the backs of his pictures,[1] his satirical style was more in keeping with the caricatures of Bunbury. The critic R. F. Johnson described him, perhaps more accurately, as 'rag-bag Rowlandson'.[2]

The fashion for felt pictures appears to have declined after about 1840, from which time few ladies' journals made any mention of the technique (and then only in the form of fringed felt covers and table-runners). Even the indispensable handbook, the *Elegant Arts for Ladies* (*c.*1856) excluded feltwork from its burgeoning list of home crafts, and while imitation fruits and flowers remained popular with Victorian housewives, they now appeared in other materials. Leather, in particular, became the preferred medium for modelling bouquets and still lifes, following its debut at the Great Exhibition of 1851.

WOODLAND AND RUSTIC DECORATIONS

Make up a party to go off on an exploring expedition, and do not forget the children, for they as much as any will enjoy a day in the woods . . . You will be surprised to learn how much lies at your feet of interest, beauty and use, which hitherto you have trodden upon as worthless. . . .

Cassell's Household Guide, 1875[1]

110. Papier-mâché dish decorated with spatterwork fern leaves and foliage, in keeping with the vogue for rustic designs during the nineteenth century. English, *c.*1870.
(Mrs Monro, London)

The vogue for rustic decorations emerged during the second half of the eighteenth century, at a time when architects and designers turned their attentions to the creation of picturesque, landscaped parks for the grounds of country estates. The schemes were executed on a grandiose scale, and adhered largely to the period tastes for Neoclassicism. Temples and summer houses fashioned out of marble and stone appeared along the banks of artificial lakes and rock pools, recalling both the splendour and sobriety of their Antique prototypes. This infusion of classicism appealed particularly to those recently returned from the obligatory Grand Tour. Additional elements of exoticism and fantasy were interspersed frequently as focal points, in keeping with the exuberant styles published in pattern books of the 1750s and 60s. W. and J. Halfpenny's *New Designs for Chinese Temples, Trium-*

111. 'Negative' fern-leaf impressions executed on the wooden panels of a flower press – a style of decoration made popular by the industrious Victorian housewife, ever keen to ornament every surface, *c.*1880.
(By courtesy of Loot, London)

phal Arches, Garden Seats, etc. embraced the latest trends for chinoiserie, while P. Decker's *Gothic Architecture Decorated* illustrated gazebos, greenhouses and garden furniture of medieval inspiration, using the tracery and vaulted ornaments characteristic of that period.

The rugged, 'back to nature' qualities of rustic interpretations provided a further source of novelty, and a departure from the otherwise contrived formality of Neoclassicism. Designs for outdoor furniture constructed from 'the limbs of Yew and Apple Trees, as Nature produces them' featured in Thomas Manwaring's *Cabinet and Chair Maker's Real Friend and Companion* (1765), with their gnarled woody branches and twigs forming the backs and sides of 'rural settees'. The style was copied during the early 1800s in cast iron, and by the Victorian period a wide range of garden furniture in 'imitation rustic' was mass-produced by factories in Europe and America.

In spite of the effects of increasing industrialization, the use of woodland materials for the construction and decoration of summerhouses and garden accessories continued to be favoured until the 1870s. Small, thatched huts and log-cabin retreats became *de rigueur* among the variety of parkland architecture commissioned by the wealthy.

Charles Hamilton Esq., of Pains Hill, for example, went as far as to employ a hermit to reside in one of his rusticated dwellings for the purposes of keeping 'the hermitage clean and to sit at the door with a book ... when any company came'.[2] The adherence to natural, organic forms and what one architect referred to as 'the effect(s) of chance'[3] were the key ingredients of rustic stylizations. A splendid example in the tradition is the so-called 'Bear's Hut', built during the early 1800s for Sir Thomas Acland, in the grounds of Killerton House, near Exeter (now open to the public). The roof is heavily thatched, and the irregular walls rendered in herringbone patterns of pine logs, bark and basketry. The ceiling in the main room is covered with matting, over which a decorative framework of pine-cone wreaths is displayed. Cobblestones appear at the entrance, while the floor of the tiny chapel is lined with hundreds of deers' knucklebones, laid in heart and diamond shapes to create a rich mosaic effect. This paragon of 'idyllic rusticity' had no resident hermit, although for a short time it was inhabited by a black bear (hence its name), which was brought from Canada by Sir Thomas's eccentric son Gilbert.

At a time when the construction of timbered pavilions and bark-covered summerhouses continued unabated on both sides of the Atlantic, the style was also taken up by ladies as a 'fascinating domestic employment'[4] – not only as a means of home embellishment, but also for the decoration of conservatories, which became an almost constant feature of middle-class suburban architecture by the middle of the nineteenth century. Mrs Loudon's well-known treatises on horticulture, such as her *Gardening for Ladies* (1841), made outdoor pursuits respectable, and she went on to suggest that the creation of garden ornaments was 'an excellent exercise for female taste'. Instructions for making rustic-style flower pots and hanging baskets from the 'twisted and gnarled boughs and roots of shrubs'[5] were included in crafts manuals of the period. Other popular items for home manufacture were picture frames constructed from twigs, dried mosses, pine cones and acorns, which made suitable surrounds for Victorian needlepoints stitched with sentimental mottoes such as 'Welcome' or 'Peace Be To This House'. Margaret Plues' popular handbook, *Rambles in Search of Flowerless Plants* (1866), became a steady companion for ladies in search of mosses and lichens. For those less keen on 'rambling', however, woodland foliage by the sackful could be purchased at Covent Garden and other nurseries. Cone work was praised as a domestic decoration, and was applied to the exteriors of baskets and ornamental wall brackets such as those illustrated in *Cassell's Household Guide* (1875): '(These) pretty and useful articles ... make not only pleasing additions to one's own home, but provide an acceptable gift to a friend'.

Victorian ladies collected autumn leaves and arranged them into fanciful collages, or took to drying ferns and other woodland plants to ornament all manner of interior 'elegancies', from doilies[6] to the drawing-room whatnot. The vogue for rustic foliage was also subscribed to by commercial manufacturers such as the Burslem Pottery in England, who produced a range of vessels in stoneware, modelled in relief with strands of entwined ivy.

Perhaps most curious of all were the ethereal, fairy-like bouquets of skeleton leaves. Instructions for creating them appeared in the usual publications devoted to women's handicrafts. In the indispensable volume *Enquire Within Upon Everything* (1875), directions for the maceration of leaves were given as follows: 'The leaves should be put into an earthen or glass vessel, and a large quantity of rain water poured over them; after this they may be left in the open air, and to the heat of the sun, without covering the vessel ... the leaves will by this means putrefy ... according to the toughness of their parenchyma'. Once the membranes had disintegrated completely, leaving only their veined skeletons behind, the leaf remnants were then 'washed with clean water, and dried between the leaves of a book'. The skeletons could then be assembled into freestanding sprays and set under the ubiquitous glass shades so favoured for Victorian parlour display.

112. Bouquet of dried foliage and skeleton leaves, mounted on red velvet and glazed for protection. English, *c.*1850.
(Mallett at Bourdon House Ltd, London)

DRIED LEAFWORK ON FURNITURE

Victorian-style serving tray in leafwork and imitation Japan

The style of ornamenting furniture and small decorative objects with dried leaves was immensely popular during the Victorian period and was used to create a variety of rustic effects. *Cassell's Household Guide* (1875) listed several ambitious leafwork 'projects', including a large folding screen, bureau and blanket box.

The technique is easily acquired and can be applied equally well to smaller surfaces such as a tray. The results are most effective if small, serrated leaves are used because of their fine detail and delicacy.

1

2

3

4

5

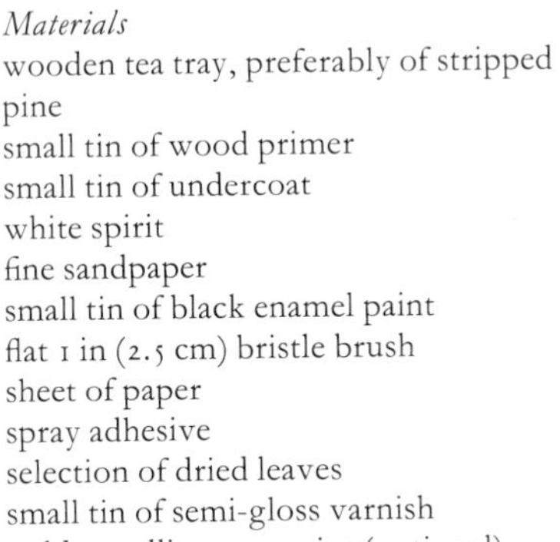
Materials
wooden tea tray, preferably of stripped pine
small tin of wood primer
small tin of undercoat
white spirit
fine sandpaper
small tin of black enamel paint
flat 1 in (2.5 cm) bristle brush
sheet of paper
spray adhesive
selection of dried leaves
small tin of semi-gloss varnish
gold metallic spray paint (optional)

Method
1. Press the leaves between sheets of newspaper under a heavy weight until completely dry (2–4 weeks). Turn them occasionally and change the newspaper if necessary to make sure they are drying evenly.
2. Prepare the tray by stripping off any old varnish or paint and sanding the surface lightly. If it is already stripped, apply one coat of primer and sand gently when dry. In either case, apply the undercoat, leave overnight to dry and sand again. Apply a coat of black paint. Leave to dry and sand lightly to remove any blemishes. Add two more black coats, sanding gently between them. Do not, however, sand the final coat.
3. Select the leaves and practise arranging them on a piece of paper to find an attractive design. They can either be left naturally coloured or their top sides spray-painted in gold to create a richer effect.
4. Once dry, spray the undersides of the leaves with adhesive and place gently onto the tray following the design already devised.
5. Making sure that the leaves are firmly in position, particularly their edges and stems, apply four coats of varnish to the tray, ensuring that each coat is thoroughly dry before applying the next, and sanding lightly after each of the first three.

DECORATIONS IN SAND AND SEAWEED

The variety of sea-weed, coralleries, pebbles and petrifactions to be met with on the rocks is very considerable . . . but persons who prefer a less fatiguing mode of collecting may purchase very good specimens in the shops of the town.[1]

From the Scarborough *Guide* book, 1813

Trips to the seaside became a popular form of entertainment for the leisured classes by the end of the eighteenth century, and provided an opportunity to explore the beaches and shorelines of the surrounding area. Collecting shells was a much-favoured diversion for gentlewomen such as the Duchess of Portland and her great friend, Mary Delany, who spent many hours by the sea in search of fine specimens.

A natural extension of shellwork was the fanciful arrangement of dried seaweed into small pictures and freestanding bouquets. Some of the earliest surviving examples in the style were created during the 1790s by the enterprising Misses Parminter for their home, *A la Ronde* (see plate 114). In a landscape picture attributed to Jane Parminter, for example, sand, seaweed and paint were combined to striking effect. The background was painted in washes of watercolour, with the avenues of trees in the foreground made up of tinted and dried seaweeds – cut into strips for the trunks, and arranged delicately into serrated strands for the leaves and branches. Thin layers of sand were applied to the ground areas, forming a harmonious blend of marine materials.

During the nineteenth century, the making of seaweed pictures, bouquets and albums was taken up by ladies as a fashionable pastime. Many of the decorations were rendered simply as collages. The varicoloured fronds were first pressed and dried between sheets of blotting paper, and then pasted in pleasing patterns onto a cloth or paper background. The designs were afterwards mounted, typically in maple and gilded frames, and hung from walls.

Perhaps more elaborate were the freestanding floral displays, in which the seaweed was arranged in tiny wicker baskets, sometimes with added foliage and shells, and set within glazed cases for protection. Many were inscribed with popular verses, such as the one attributed to Miss Elizabeth Aveline of Lyme Regis:

Oh, call us not weeds, but flowers of the sea,
For lovely and gay and bright-tinted are we,
Our blush is as deep as the rose in thy bowers,

113. Page from an album of dried seaweeds, believed to have been assembled by Mary Eleanor Bowes, Countess of Strathmore, *c.*1780–1800.
(The Bowes Museum, Barnard Castle, Co. Durham, UK)

Then call us not weeds – we are ocean's
gay flowers.

For those lacking inspiration, Mrs Gatty's best-selling book, *British Seaweeds* (1862) provided a list of useful 'Rules for the Preserving and Laying-out of Seaweeds', while the earlier volume, *A Popular History of Seaweeds* (1849) by the Revd Lansborough, assisted in the classification of specimens. Collections of dried seaweed were also mounted in special albums – a practice which appealed to devotees of the popular Victorian hobby of amassing paper scraps and mementos (see pp. 78–83).

Pictures ornamented with coloured sand enjoyed a considerable vogue during the late 1700s, and received royal patronage under George III and his son, Prince Frederick. The king employed a number of 'table-deckers' at Windsor, who were commissioned for formal banquets to devise elaborate centrepiece displays using powdered sugar, sand and marble dust. The 'marmotinto' designs, as they were then referred to, were afterwards swept away. However, it was not long before a more enduring decorative format was developed, by which the patterns could be fixed permanently to the surface. The discovery of suitable adhesives during the late

114. Collage picture of a rural landscape made by a member of the Parminter family for A la Ronde, late eighteenth century.
(A la Ronde, Exmouth)

1780s resulted in the creation of sand pictures, in which fine layers were scattered, section by section, over the surface to be covered, according to the coloured outlines of the composition.

Talented amateurs, such as Jane Parminter, soon worked their own pictorial displays in coloured sand, and during the Victorian period a number of ladies found inspiration in the novelty aspects of the medium. Once the sand was collected, the desired scene was painted or drawn on a background of paper, card or millboard, and small areas of the composition glued. The appropriate shade of sand was then sifted over the surface and adhered to the designated portions. The process was then repeated until the entire design was covered.

Directions for making sand and seaweed pictures were included in Victorian journals devoted to the 'minor arts'. In the *Elegant Arts for Ladies* (*c.*1856), for example, 'easy instructions' were included '. . . to convert . . . the scraps of weed, sponge, etc. . . . into elegant ornaments . . . using all the varieties that can be collected.'

Marine collages and sand-covered landscapes, however, have not survived in large number: for all their adhesives were strong enough, many were nevertheless discarded following the demise of the cluttered Victorian parlour.

LETTER RACK

Decorated with pressed seaweed

Seaweed can be found in a surprisingly wide variety of colours, shapes and textures. Once dried, it can be used as an unusual and striking addition to dried flower arrangements. Alternatively, it can be pressed and mounted on paper, fabric-covered card or wood, in floral or abstract designs.

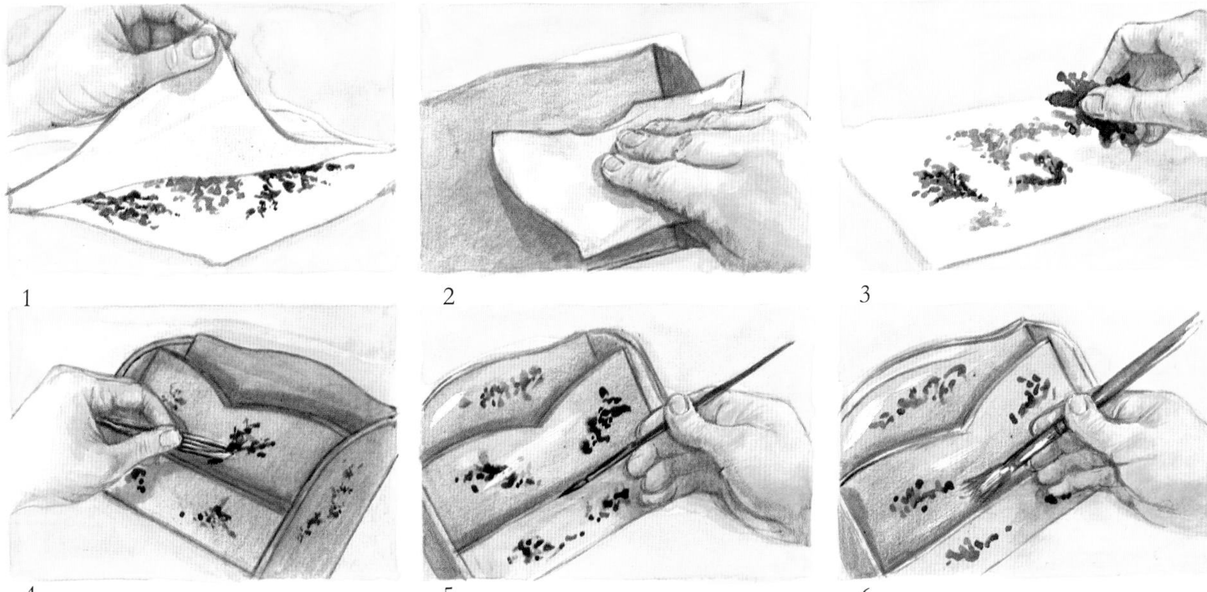

Materials
selection of small sprigs and fronds of seaweed
blotting paper
heavy weight such as a pile of books
letter rack made of stripped, fine-grained wood (found in many department stores or gift shops)
fine sandpaper
soft cloth
four sheets of plain paper
sharp scissors
tweezers
clear spray adhesive
flat 1 in (2.5 cm) bristle brush
fine sable brush
tin of semi-gloss varnish
salt

Method
1. Wash the seaweed in a weak salt solution and dry carefully using a soft cloth or paper towel. Place the pieces between sheets of blotting paper making sure they do not overlap and press under a heavy weight until completely dry – 1–2 weeks.
2. Sand the letter rack lightly to remove any blemishes. Wipe the entire surface with a damp cloth to remove dust and leave to dry at room temperature. Do not immerse the rack in water or leave to dry in too warm a room, as the bare wood will warp or crack.
3. When the seaweed is completely dry, plan decorative arrangements for the front and sides of the rack, practising on pieces of paper first, cut to the size of each panel.
4. Once suitable designs have been found, take each piece of seaweed, spray the underside with glue and mount on the panels following the pattern. Use tweezers to place delicate fronds if necessary. Press each sprig down lightly, making sure that the ends in particular are firmly fixed.
5. When all the panels have been covered, apply a coat of varnish. Use the fine brush and stroke gently over the seaweed so as not to pull or break any of the sprigs.
6. Start with the internal walls of the rack and then varnish the outside, so that the seaweed is protected from the outset. Leave to dry and apply two further coats for protection.

CORK CASTLES AND STRAW BOUQUETS

... Her daughter's boudoir ... was full of girlish treasures – evidencies of fancies that had passed like summer clouds – accomplishments begun and abandoned – an easel in front of the window – a gigantic rush-work basket ... crammed ... with scraps and unfinished undertakings.

Miss Braddon, *The Day Will Come*, 1890

The novel techniques of straw- and corkwork came under that ubiquitous category known to every Regency and Victorian lady as 'fancy work'. As women tired of their needles, paintbrushes and scissors, so crafts manuals endeavoured to provide their readers with new materials, which they pronounced 'hitherto unrealised', in the name of Art.

Despite the boastful, self-congratulatory sentiments expressed in the majority of ladies' magazines, each claiming to discover a novel trend, or anticipate a new fashion, straw work was not invented by the doyennes of 'good taste'. Its decorative use as marquetry was known during the seventeenth century when French craftsmen turned to the method in imitation of wood inlays. Straw marquetry was later brought to England during the 1760s by French prisoners of war, who ornamented tea caddies, boxes, book covers and trinkets in the style, which they sold for pocket money to supplement their rations. The pieces of straw were first split and flattened, and when opened up could be cut with a penknife either into tiny segments (to resemble flowers and naturalistic forms) or simply into sticks, diamonds, triangles and other geometric shapes. The pieces were then assembled into intricate mosaic or pictorial patterns, and glued to the flat surface of the object.

Amateurs soon tried their hands at strawwork, although it would appear that female enthusiasts preferred another version of the handicraft – the creation of

115, 116. *Left and opposite,* nineteenth-century boxes inlaid with natural and coloured cut and flattened straw. *(Halcyon Days, London)*

117. Intricate cut-straw framed flower arrangement, *c.*1810. *(Alistair Sampson Antiques Ltd, London)*

freestanding floral bouquets. The flattened straw was cut with a penknife to form individual petals, leaves and stalks, and each was ornamented in considerable detail. The petals of carnations, for example, were snipped into ridged patterns using sharp scissors, while lilies were broadly curled on the edge of the blade. Leaves were incised to convey veining, tulips over-painted with fine stripes to highlight their contrasting tints, and primulas gently serrated and given brightly coloured centres. Each blossom was wired to a stem and gathered into naturalistic sprays, which were sometimes held by lengths of straw tied into elegant ribbons and bows.

The fashion for corkwork emerged during the early Victorian period, when ladies resorted again to their trusty penknives for cutting sheets of cork into low-relief landscape collages. The vogue for 'the picturesque', be it crumbling ruins or castellated 'Gothick' towers, was encapsulated in the novels of Sir Walter Scott, and the Romantic Revivalists. By the 1830s, the imagery was translated into pictures dotted with gloomy medieval fortresses perched on rocky precipices, above valleys of densely wooded forest. Cork, as a material, was ideal for the purpose, being inexpensive, easy to cut and, above all, novel. Its immense versatility enabled it to be worked either in sheet form, pierced into openwork designs, or crumbled into irregularly-shaped fragments, which were glued onto the background.

The substance could be purchased in flat sheets from the handiwork repositories or 'Temples of Fancy', which stocked the full range of materials required for parlour pastimes. Since so little in the way of equipment was necessary for the exercise, the writers of *Enquire Within* (1875) encouraged readers to bring their cork 'kits' with them on their journeys abroad, to compose souvenirs *in situ* of the places they visited. Hence, like their mothers and grandmothers before them who travelled the well-worn routes of the Grand Tour with their paintbox and sketchbook in hand, so the Victorian lady ventured into the wide world with her cork, penknife and pot of gum.

PRESSED FLOWERS AND LEAF PRINTS

Open any thick volume of the period, open any untouched casket
of love letters, and you will disinter the brownish fragments
of what were once gay and living flowers . . . faded, formless blossoms
still linked together with a time-stained scrap of thread.

Frances Lichten, *Decorative Art of Victoria's Era*, 1950

With the rise of floriculture and botany as popular pursuits, made fashionable by publications such as Mrs Loudon's *The Ladies' Companion to the Flower Garden* (1841) and Mrs Brightwen's *Rambles with Nature Students*, the Victorian gentlewoman was encouraged to venture outdoors in search of flowering plants, ferns and mosses. She learned to cultivate the ornamental 'carpet' beds which greeted her from the French doors of the morning room (keeping well away from the kitchen garden which came strictly under the domain of servants) and to assemble flowers into elegant arrangements and posies to decorate her home or her *porte-bouquet*. The writers of *Cassell's Household Guide* (1875) recommended woodland expeditions to gather colourful autumn foliage and twigs with which to create all manner of interior ornaments, from fern-leaf spattered lampshades (see pp. 40–43) to rustic hanging baskets for the conservatory. As women rambled around the countryside and parklands with their pocketbook manuals in hand, and baskets overflowing with hand-picked specimens, here was ample opportunity to observe Nature – and to *preserve* it, whether through paintings and sketches, or as precious keepsakes in the pages of albums.

The vogue for pressed floral pictures emerged out of this milieu of 'female cultivation', and while the amateur botanist went about drying and cataloguing her collection into a vast compilation, or *hortus siccus*, the budding artist preferred pictorial collages of gracefully arranged leafy sprays. Some were mounted and glazed as wall pictures and featured home-made rustic frames composed of gnarled twigs, pine cones and acorns; others were safeguarded in token albums, scattered among memorabilia of handwritten poems, autographs and souvenirs. The flattened bouquets of ferns, flowers and 'skeleton leaves' (see pp. 156–7) were often tied with ribbons. Some incorporated relief-embossed paper scraps of blossoms and cupids in the manner of valentine cards, complete with sentimental inscriptions alluding to love, hope and romance. Landscape scenes were also popular. Dried foliage in imitation of trees towered above hand-painted figures clothed in gowns of pressed butterfly wings. Memorials were made of ivy-leaf wreaths, and religious themes conveyed by floral crucifixes. All found a ready place in the Victorian lady's scrapbook.

A novel variation of pressing leaves to create negative prints appeared in *Enquire Within Upon Everything* (1875):

'Hold oiled paper in the smoke of a lamp or of pitch, until it becomes coated with the smoke; to this paper apply the leaf of which you wish to make an impression, having previously warmed it between your hands, that it may be pliable. Place the lower surface of the leaf upon the blackened surface of the oil-paper, that the numerous veins, which are so prominent on this side, may receive from the paper a

118. Pressed flower picture from a late nineteenth-century album bound in olive wood, entitled 'Flowers from Palestine' – a religious keepsake popular during the period *c.* 1870–90. *(The Bowes Museum, Barnard Castle, Co. Durham, UK)*

119. Victorian bouquet of pressed flowers and leaves, from an album entitled 'Fleurs du Terre Sainte'.
(By courtesy of the Trustees of the British Museum, London)

portion of the smoke. Lay a paper over the leaf, and then press it gently upon the smoked paper with the fingers, or with a small roller covered with a woollen cloth, or some similarly soft material, so that every part of the leaf may come in contact with the sooted oil-paper. A coating of the smoke will adhere to the leaf. Then remove the leaf carefully, and place the blackened surface on a sheet of white paper, or in a book prepared for the purpose, covering the leaf with a clean slip of paper, and pressing upon it with the fingers, or roller, as before. With care excellent impressions may be thus obtained'.

Bookmark Decorated With Pressed Flowers

Pressing flowers and leaves requires little in the way of equipment and, depending on the time of year, a wide selection of plants, leaves and grasses can usually be collected. After pressing, the specimens can be arranged into bouquets for display on greeting cards, bookmarks or wall hangings. Alternatively, they can be glued into albums with hand-painted watercolour surrounds.

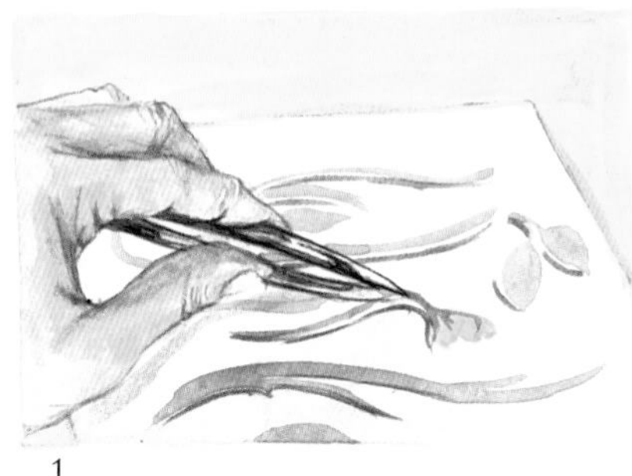
1

2

3

Materials
old telephone directory
stack of heavy books or weights
sheets of blotting paper
adhesive tape
tweezers
sharp scissors or craft knife
fabric adhesive
selection of small flowers, leaves and grasses
piece of stiff card $1\frac{1}{2} \times 9$ in (3.75 × 22.5 cm)
piece of raw silk $3 \times 9\frac{1}{2}$ in (17.5 × 23.75 cm) in a shade that will complement the colours of the plants
piece of clear sticky-back plastic or fablon $3 \times 9\frac{1}{2}$ in (7.5 × 23.75 cm)

Method
1. Arrange the flowers, leaves and grasses on a piece of blotting paper, making sure that each specimen is laid separately, without touching any of the others. Tweezers will help to position them and tiny pieces of adhesive tape can be used to hold stems in place if necessary. Cover the plants carefully with another sheet of blotting paper and place between the pages of the directory. The directory can hold several such layers, but they should be well separated so that the plants dry evenly. Place the directory under a heavy weight and leave until the plants are completely dry – 4–6 weeks. Examine them every 4–5 days, replacing the blotting paper if it has become excessively moist.
2. To make the background of the bookmark place the card in the centre of the piece of silk. Mitre each corner of the cloth, fold the edges round the card and glue firmly into place on the back.
3. Once the plants are completely dry remove them from the directory and arrange them on the front of the silk strip using the tweezers. Glue into place using as little adhesive as possible and just enough pressure to position them firmly. Protect the flowers by covering the bookmark with the sticky-back plastic.

HAIRWORK

... Of all the various employments devised for the fingers of our fair countrywomen, the manufacture of ornaments in hair must be one of the most interesting ... (and) truly feminine ... occupations.[1]

Elegant Arts for Ladies, c. 1856

The somewhat macabre notion of preserving the hair of a departed relative or companion appealed greatly to the Victorians. Expressions of eternal love and everlasting friendship were appropriate to an era which doted on 'the sentimental treasures of the heart',[2] and undertook an almost ritualistic observance of lengthy periods of bereavement. In the decorative arts, the fashion for mourning was interpreted by the appearance of embroidered memorials, the majority of which were worked by young girls both in Europe and America during the early years of the nineteenth century. The grieving families were depicted beneath the 'weeping' branches of willow trees, in a limited repertoire of set patterns which were stitched in threads of silk and occasional strands of hair. By the 1830s, the decorative potential of hair as an artistic medium was explored beyond its mere application to needlework, and its methods of working were already sufficiently well documented for amateurs to take up the techniques at home.

Hairwork ornaments were produced in great variety, from floral pictures, wreaths and free-standing trophies, to items of jewellery adorned with minute swags and sprays of curled hair. The most ambitious *memento moris* combined the family locks of several generations, using the hairs of its deceased members and those still living. These curious amalgams were presented frequently in the form of trees, using the grey or white hairs of grandparents and elders for the trunk and low-lying branches, and children's tresses for the higher twigs and foliage.

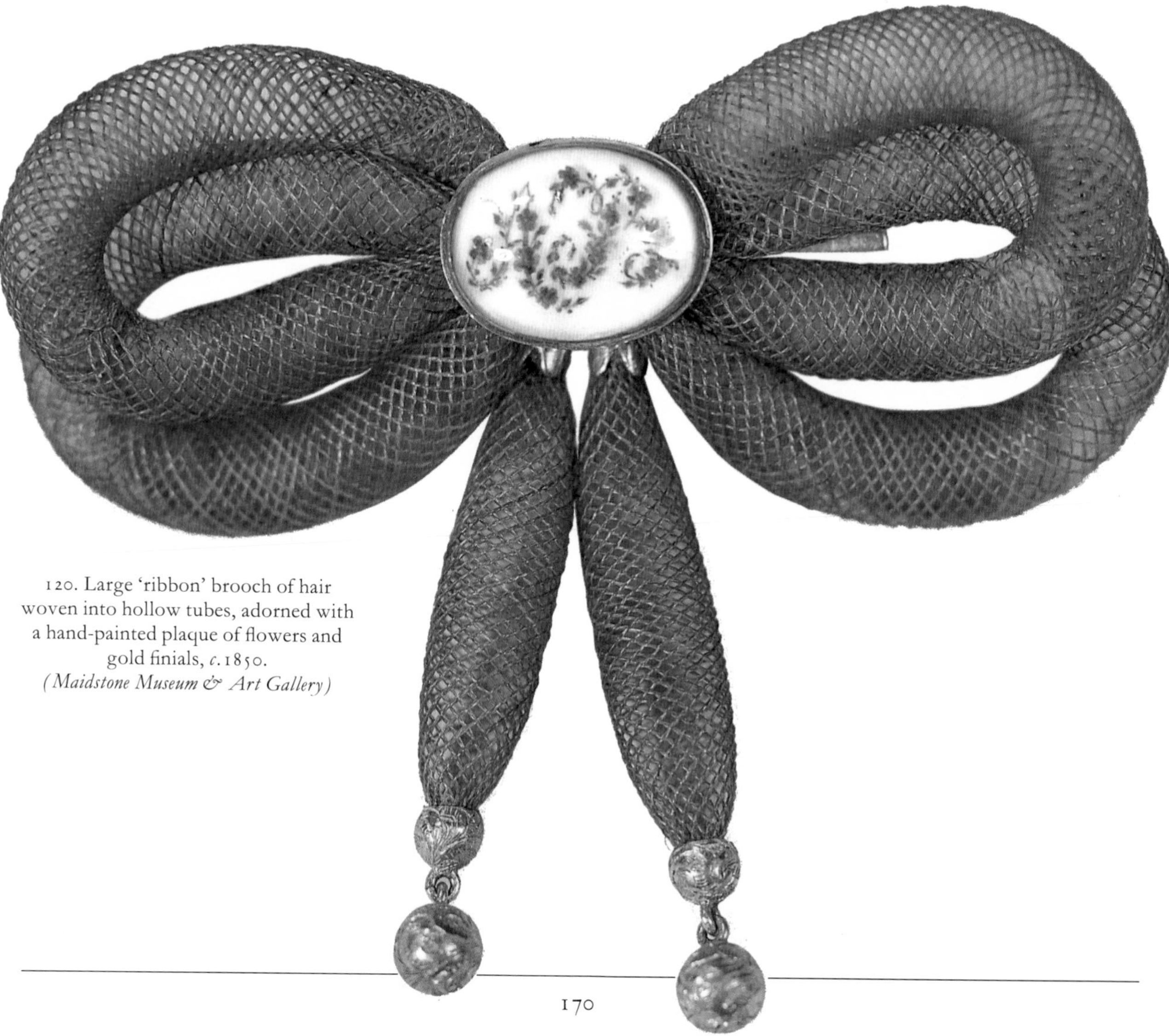

120. Large 'ribbon' brooch of hair woven into hollow tubes, adorned with a hand-painted plaque of flowers and gold finials, *c.* 1850.
(Maidstone Museum & Art Gallery)

121. Woven and plaited hairwork bracelet fitted with a gold clasp, *c.*1850.
(Maidstone Museum & Art Gallery)

Elegant mourning jewels were *de rigueur* during the period *c.*1840–80 (especially following the death of Prince Albert in 1861, when the nation was plunged into bereavement, following the example of Queen Victoria). Fashionable mourning dress was accompanied by large lockets, brooches, pendants and rings, on which the carefully assembled strands of the deceased's hair were arranged under bevelled glass plaques. The hairwork itself was executed by both amateurs and professionals (the services of the latter were, in any case, required for mounting the finished panels into frames of gold or pinchbeck).

The decorative arrangement of hair into minute plaits, basket patterns, feathered curls and simple pictorial devices could be executed readily, following the illustrations published in Victorian magazines. The only tools required for the task were tweezers, a sharp penknife, curling-tongs, gum and 'a firm, smooth, square cushion'[3] upon which to work. More difficult to assemble, however, were the mourning necklaces, bracelets and pendant earrings made entirely of woven strands of plaited hair. This style of jewellery was immensely popular by the middle of the nineteenth century, but in view of its intricate designs, its construction was entrusted frequently to reputable craftsmen.

While the most artistic pieces were undoubtedly created by professionals, woven hairwork was nevertheless recommended as a challenging pursuit for young ladies of accomplishment. Instructions for making rouleau headdresses, ribboned brooches, serpent bracelets, finger rings and beaded hairnets were all included in the crafts manuals devoted to the 'Weaving or Plaiting of Hair Ornaments'. For projects at home, an extensive list of equipment was required, the most essential of which was described as a 'proper hair-work table . . . about three feet in height . . . having a circular hole in the centre of the top'.[4] Other paraphernalia included 'about three dozen leaden weights, a skein of strong silk or twist, a little shellac melted and rolled into a stick, and a brass tube or wire of the proper size for the pattern' – not to mention a substantial quantity of hair! Fortunately, the use of one's own hair (or that of a living relation's) was deemed suitable for the exercise, as the jewellery was offered to family and friends as 'tokens of affection'.

By the mid-1880s, the vogue for hairwork ornaments and jewellery subsided. For the new generation of Arts and Crafts designers, the once 'cherished mementos' were dismissed instantly as hideous reminders of a bygone age. Even today, hairwork is regarded with a certain degree of diffidence, in spite of the popular revival of Victoriana.

MODELLING IN WAX

The advantage of wax-modelling over other fancy work is that the sight is not likely to be injured ...
nor need the body be bent – a matter of much importance with growing girls, many having
suffered affections of the chest, and others disfigured for life,
through continually stooping to frame-work.

Mrs Emma Peachey, *The Royal Guide to Wax Flower Modelling*, 1856

122. *Above*, wax model of Queen Anne, the figure and background covered with glittering paper filigree swirls. English, *c.*1710. *(Lady Lever Art Gallery, Port Sunlight)*

123. *Right*, Victorian wax fruit decoration. *(Museum of London)*

Glass domes brimming with wax fruits and flowers were immensely popular during the Victorian period, when every middle-class drawing room 'with any pretentions to good taste' featured at least one shade amongst its clutter of home-made knick-knacks.

John and Horatio Mintorn's *Modelling Wax Flowers* (1844) was one of the first volumes to instruct the 'fair hands' of lady amateurs, followed some years later by Mrs Peachey's *The Royal Guide to Wax Flower Modelling* (1856). A small handbook entitled *The Art of Modelling and Making Wax Flowers*, by Charles Pepper, was another invaluable source, and could be purchased by mail order for 1s 6d.

During the period *c.*1855–80, patterns for wax fruits and flowers appeared in ladies' magazines on both sides of the Atlantic in response to their readers' popular requests for articles devoted to the very latest trends in interior decoration. *The Ladies' Book of the Month* (1867) published directions for making a white clematis using sheets of wax, which could be purchased from outlets such as J. Barnard and Son of Oxford Street, London. The wax sold for 6s per gross of sheets, and came in two standard thicknesses. Other requisite materials included a selection of powdered paints in a variety of colours, silk-covered wires, scissors, a dozen or so 'poonah' brushes, steel curling pins and special moulding tools fashioned out of boxwood or ivory.

Despite the problems of working with such sundry materials and tools – not to mention the ensuing mess – Mrs Peachey suggested that '... the most elegant drawing-room might be used, without suffering in its appearance during ... operations'.[1] Once all the paraphernalia had been assembled, the worker used any number of paper patterns to mark and cut the sheets of wax into a variety of leaves and petals. Each piece was then rolled and twisted on curling sticks until the desired shape was achieved. Fruits such as oranges, plums and apples usually required the use of hinged moulds, into which hot wax was poured and cast to create three-dimensional forms. Grapes were made by coating glass marbles with wax. Each fruit was afterwards hand-coloured, and occasionally incised over the surface to achieve as realistic an effect as possible. Frances Lichten, in her book *Decorative Art of Victoria's Era*, described how the most dedicated workers strived to reproduce 'Nature's accidentals – the bruise on a pear, the bee in the throat of a blossom, (and) the browning edge of a leaf'. Indeed, for those who excelled in the art, modelling in wax was as much an exercise in clever botanical observation as it was in sculpture and painting.

The wax bouquets and still lifes of fruit were usually arranged under glass shades (or domes) – a presentation which the Mintorns considered 'absolutely essential ... to preserve the work'. However, they also recommended the use of alabaster vases as 'the most suitable backgrounds for the varied hues of the flowers'. These could all be purchased 'on the most reasonable terms' from their counter in the Pantheon, Oxford Street, or from their home in nearby Soho Square.

In spite of Mrs Peachey's earnest assurances that the art of wax-modelling could be executed readily by 'the fairy touch of a delicate hand',[2] the technique was undoubtedly difficult and time-consuming. Moreover, it was an expensive exercise, and as such its appeal as a parlour diversion was almost certainly limited to the reasonably well-off. By the late 1870s, the fashion for wax fruits and flowers declined in favour of whimsical food displays, in which a selection of wax cheeses, blancmanges, sweetmeats and canapés were arranged on tiered salvers to adorn the dining room sideboard. These peculiar, inedible creations bore little resemblance to their counterparts of previous years, and what once had been regarded elegant had now degenerated into something ungainly, if not foolish.

LEATHERWORK

The student should bear in mind that leatherwork is
an art by itself, and should never be regarded as
imitating wood or anything else.
C.G. Leland, *The Minor Arts*, *c.*1880

At the Great Exhibition held in 1851 at Crystal Palace, a selection of leather relief-moulded frames, floral swags and wall friezes was displayed. The pieces attracted considerable attention, being both a novel decoration and one which could be '... readily mistaken for wood carvings', as described in the accompanying catalogue.[1] Indeed, the immense versatility of the medium was praised, and the 'excellent specimens' manufactured by the firm of Messrs Esquilant recommended for '... their applicability for the internal decoration of houses, and for the saloons of steam ships'.

It was not long before amateurs turned their hands to the modelling of leather, in keeping with the latest trends in interior furnishing that encouraged that every surface, nook and cranny be ornamented, preferably with the homespun creations of the lady of the house. Directions for leatherwork appeared in numerous journals both in Britain and America and, thus inspired, ladies cleared their worktables of feathers, shells and yarns to make room for the leather scraps required for the exercise.

Cassell's Household Guide (1875) was one of several manuals to pronounce leather the ideal material for decoration, since 'it improves with age, does not break or chip and is not readily affected by heat or damp . . . it can be gilt, silvered or stained'. Beginners were urged to commence working with small pieces of leather, assembled invariably into the sprays of foliage so favoured during the period, and to adorn wall brackets and picture frames. The stems, leaves and petals could all be cut from paper patterns fastened to damp sheets of goat- or sheepskin (sponged previously with cold water). The moist leather pieces were then stamped or incised with special tools to create areas of shallow patterning, or simply manipulated into 'natural' forms by moulding, twisting or pinching them in the hand. Stems were wrapped tightly into long coils and afterwards stiffened with lengths of wire, while small berries could be constructed from thin leather shavings which, when wet, could be rolled between the fingers into tiny roundels. Once all the various parts had been made, they could be glued or wired together to form flowers or leafy branches. After drying, the leather was coated with a liquid mixture of 'Australian red gum, orange shellac and spirit of wine', which was applied thinly and evenly to the surface with a camel-hair brush to achieve a hard, varnished effect. Finishing touches, such as the veins of leaves, could be added by painting or gilding over the exterior using powdered pigments or sheets of gold leaf. Finally, the leather ornaments were glued to the surface of the picture frame or wall bracket – leaving only 'the burden of dusting'.[2]

In *The Elegant Arts for Ladies* (*c.*1856), instructions for decorating wall brackets and 'card baskets' with gilt-leather lily leaves, vines and grapes were included as introductory exercises for beginners. For those experienced in modelling techniques, however, the authors suggested several new and exotic presentations '. . . never yet been attempted in leather . . . as far as we are aware'.[3] Projects for small-scale designs consisted of low-relief wall medallions and little figurines for the mantelshelf, while flamboyant tastes were catered for by massive centrepiece trophies, Grecian vases, caryatid heads for columns, and novelty stands for goldfish bowls.

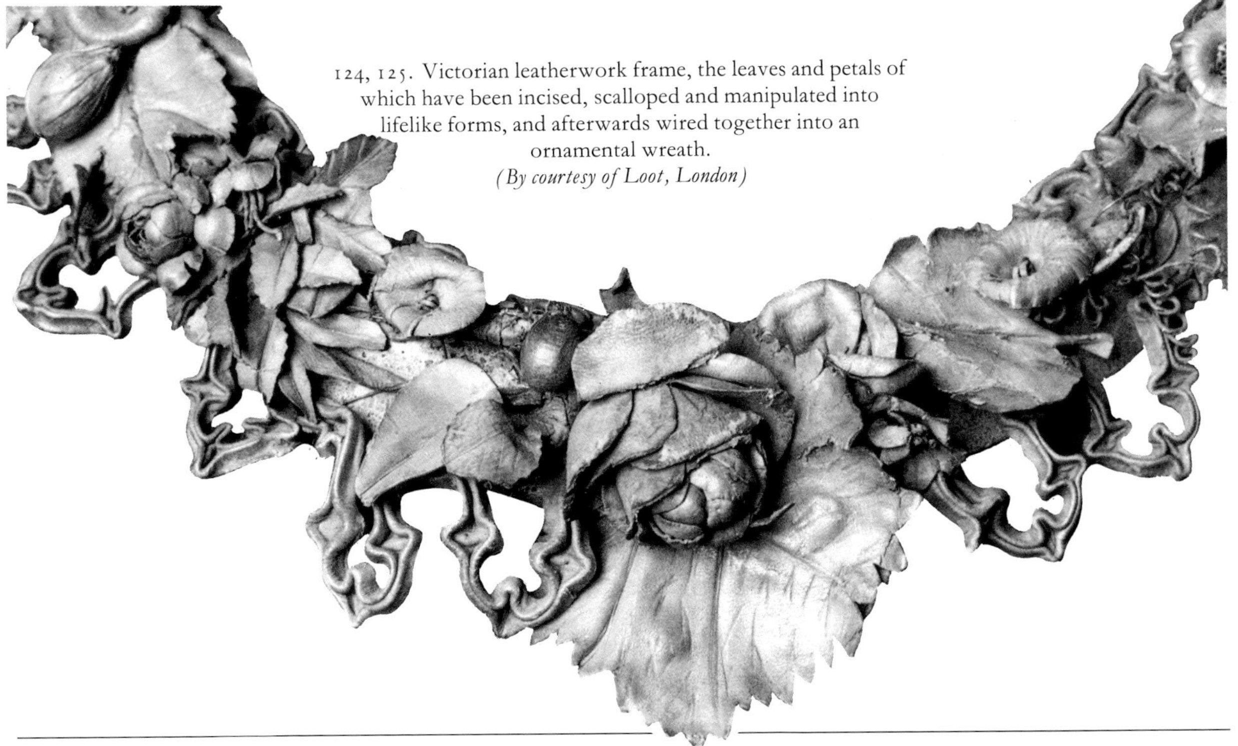

124, 125. Victorian leatherwork frame, the leaves and petals of which have been incised, scalloped and manipulated into lifelike forms, and afterwards wired together into an ornamental wreath.
(By courtesy of Loot, London)

LEATHERWORK NEEDLECASE

The technique of sewing leather was described in C. G. Leland's *Minor Arts* in 1880, in which instructions were given for making a 'tobacco pouch, to be hung with a pipe'. This would undoubtedly have held some appeal for the Victorian housewife, whose chief inspiration for all her 'fancy work' was to please her husband. Today, leather can be used to both practical and decorative effect to make purses, belts, bookmarks, collage pictures and much more. The needlecase described here is made from soft sheepskin, which can be found in any good craft shop. Like all animal skin, it contains occasional blemishes, and will be thinner at the edges, so care should be taken when choosing and cutting the pieces to ensure that they are as even as possible. Being soft, the only tools needed for cutting and sewing are a good pair of sharp scissors, a leatherwork needle and pure silk or synthetic thread, which, like the skin, is slightly elastic.

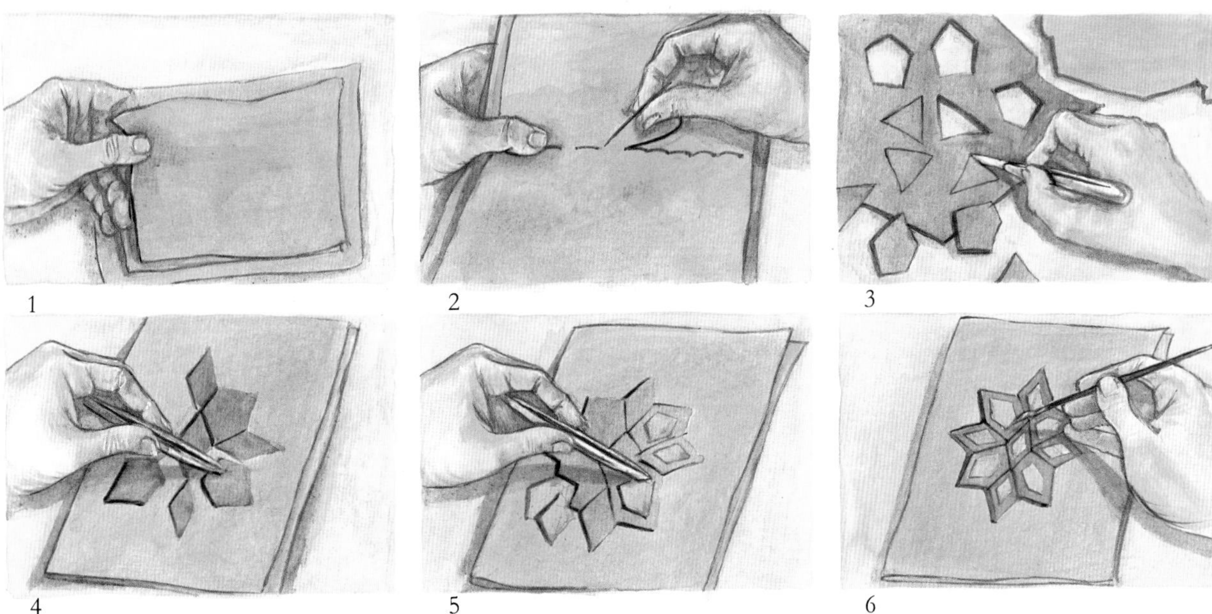

Materials
piece of basil leather (vegetable-tanned sheepskin) 6 × 4 in (15 × 10 cm)
2 pieces of thin felt each measuring 5½ in × 3½ in (14 × 9 cm)
double-sided adhesive tape
dressmaker's chalk
ruler
sharp leatherwork needle
silk or synthetic buttonhole thread
2 pieces of basil leather each 2 × 2 in (5 × 5 cm) in contrasting shades
Copydex glue
tweezers
gold acrylic paint (optional)
fine sable brush
sharp scissors or craft knife

Method
1. With the large piece of leather face downwards, place the two pieces of felt together in the centre, leaving ¼ in (1 cm) margin all round. Hold the three layers in place with double-sided tape between them. Do not pin or tack the layers together as this will mark the leather.
2. Draw a seam line with the chalk down the centre of the top layer of felt. Sew the three layers together along the chalk line using a small double-running stitch – i.e. sew in running stitch from top to bottom, turn and sew in running stitch again, filling in the spaces left by the first seam. Peel off the tape to separate the needlecase's felt 'pages' from its leather 'cover'.
3. Next, take the two smaller pieces of leather and, following the pattern shown here, cut five equal diamonds and four equal pentagons from one piece. Repeat with the second piece, but cut the shapes slightly smaller.
4. Placing the booklet leather-side up, mark the centre of the front cover lightly with chalk. Then, taking the larger diamonds and pentagons first and working from the centre outwards, glue sparingly and stick each shape into place, using tweezers to position them.
5. Then place the smaller pieces in the centre of each of the larger ones and stick down.
6. The edges of the diamonds can be outlined in gold paint to give an 'embossed' effect. Use acrylic paint, which will not crack, and apply it lightly to only a few of the edges to produce a rich effect.

NOTES

THE PAINTING PORTFOLIO

INTRODUCTION

1. *Winchilsea Poems*, with an introduction by Myra Reynolds; in Antonia Fraser, *The Weaker Vessel* (see bibliography), p. 322.
2. Fraser, *The Weaker Vessel*, p. 343.
3. Germaine Greer, *The Obstacle Race* (see bibliography), p. 91.
4. Vol. XII (July 1828).
5. Published under the heading 'The Industrious Housewife' (September 1813), p. 155.
6. Man in a Club Window, *The Habits of Good Society* (1859); in Pamela Gerrish Nunn, *Victorian Women Artists* (see bibliography), p. 8.
7. John Ruskin to Sophia Sinnett, 1858; in Gerrish Nunn, *Victorian Women Artists*, p. 16.
8. Candace Wheeler, *Yesterdays in a Busy Life* (Harper and Brothers, New York, 1918), p. 211; in Isabelle Anscombe, *A Woman's Touch* (see bibliography), p. 38.
9. In her article 'The Future of Englishwomen', *Nineteenth Century* (June 1878); in Gerrish Nunn, *Victorian Women Artists*, p. 21.

THE AMATEUR ARTS

1. From the edition published by Nelson Doubleday Inc. (New York), p. 123.
2. Marina Warner, *Queen Victoria's Sketchbook* (see bibliography), p. 20.
3. Flora Fraser, *The English Gentlewoman* (see bibliography), p. 78.
4. Fraser, *The English Gentlewoman*, p. 104.
5. Her works, signed 'P.C.', are not widely known today; see Daphne Foskett, 'The Modest Miniatures of Penelope Carwardine', *Antique Collector* (June 1985).
6. From the title of a plate which appeared in Ackermann, *The Repository of Arts* (July 1815).
7. Dated 1799; Honoria D. Marsh, *Shades from Jane Austen* (see bibliography).
8. The only extant piece attributed to her hand is a self-portrait silhouette, which she inscribed 'Done by Herself in 1815'.
9. Vol. III, November 1889–October 1890 (Cassell and Co. Ltd., London).
10. In the chapter 'Oil Painting', *Elegant Arts for Ladies* (*c.*1856), p. 93.

PAINTING ON GLASS

1. While published at this date, the story is set in the 1820s–30s.
2. Vol. XI, April 1828, in the article 'Painting on Glass'.

PAINTING ON VELVET

1. Fraser, *The English Gentlewoman*, p. 100.
2. In the Julia Munson Sherman Collection.
3. Judith R. Weissman and Wendy Lavitt, *Labors of Love: America's Textiles and Needlework 1650–1930* (see bibliography), p.131.
4. As described in a letter dated 20 January 1850, to Mrs Sherman; in Jean Lipman, *American Primitive Painting* (see bibliography), p. 100.

PENWORK

1. The similarity between graphic and embroidery designs was fully recognized during the period and in Ackermann, *The Repository of Arts* (December 1816) it was suggested that '... many of the borders will, according to taste, be as well adapted for muslin patterns, as painting'.

STENCILLING AND SPATTERWORK

1. p. 169. The phrases are adapted from an article which appeared in *Harper's Bazar* (17 May 1873).

PAPER PURSUITS

SILHOUETTES

1. Peggy Hickman, *Two Centuries of Silhouettes* (see bibliography), p. 17.
2. For a more detailed list of amateur silhouettists, see Mrs E. Nevill Jackson, *Silhouettes: A History and Dictionary of Artists* (see bibliography).
3. The silhouettes have since been destroyed, but appear as illustrations in Nevill Jackson, *Silhouettes: A History and Dictionary of Artists*.

PAPER CUTOUTS AND PINPRICKING

1. Ruth Hayden, *Mrs Delany, Her Life and Her Flowers* (see bibliography), p. 51.
2. Described in *Mortimer's Director* (1763); in June Field, *Collecting Georgian and Victorian Crafts* (see bibliography), p. 15.
3. R.Brimley Johnson, *Mrs Delany at Court and among the Wits* (Stanley Paul, London, 1925).
4. Dated May 1782; in Hayden, *Mrs Delany, Her Life and Her Flowers*, p. 158.

THE ART OF PAPER FLOWERS

1. Jane Toller, *Regency and Victorian Crafts* (see bibliography), p. 49.
2. For a satirical account of charity bazaars, see Mrs Trollope, *Domestic Manners of the Americans* (1828).

DECORATIVE PAPER SCRAPS

1. From an advertisement for William Cole's 'Superior Lithographic Drawings', illustrated in Alistair Allen and Joan Hoverstadt, *The History of Printed Scraps* (see bibliography), p. 18.
2. From the lithograph by E. Purcell, illustrated in Allen and Hoverstadt, *The History of Printed Scraps*, p. 22.
3. Lichten, *Decorative Art of Victoria's Era*, p. 188.
4. From a volume published in 1859; in Lichten, *Decorative Art of Victoria's Era*, p. 170.
5. From the firm's original advertisement, illustrated in Allen and Hoverstadt, *The History of Printed Scraps*, p. 158.
6. From the chapter 'Potichomanie' (*c.*1856), (see bibliography), p. 150.

THE LADY'S WORKBOX

SAMPLERS

1. Created by Patty Polk of Kent County, Maryland; in Elisabeth Donaghy Garrett, 'American Samplers and Needlework Pictures in the DAR Museum: Part I, 1739–1806', *Antiques* (February 1974).
2. Joan Edwards, *Crewel Embroidery in England* (see bibliography), p. 53.
3. *A Booke of Curious and Strange Inventions called the first part of Needleworkes*, pub. William Barley (1596).
4. Betty Ring, *American Needlework Treasures: Samplers and Silk Embroideries from the Collection of Betty Ring* (see bibliography), p. 1.

STUMPWORK & ENCRUSTED EMBROIDERY

1. This description also appears later in Lady Marian Alford, *Needlework as Art* (1886).

2. Lanto Synge, *Antique Needlework* (see bibliography), p. 80.
3. Synge, *Antique Needlework*, p. 80.
4. In the second edition.
5. Muriel Baker, *Stumpwork, The Art of Raised Embroidery* (see bibliography), p. 26.
6. *Diary and Correspondence of John Evelyn*, ed. William Bray, four vols (1850).

BEADWORK

1. Fraser, *The Weaker Vessel*, p. 327.
2. Marjorie Henderson and Elizabeth Wilkinson, *Cassell's Compendium of Victorian Crafts* (see bibliography), p. 80.

CREWEL EMBROIDERY

1. Quoted in several sources, among them *The Complete Guide to Needlework*, ed. Mary Gostelow (see bibliography), p. 154; and Erica Wilson, *Embroidery Book* (see bibliography), p. 6.

BLACKWORK

1. Alford, *Needlework as Art* (see bibliography), p. 383.
2. Sonnets in 'memory of Queenes and great Ladies'.
3. Mary Gostelow, *Blackwork* (see bibliography), p. 68.
4. A pagan symbol of fertility and, later, purity.
5. *The Hardwick Hall Inventories of 1601*, ed. Lindsay Boynton (The Furniture History Society, London, 1971), p. 23.
6. Gostelow, *Blackwork*, p. 35.

WHITEWORK

1. John Taylor, *The Prayse of the Needle* (*c.*1636).
2. Weissman and Lavitt, *Labors of Love*, p. 73.

SILK EMBROIDERED PICTURES

1. As listed in the curriculum of Susanna Rowson's Academy in Boston, 1803; in Jane C. Giffen, 'Susanna Rowson and her Academy', *Antiques* (September 1970).
2. This appeared in the *American and Commercial Daily Advertiser* (Baltimore, 29 March 1814); in Weissman and Lavitt, *Labors of Love*, p. 127.
3. Advertised in the *Columbian Centinel* (Boston, 19 July 1809).

QUILTING AND PATCHWORK

1. Lichten, *Decorative Art of Victoria's Era*, p. 172.
2. Weissman and Lavitt, *Labors of Love*, p. 44.
3. Florence Peto, *Historic Quilts* (for the American Historical Company, New York, 1939).

KNITTING AND CROCHET

1. Anne L. Macdonald, *No Idle Hands: The Social History of American Knitting* (see bibliography), p. 150.
2. Macdonald, *No Idle Hands*, p. 57.
3. Published by Weldon and Co., London, *c.*1895.

DECORATIVE RUGS

1. C. Kurt Dewhurst and Betty and Marsha MacDowell, *Artists in Aprons* (E.P. Dutton, New York, 1979), p. 100.
2. In the *Descriptive Catalogue of E.S. Frost and Co.'s Hooked Rug Patterns* (Greenfield Village and Henry Ford Museum, Dearborn, Michigan, 1970).

BERLIN WORK

1. Lichten, *Decorative Art of Victoria's Era*, p. 13.
2. *Art Journal* (January 1851).
3. British canvases 'stamped in colours' were shown at the Great Exhibition of 1851; see Lichten, *Decorative Art of Victoria's Era*, p. 12.
4. Molly G.Proctor, *Victorian Canvas Work* (see bibliography), p. 10.
5. See Lichten, *Decorative Art of Victoria's Era*, p. 14.
6. M.T. Morrall, *A History of Needlemaking* (1852).

FANCY WORK

FEATHERWORK

1. Toller, *Regency and Victorian Crafts*, p. 57.
2. Toller, *Regency and Victorian Crafts*, p. 62.
3. Mrs H.R. Haweis, *The Art of Beauty* (1878).

SHELLWORK

1. Bea Howe, *Antiques from the Victorian Home* (see bibliography), p. 142.
2. Hayden, *Mrs Delany, Her Life and Her Flowers*, p. 10.
3. Hayden, *Mrs Delany, Her Life and Her Flowers*, p. 48.
4. Dated October 1761; in Hayden, *Mrs Delany, Her Life and Her Flowers*, p. 101.
5. From the reprinted edition, pp. 52–6.
6. p. 16.

FELTWORK

1. The key phrase was 'Sure Ruben's There', quoted in the exhibition catalogue *American and British Folk Art* (1–31 July 1976, see bibliography).
2. From an article by that title, in *Country Life* (15 September 1960).

WOODLAND AND RUSTIC DECORATIONS

1. Henderson and Wilkinson, *Cassell's Compendium of Victorian Crafts*, (see bibliography), p. 137.
2. Guimond Mounter, 'The Teddy Bear's Picnic Hut', *The World of Interiors* (November 1988).
3. James Hatton, essay entitled 'British Cottage Architecture' (1798).
4. Lichten, *Decorative Art of Victoria's Era*, p. 207.
5. C.G. Leland, *The Minor Arts* (1880), (see bibliography), p. 130.
6. Instructions for which were included in *Cassell's Household Guide* (1875).

DECORATIONS IN SAND AND SEAWEED

1. Sarah Howell, *The Seaside* (see bibliography), p. 90.

HAIRWORK

1. In the chapter 'Weaving or Plaiting Hair Ornaments', p. 3.
2. Lichten, *Decorative Art of Victoria's Era*, p. 192.
3. *Elegant Arts for Ladies*, p. 12.
4. *Elegant Arts for Ladies*, p. 4. The individual strands of hair were weighted and placed over the table, with one end passed through the hole and the other draped over the side, to avoid them becoming twisted or knotted.

MODELLING IN WAX

1. Mrs Emma Peachey, *The Royal Guide to Wax Flower Modelling* (1856)
2. Peachey, *The Royal Guide to Wax Flower Modelling* (1856), Editor's preface.

LEATHERWORK

1. *The Illustrated Catalogue of the Exhibition of the Industry of All Nations, 1851* (George Virtue, London 1851), p. 74.
2. Lichten, *Decorative Art of Victoria's Era*, p. 175.
3. In chapter 'Ornamental Leatherwork', p. 169.

GLOSSARY

antimacassar Cover used to protect the back or arms of furniture.
appliqué Decoration of one piece of material sewn or otherwise attached to another.
art needlework Revival of traditional embroidery styles and methods, instigated by William Morris and his followers during the second half of the ninteenth century.
baste Sew with long stitches to hold fabric in place temporarily; after final stitching, the basting is removed.
block Piece of cloth, often square-shaped, sewn onto the surface of a patchwork quilt as an individual design element (see *appliqué*).
bobbin lace Lace made by weaving threads on bobbins, rather than with needle and thread (see *needle lace*).
bonbonnière Small decorative box to hold sweets.
bradawl Small boring tool.
broderie perse Style of appliqué using chintz and other printed fabric cutouts, which are sewn onto a white background and then quilted and embroidered in imitation of Persian textiles; popular during the eighteenth century.
buckram Coarse cotton or linen cloth stiffened with paste.
bugle Long, cylindrical-shaped bead.
buttonhole stitch Reinforcing, looped stitch used for edgings, and decoratively for fillings.
calico Fine white linen material; imitations were made of hand-spun cotton yarn.
candlewick spread Bedcover, usually of white cotton, having embroidered or woven designs, sometimes with surface pile sheared; popular from the early nineteenth century onwards.
cartouche Ornamental scroll, medallion or other shape reserved for inscriptions or pictorial devices, found commonly on engravings and needlework panels.
celadon Green, glazed stoneware or ceramic produced in the Orient from the eleventh century onwards, ranging in shade from pale grey-green or blue to deep olive.
chain stitch One of the oldest stitches, used to create various patterns, among them interlocking, flat chains. Can be used as a line or filling stitch.
chemise Lady's undergarment or shift.
chenille Thick, soft, tufty silk or worsted velvet cord or yarn.
chinoiserie European interpretation of Chinese decoration depicting pseudo-oriental figures, pagodas, beasts and foliage; popular from the late seventeenth century onwards.
chintz Plain-weave, printed cotton fabric with glazed finish.
coif Small, fitted cap worn informally by men and women during the sixteenth and seventeenth centuries.
collage Cutouts of paper or other materials, assembled and glued into decorative compositions.
couching Method of embroidery in which the thread is caught down at intervals by another thread passed through the material from beneath.
coverlet Woven bedcover, usually of wool and cotton.
crosshatching Shading in two layers of parallel lines, with one layer crossing the other at an angle.
cross-stitch Also known as *gros point*. Usually worked over two vertical and two horizontal threads of the canvas foundation, forming a crisscrossed pattern.
cut-and-drawn-work Process of cutting out sections of fabric, and subsequently filling the spaces with threads in crisscross or lace-like patterns.
cutwork Used in needlework to describe the process of cutting out sections of fabric to create patterns; also used generally for cut-paper decoration.
damask Rich, reversible silk material with a pattern woven into it.
découpure French term meaning 'cut out', and used in France to describe paper cutwork.
diaphanie Decorative process of imitating stained glass by painting onto a sheet of glass, muslin or silk in bright, translucent colours; popular during the Victorian period for ornamenting windows, lampshades, handscreens and conservatories.
distemper Powdered colours mixed with a glutinous substance soluble in water – an inexpensive but impermanent method of painting.
dog of fō Fantastic lion-like creature – symbol of valour and energy – employed decoratively in Chinese architecture, sculpture and painted porcelain designs.
eyelet Hole made in fabric for passing a lace or point through, or used purely for ornamental purposes as found, for example, in broderie anglaise.
fancy work General term used commonly during the Victorian period to describe ornamental needlework and handicrafts.
fichu Triangular piece of cloth, often lace or muslin, worn by women to cover the neck, throat and shoulders.
Florentine stitch Used in florentine embroidery (also known as *bargello work*), this upright, straight stitch is usually taken up over four threads and down two threads according to the design, to form a variety of zigzag and chevron patterns.
folly Decorative (and often whimsical) building, tower or other structure used to ornament a landscaped park or other outdoor scheme, intended as a conversation piece during the eighteenth century.
foundation Underlying base fabric for needlework and rug-hooking, into which the yarn or thread is worked.
fretwork Decorative, interlaced patterns used in architecture, interior design and to adorn the surfaces of objects and furnishings, from metalware to needlework.
gesso The ground used for tempera painting, possessing a high degree of absorbancy and densely white brilliance.
gouache Painting technique using opaque colours ground in water and mixed with gum, honey or other binding agent.
grisaille Colouring in grey monotone to imitate low-relief sculpture, or to achieve effects of shadowing.
grotesque Fantastic creature or exaggerated human figure conveyed in flamboyant style, in keeping with Rococo tastes.
grotto Cave or cavern adorned internally with shellwork and/or rocks, in keeping with the grandiose schemes of eighteenth-century landscape architecture.
Hungarian stitch One of several grounding stitches used in counted-thread embroidery.
Indian General term used during the seventeenth and eighteenth centuries to describe an exotic design – Indian, Chinese or Japanese – regardless of origin.
isinglass Gelatin substance obtained from the bladders of certain freshwater fish, or animal skins and hooves, used as an adhesive. An early recipe appeared in Stalker and Palmer's *A Treatise of Japanning and Varnishing* (1688).
japanning English and American term used since the late seventeenth century to describe imitation oriental lacquer (often combining découpage decoration); today, the term is used indiscriminately to describe almost any shiny black surface – wood or metal – regardless of origin.
jasper ware Fine, unglazed stoneware or ceramic invented by Josiah Wedgwood in 1764, stained various colours including blue, green, yellow, pink and brown; used for decorative ornaments and jewellery.
lampblack Black pigment made from soot, often added to black paint for greater density.

lappet Loose or overlapping panel on a garment.
latticino Clear glass embedded with decorative threads of glass, often coloured white.
lawn Fine linen material, similar to cambric.
lead white Compound of lead carbonate and hydrated oxide of lead, used as a white pigment.
limning Seventeenth-century term for painting in watercolours or distemper.
marbling Technique of imitating marble by painting or staining, which was used to decorate walls, furniture and paper; also known by the French term *faux marbre*.
marquetry Decorative veneering using wood, ivory, mother-of-pearl, straw or other materials, in which thin sheets are cut and applied to the exteriors of furniture and objects in delicate patterns.
millboard Specially prepared board made of layers of paper or paper pulp stuck together, used as a ground for sketching and decorative work.
motif Decorative element used alone or as a recurring part of a design
muslin Delicately woven cotton fabric.
neckerchief Large square of material, folded lengthways and worn as a neck collar or shawl.
needle lace Lace made by sewing with a needle and thread.
neoclassicism Revival of antique Greek and Roman styles, popular during the third quarter of the eighteenth and early nineteenth centuries, characterized by formal designs.
nosegay Small bouquet or posy of flowers.
organdie Very fine, slightly stiff, translucent muslin.
palampore Hand-painted (and later printed) Indian cotton hanging or bedcover, usually decorated in bright colours with the 'tree of life' or other pattern, made for the European market during the eighteenth century.
paper mosaic Decorative art of cutting paper into tiny pieces and assembling them into compositions, mosaic-fashion; practised with immense skill by the eighteenth-century gentlewoman Mary Delany in studies of flowers and plants.
papier mâché French term for mashed paper: the pulp was mixed with glue, chalk and occasionally sand or sawdust, then shaped and hardened by baking. Popular during the eighteenth and nineteenth centuries for furniture and small objects, of which many examples were japanned, gilded or hand-painted, and/or inlaid with mother-of-pearl.
pastel Powdered colour pigment mixed with gum-water and formed into small sticks for drawing.
pattern-drawer Usually a professional employed to draw patterns onto fabric, for subsequent embroidery.
Pennsylvania-German Also known as Pennsylvania-Dutch, a term used to describe the decorative style developed by German settlers in Pennsylvania, characterized by bright colours and recurrent stylized motifs such as tulips, hearts and 'tree of life' designs.
piecework Piecing together fabric remnants, as in patchwork.
pinchbeck Imitation gold metal – an alloy of copper and zinc – invented *c.*1720 by Christopher Pinchbeck and used to manufacture a range of inexpensive jewellery and personal accessories.
pole screen Fire screen with a shield attached to a central pole: the height of the shield could be adjusted as desired.
polonaise Woman's fashionable dress or over-dress, popular during the late eighteenth century, consisting of a tight bodice and a full skirt, which was drawn back from the waist to reveal a petticoat underneath.
potichomanie French term for decorating the interior walls of hollow glass vessels with paper cutouts, in imitation of costly European and Oriental porcelain.
prie-dieu chair Low-seated chair with a tall sloping back, used for praying; popular during the Victorian period.
primitive Unsophisticated or naive, as represented by folk-art decoration.
pulled work Drawn-thread work (see *cut-and-drawn-work*).
purl Thread or cord made from twisted gold or silver wire, used for embroidery.
quill-work American term for paper filigree decoration using coils of paper to ornament the exteriors of small boxes, candle sconces, picture frames, etc.; popular during the late seventeenth and eighteenth centuries.
reticella Needle lace worked on a geometric grid by drawing threads from a woven cloth and working them into patterns using buttonhole stitch.
rococo Derived from the French *rocaille*, an elaborate style of decoration and architecture consisting chiefly of flowing arabesques and curvilinear forms, profuse foliage, flowers, shells and rock-work, popular in France *c.*1740–60 and in England *c.*1745–65.
rouleau Decorative trimming, or part of an article which has been rounded or rolled, as found on fashionable costume and accessories during the nineteenth century.
sepia Rich brown pigment made from the inky secretion of the cuttlefish, used in monochrome watercolour painting.
shade Glass dome used for display purposes; popular during the Victorian period to cover and protect delicate handiwork.
shellac Resinous substance secreted by the lac insect which was made into thin sheets and dissolved in alcohol to make varnish or a lacquer finish.
skeleton leaves Decorative process of decomposing leaves to skeletons; popular during the Victorian period when examples were described as 'phantom bouquets'.
spangle Small, thin, metallic disc pierced with a central hole, used for lavish embroidery from the sixteenth century onwards.
strap work Decoration consisting of interlaced bands or straps (sometimes with foliage); popular during the late sixteenth and seventeenth centuries for interior mouldings and furnishings.
tempera Quick-drying painting medium using egg as a binding agent.
template Pattern cut from paper, card or thin metal sheet, used for tracing and cutting outlines.
tent stitch Also called *petit point*, a small diagonal stitch used for fine work on single-thread canvas, executed in horizontal or diagonal rows.
tôle French term for japanned metalware.
tremblant French term for a brooch, pendant or hair ornament supported on a wire framework or springs, which 'trembled' as the wearer moved.
trompe l'oeil Pictorial illusions, using perspective and fore-shortening to create a convincing sense of reality; popular from the eighteenth century onwards for murals and furniture decoration.
Tunbridge ware Small items of furniture and wooden objects adorned with mosaic veneers formed into geometric or pictorial patterns, using both naturally coloured and dyed pieces of wood; popular in England during the nineteenth century.
varnish Resinous solution, transparent or tinted, applied to the exteriors of furniture and objects to give a hard, protective finish, drying glossy or matt.
vignette Small ornamental design whose edges shaded to merge with the surrounding background, as found commonly on eighteenth-century engravings.
volute Spiral scroll, curve or other decorative twist, as found in architecture and interior design.

SELECT BIBLIOGRAPHY

GENERAL CRAFTS AND HISTORICAL BACKGROUND

Ackermann, Rudolf, *The Repository of Arts, Literature, Fashions*, 3rd series, vols. XI and XII, London, 1828
Andrew, H.E. Laye, *The Batsford Encyclopedia of Crafts*, Batsford, London, 1978
Anscombe, Isabelle, *A Woman's Touch*, Virago Press, London, 1984
Ashelford, Jane, *Dress in the Age of Elizabeth I*, Batsford, London, 1988
Black, J. Anderson, *A History of Jewels*, Orbis, London, 1974
Briggs, Asa, *Victorian Things*, Batsford, London, 1988
Buck, Anne, *Dress in 18th Century England*, Holmes & Meier, New York, 1979
Burton, Elizabeth, *Georgians at Home*, Longman, London, 1967
Cooper, Nicolas, *The Opulent Eye: Late Victorian and Edwardian Taste in Interior Design*, The Architectural Press, London, 1976
Cramer, Edith, *Early American Decoration Made Easy*, Dover Publications Inc., New York, 1985
Elegant Arts for Ladies, Ward Lock, London, *c.*1856
Fairbanks, Jonathan L., and Bates, Elizabeth Bidwell, *American Furniture: 1620 to the Present*, Richard Marek, New York, 1981
Field, June, *Collecting Georgian and Victorian Crafts*, Heinemann, London, 1973
Flower, Margaret, *Victorian Jewellery*, Cassell, London, 1951
Ford, Marianne, *Copycats and Artifacts*, David R. Godine, Boston, 1986
Fraser, Antonia, *Mary Queen of Scots*, Weidenfeld and Nicolson, London, 1969, 1978
The Weaker Vessel: Woman's Lot in Seventeenth-Century England, Weidenfeld and Nicolson, London, 1984
Fraser, Flora, *The English Gentlewoman*, Barrie & Jenkins, London, 1987
Hayward, Helena (ed.), *World Furniture*, Paul Hamlyn, London, 1965
Henderson, Marjorie, and Wilkinson, Elizabeth, *Cassell's Compendium of Victorian Crafts*, Cassell, London, 1977
Howe, Bea, *Antiques from the Victorian Home*, Batsford, London, 1973
Howell, Sarah, *The Seaside*, Studio Vista, London, 1974
Hughes, Therle, *Small Decorative Antiques*, Lutterworth Press, London, 1959
Ickis, Marguerite, and Esh, Reba Selden, *The Book of Arts and Crafts*, Dover Publications Inc., New York, 1965
Illustrated Catalogue of the Exhibition of the Industry of all Nations, 1851, George Virtue, London, 1851
Ireson, Barbara, *Cottage Crafts*, Faber and Faber, London, 1975
Jackson, Valerie, *Crafts: Yesterday's Crafts for Today*, Lutterworth Press, 1979
Lasdun, Susan, *Victorians at Home*, Weidenfeld and Nicolson, London, 1981
Latham, Jean, *Victoriana*, Frederick Muller, London, 1971
Leland, Charles G., *The Minor Arts*, Macmillan, London, 1880
Lichten, Frances, *Decorative Art of Victoria's Era*, Bonanza Books, New York, 1950
Lipman, Jean, and Winchester, Alice, *The Flowering of American Folk Art 1776–1876*, Thames and Hudson, London, 1974
Lofts, Norah, *Domestic Life in England*, Weidenfeld and Nicolson, London, 1976
Petersen's Magazine, Vol. XIX, Philadelphia, 1851
Reader's Digest Manual of Handicrafts, Reader's Digest, London, 1980
Rees, Barbara, *The Victorian Lady*, Gordon and Cremonesi, London and New York, 1977
Rome, John (ed.), *The Blandford Book of Traditional Handicrafts*, Blandford Press, Dorset, 1981
Seymour, John, *The National Trust Book of Forgotten Household Crafts*, Dorling Kindersley, London, 1987
Toller, Jane, *Regency and Victorian Crafts*, Ward Lock, London, 1969
White, Cynthia L., *Women's Magazines 1693–1968*, Michael Joseph, London, 1971
Wilde, Oscar (ed.), *The Woman's World*, Vol. III, Cassell, London, 1890

THE PAINTING PORTFOLIO

American and British Folk Art, catalogue American Museum in Britain, Bath, 1976
Bishop, Adele, and Lord, Cile, *The Art of Decorative Stencilling*, Thames and Hudson, London, 1976
Bourne, Jonathan, *Lacquer: An International History and Collector's Guide*, The Crowood Press, Marlborough, 1984
Dampièrre, Florence de, *The Best of Painted Furniture*, Weidenfeld and Nicolson, London, 1987
Davidson, Alex, *Interior Affairs: The Decorative Arts in Paintwork*, Ward Lock, London, 1987
Davidson, Caroline, *Women's Worlds: The Art and Life of Mary Ellen Best 1809–1891*, Crown Publishers Inc., New York, 1985
Greer, Germaine, *The Obstacle Race*, Secker and Warburg, London, 1979
Innes, Jocasta, *Paint Magic*, Windward, London, 1981
Lipman, Jean, *American Primitive Painting*, Dover Publications Inc., New York, 1969
Lipman, Jean, and Black, Mary, *American Folk Painting*, Bramhall House, New York, 1987
Nunn, Pamela Gerrish, *Victorian Women Artists*, The Women's Press, London, 1987
O'Neil, Isabel, *The Art of the Painted Finish for Furniture and Decoration*, William Morrow and Co. Inc., New York, 1971
Stalker, John, and Parker, George, *A Treatise of Japanning and Varnishing*, 1688, reprinted with an introduction by H.D. Molesworth, Alec Tiranti, London, 1960, 1971
Warner, Marina, *Queen Victoria's Sketchbook*, Macmillan, London, 1979

PAPER PURSUITS

Aaron, Elizabeth, *Quilling, The Art of Paper Scroll Work*, Batsford, London, 1976
Allen, Alistair, and Hoverstadt, Joan, *The History of Printed Scraps*, New Cavendish Books, London, 1983
Doeser, Linda, *Paper*, Marshall Cavendish Books Ltd., London, 1975
Harrower, Dorothy, *Découpage, A Limitless World in Decoration*, M.Barrows and Co., New York, 1958
Hayden, Ruth, *Mrs. Delany, Her Life and Her Flowers*, Colonnade Books, London, 1980
Hickman, Peggy, *Two Centuries of Silhouettes – Celebrities in Profile*, A.&C.Black, London, 1971
Jackson, Mrs E. Nevill, *Silhouettes: A History and Dictionary of Artists*, Dover Publications Inc., New York, 1981
Lister, Raymond, *Silhouettes*, Pitman, London, 1953
Marsh, Honoria D., *Shades from Jane Austen*, Parry Jackson Ltd., London, 1975

THE LADY'S WORKBOX

Alford, Lady Marion, *Needlework as Art*, Sampson Low, 1886; EP Publishing, 1975
Baker, Muriel, *Stumpwork*, Bell and Hyman, London, 1978

Betterton, Shiela, *Rugs from the American Museum in Britain*, Bath, 1981

Quilts and Coverlets from the American Museum in Britain, Bath, 1978

Bishop, Robert, *Quilts, Coverlets, Rugs and Samplers*, Alfred A. Knopf Inc., New York, 1982

Edwards, Joan, *Crewel Embroidery in England*, Batsford, London, 1975

Embroiderer's Guild, *Needlework School, The Embroiderer's Guild Practical Study Group*, Windward, London, 1984

Felcher, Cecelia, *The Complete Book of Rug Making*, Robert Hale, London, 1975

Gostelow, Mary (ed.), *The Complete Guide to Needlework*, Quill Publishing Ltd., London, 1982; Fraser Stewart, Hertford, 1988

Blackwork, Batsford, London, 1976

Macdonald, Anne L., *No Idle Hands: The Social History of American Knitting*, Ballantine Books, New York, 1988

Proctor, Molly G., *Victorian Canvas Work*, Batsford, London, 1972

Puls, Herta, *The Art of Cutwork and Appliqué*, Batsford, London, 1978

Ring, Betty, *American Needlework Treasures*, E.P. Dutton, New York, 1987

Needlework, An Historical Survey, A New and Expanded Edition, The Main Street Press, New Jersey, 1984

Rosenstiel, Helene Von, *American Rugs and Carpets from the Seventeenth Century to Modern Times*, Barrie & Jenkins, London, 1978

Sebba, Anne, *Samplers – Five Centuries of a Gentle Craft*, Thames and Hudson, New York, 1979

Swain, Margaret, *The Needlework of Mary Queen of Scots*, Van Nostrand Reinhold Co., New York, 1973

Synge, Lanto, *Antique Needlework*, Blandford Press, Dorset, 1972

The Royal School of Needlework Book of Needlework and Embroidery, William Collins, London, 1986

Weinstein, Florence, *Victorian Crochet by Weldon and Company*, Dover Publications Inc., New York, 1974

Weissman, Judith Reiter, and Lavitt, Wendy, *Labors of Love: America's Textiles and Needlework 1650–1930*, Studio Vista, London, 1988

Wilson, Erica, *The Craft of Crewel Embroidery*, Faber and Faber, London, 1977

Embroidery Book, Charles Scribner's Sons, New York, 1973

FANCY WORK

Albert, Lillian Smith, and Adams, Jane Ford, *The Button Sampler*, Gramercy Publishing Co., New York, 1951

Haddon, Celia, *Gifts from your Garden*, Michael Joseph, London, 1985

Haragan, Christine, *Shell Designs*, Midas Books, 1980

Jeffrey, Vera, *Handmade Flowers*, Hamlyn, London, 1980

Pettit, Florence H., *Whirligigs and Whimmy Diddles and other American Folkcraft Objects*, Thomas Y. Crowell Co., New York, 1972

Scott, Margaret Kennedy, and Beazley, Mary, *Making Pressed Flower Pictures*, Batsford, London, 1979

Wood, Emma, *Flower Crafts*, Orbis, London, 1982

SUPPLIERS

Apart from the stockists listed below, materials can also be purchased at department stores, local needlecraft and art shops and D.I.Y. outlets. Shells and seaweed are sold by seaside tourist shops. Up-to-date lists of suppliers and manufacturers are published regularly in the following magazines:
Embroidery (published by The Embroiderer's Guild, Hampton Court, Surrey); *Crafts* (published by The Crafts Council, 1 Oxenden Street, London SW1); and *The Artist's and Illustrator's Magazine* (4 Brandon Road, London N7).

GENERAL CRAFTS

Fred Aldous Ltd.,
Dept. C37,
Lever Street,
Manchester M60 1UX

E. J. Arnold,
Butterley Street,
Leeds LS10 1AX

Arts and Interiors,
48 Princes Street,
Yeovil,
Somerset

Beckfoot Mill,
Prince Street,
Dudley Hill,
Bradford BD4 6HQ

Bits and Bobs,
18 Lodge Road,
Holt,
Wimbourne,
Dorset BH21 7DN

Dryad,
P.O. Box 38,
Northgates,
Leicester LE1 9BU
(contact for stockists of a wide selection of materials)

Griffin Fabrics Ltd.,
The Crafts Centre,
97 Claremont Street,
Aberdeen AB1 6QR

W. Hobby Ltd.,
Knight's Hill Square,
London SE27 0HH

Model and Craft Centre,
260 Dewsbury Road,
Wakefield WF2 9BY

Pastimes,
853 Chesterfield Road,
Woodseats,
Sheffield S8 0SQ

Pretty Things (Crafts) Ltd.,
7 Greenfield Road,
Harbourne,
Birmingham B17 0ED

The Tropical Shell Company,
22 Preston Road,
Brighton,
Sussex BN1 4QF

Williams Adhesives,
247 Argyll Avenue,
Slough,
Berks SL1 4HA

PAINTS, VARNISHES AND ARTISTS' MATERIALS

Aitken Dott and Son,
26 Castle Street,
Edinburgh

Acorn Art Shop,
28 Colquoun Street,
Glasgow

Brodie and Middleton Ltd.,
Theatrical Suppliers,
68 Drury Lane,
London WC2
(gold paints and glitters)

Cornelissen and Son Ltd.,
105 Great Russell Street,
London WC1 3RY

Crafts Unlimited,
21 Macklin Street,
London WC2

Green and Stone,
259 King's Road,
London SW3 5EL

Liverpool Fine Arts,
85A Bold Street,
Liverpool

Reeves Art Materials,
178 Kensington High Street,
London W8

George Rowney and Co. Ltd.,
10–11 Percy Street,
London WC1

Russell and Chapple Ltd.,
23 Monmouth Street,
London WC2H 9DF
(canvases)

READY-MADE STENCILS AND MATERIALS

Laura Ashley, branches nationwide.

Lyn le Grice Stencil Design Ltd.,
Bread Street,
Penzance,
Cornwall TR18 2EQ
(mail order)

Carolyn Warrender,
91 Lower Sloane Street,
London SW1W 8DA

PAPER

Compton Marbling,
Tisbury,
Salisbury,
Wilts SP3 6SG

Susan Doncaster,
26 Clayton Park Square,
Jesmond,
Newcastle-upon-Tyne NE2 4DP

G.P. Inveresk Corp.,
Belgrave House,
Greyfriars,
Northampton NN1 2LS

The Italian Paper Shop,
11 Brompton Arcade,
London SW3

Mastercraft Papers Ltd.,
Paper Mews,
Dorking,
Surrey RH4 1QX

Paperchase,
216 Tottenham Court Road,
London W1

Paperpoint,
130 Long Acre,
London WC2E 9AL

Papyrus,
25 Broad Street,
Bath,
Avon BA1 5LW

Rampant Lions Press,
12 Chesterton Road,
Cambridge CB4 3AB

NEEDLECRAFTS

Laura Ashley, branches nationwide
(sampler kits, patchwork, needlepoint)

Applebees Craft Centre,
2–4 Crown Street,
Castle Hedingham,
Essex CO9 3DB
(spinning, weaving and lace-making)

The Campden Needlecraft Centre,
High Street,
Chipping Campden,
Glos GL65 6AG

Colourspun,
18A Camden Road,
London NW1 9HA
(knitting yarns)

Country Yarns,
13 Lichfield Drive,
Prestwich,
Manchester M25 8HX
(sampler kits)

The Irish Linen Depot,
39 Bond Street,
London W5 5AS
(linen, lace, frames)

Leven Crafts,
23 Chaloner Street,
Guisborough,
Cleveland TS14 6QD

L. Lockhart and Son Ltd.,
Linktown Works,
Kirkaldy,
Fife
(linen)

Mace and Nairn,
89 Crane Street,
Salisbury,
Wilts SP1 2PY

Roderick Owen,
38 Argyle Street,
Oxford OX4 1SS
(pattern-books)

The Patchwork Dog and The Calico Cat,
21 Chalk Farm Road,
London NW1
(templates, patchwork, quilting, etc.)

Pioneer Patches – The Store,
Marsh Mills,
Luck Lane,
Huddersfield HD3 4AB
(cotton)

The Royal School of Needlework,
5 King Street,
London WC2 8HN

Strawberry Fayre,
Chagford,
Devon TQ13 8EN
(patchwork)

Sutton Needlecraft Centre,
40 Birmingham Road,
Sutton Coldfield,
W. Midlands
(patchwork, quilting, etc.)

Up Country,
12 Towngate,
Holmfirth,
W. Yorks
(yarns amd appliqué)

The Voirrey Embroidery Centre,
Brimstage Hall,
Wirral L63 6JA

BEADS AND BUGLES

The Bead Shop,
43 Neal Street,
London WC2

Cotswold Craft Centre,
Dept. E,
5 Whitehall,
Stroud,
Glos GL5 1HA

Ellis and Farrier Ltd.,
5 Princes Street,
London SW1

The Handworker's Market,
18 Chapel Yard,
Albert Street,
Holt,
Norfolk

Jewellery Craft Supplies,
Kernowcraft,
Bolingey,
Perranporth,
Cornwall

Kaleidoscope,
3 Grove Park,
Brislington,
Bristol BS4 3LG

The Needlewoman,
21 Needless Alley,
Birmingham B2 5AE

Teazle Embroideries,
35 Boothferry Road,
Hull HU3 6UA

The Warehouse,
39 Neal Street,
London WC2

DRIED FLOWERS AND FLOWER CRAFTS

Collections,
4–5 Green Street,
Bath,
Avon

The Conran Shop,
77 Fulham Road,
London SW3

Cullens Florist,
88–92 Henrietta Street,
Aston-under-Lyne,
Lancs

Culpepper Ltd.,
21 Bruton Street,
London W1

Hay Fever Dried Flowers,
4 Cathedral Close,
Exeter,
Devon EX1 1EX

Jenners,
Princes Street,
Edinburgh

Flora Products Mail Order,
5 Parkside,
Christchurch Road,
Ringwood,
Hants BH24 3SH

Flowers Unlimited,
1 Bank Street,
Hythe,
Kent

National Trust shops nationwide

LEATHER

Alma Leather Co.,
17 Wakeley Street,
London EC1

Cuyahoga Studio,
17A Hastings Road,
Bexhill-on-Sea,
E. Sussex TN40 2HJ

W. Jeffrey Co. Ltd.,
88–90 Weston Street,
London SE1

John P. Milner,
Cilycwm,
Llandovery,
Dyfed 5A20 0SS

ACKNOWLEDGEMENTS

AUTHOR'S ACKNOWLEDGEMENTS

Many friends and colleagues have helped enormously in the writing of this book but, in particular, I should like to express my thanks to the following: Vanessa Nicolson, for her diligent picture research; Denny Hemming, of Weidenfeld and Nicolson, for her careful supervision of the text; Alice Williams for her editorial research, and Lesley Baxter, whose tremendous enthusiasm for the subject, skilful editing and assistance with the projects have been invaluable. Finally, I am deeply grateful to my husband, Stephen, for his untiring advice and support, and without whose encouragement I should not have been able to pursue my own pastimes.

Felice Hodges, London, 1989

PHOTOGRAPHIC ACKNOWLEDGEMENTS

The author and publishers would like to thank the following for supplying and granting permission to reproduce illustrations, listed by plate number. Unnumbered pictures are referred to by the page numbers on which they appear:

A la Ronde 39, 105, 106, 114; Alistair Sampson Antiques Ltd 23, 84, 108, 109, 117 (*photos John Miller*); The American Museum in Britain 4, 9, 14, 15, 21, 26, 59, 78, 85, 86, 87, 88, 94, 95, 96, p.191; *Antique Collector* Magazine 55; The Bowes Museum 113, 118; The Bridgeman Art Library p. 4, p. 5; City of Bristol Museum and Art Gallery 6; The British Museum 18, 41, 42, 44, 119; Dr A. K. Brown 8; The Burrell Collection 76; Cecil Higgins Art Gallery 43, 48; Christie's 30, 51, 53; The Crane Gallery 1, 3, 25, 27, 81, 89, 90 (*photos John Miller*); Elizabeth Bradley Designs 99, 100; Halcyon Days 5, 16, 17, 19, 20, 82, 115, 116, p.4; Ian G. Hastie 45, 47; Lady Lever Art Gallery 33, 122; Museum of London 49, 101, 123; Loot 46, 103, 111, 124, 125 (*photos John Miller*); Maidstone Museum & Art Gallery 120, 121; Mallett at Bourdon House Ltd 12, 52, 54, 112 (*photos John Miller*); Mallett and Son (Antiques) Ltd 7, 32, 35, 63, 66, 67, 68, 70, 71; Manchester City Art Galleries 74; The Mansell Collection 56, p.9 (inset); The Mary Evans Picture Library 91, pp.45, 85, 141 (insets); Mayorcas 69, 92; Mrs Monro 22, 40, 50, 98, 104, 107, 110 (*photos John Miller*); Ornamenta 36, 37, 38; Phillip's 34, 60; Private collection 10, 11; Royal Library 31; Royal Museum of Scotland 58; Shelburne Museum 28, 29, 65, 72, 79, 80; Stair and Co. 62, p.5; The Tate Gallery 102; Victoria and Albert Museum 13, 24, 57, 73, 75, 77, 93, 97; Weidenfeld and Nicolson Archive 64, 83; Whitworth Art Gallery 61; York City Art Gallery 2

We are grateful to the following galleries and antique shops for granting permission to photograph objects in their collections:

Alistair Sampson Antiques, 156 Brompton Road, London SW3
The Crane Gallery, 171A Sloane Street, London SW1
Loot, 76–78 Pimlico Road, London SW1
Mallett at Bourdon House Ltd, 2 Davies Street, London W1
Mrs Monro Ltd, 11 Montpelier Street, London SW7

Our thanks to the galleries, institutions and shops listed below for lending articles photographed on the jacket, half-title and title pages and pp.8–9, 44–5, 84–5, 140–1:

The Antique Textile Company, 100 Portland Road, London W11
Carolyn Warrender, 91 Lower Sloane Street, London SW1
Charles Beresford Clark, 558 King's Road, London SW6
Forty-Eight Walton Street, London SW3
Gilani Antiques, 30–31 Islington Green, London N1
Green and Stone, 259 King's Road, London SW3
Hilary Batstone, 336 King's Road, London SW3
Joanna Wood, 48a Pimlico Road, London SW1
Kenneth Turner Flowers, 35 Brook Street, London W1
Keith Skeel Antiques, 35 Brook Street, London W1
Linda Gumb, 9 Camden Passage, London N1
Lindsay Antiques, 99 Kensington Church Street, London W8
Lunn Antiques, 86 New King's Road, London SW6
Monro Heywood Antiques Ltd, 336 King's Road, London SW3
Rogers de Rin Antiques, 76 Royal Hospital Road, London SW3
The Rowley Gallery, 115 Kensington Church Street, London W8
The Royal School of Needlework, 5 King Street, London WC2
Shepherds Bookbinders Ltd, 76b Rochester Row, London SW1
Stephen Long Antiques, 348 Fulham Road, London SW10
Valerie Wade, 108 Fulham Road, London SW3
Virginia Antiques, 98 Portland Road, London W11
556 Antiques, 556 King's Road, London SW6

Jacket photograph: John Miller
Half-title, title, pp.8–9, 44–5, 84–5, 140–41 photographs: Charlotte Wood
Stylist: Janie Jackson

Project illustrations: Pauline Hazelwood

Every effort has been made to trace and acknowledge the copyright owners of the photographs illustrated. If by chance there is an incorrect or missing credit the author and publisher would like to apologise most sincerely and will be happy to correct the entry in any future edition.

INDEX

A

B

C

D

E

F

G

First published in Great Britain in 1989 by
George Weidenfeld & Nicolson Ltd
91 Clapham High Street
London SW4 7TA

ISBN 0 297 79631 3

Phototypeset by Keyspools Ltd, Golborne, Lancashire
Printed by Printers Srl, Trento
Bound by L.E.G.O., Vicenza

Colour separations by Newsele Litho Ltd